Paddling Idaho

Paddling Idaho

A Guide to the State's Best Paddling Routes

Greg Stahl

FALCONGUIDES

GUILFORD, CONNECTICUT

An imprint of Rowman & Littlefield

Falcon and FalconGuides are registered trademarks and Make Adventure Your Story is a trademark of Rowman & Littlefield.

Distributed by NATIONAL BOOK NETWORK

British Library Cataloguing-in-Publication Information available

Library of Congress Cataloging-in-Publication Data
Names: Stahl, Greg, author.
Title: Paddling Idaho : a guide to the state's best paddling routes / Greg
    Stahl.
Description: Guilford, Connecticut : FalconGuides, [2016] | "Distributed by
    NATIONAL BOOK NETWORK"—T.p. verso. | Includes bibliographical
references,   webography and index. | Description based on print version
record and CIP   data provided by publisher; resource not viewed.
Identifiers: LCCN 2016009280 (print) | LCCN 2016006927 (ebook) | ISBN
    9781493027088 (e-book) | ISBN 9781493008438 (paperback)
Subjects: LCSH: Canoes and canoeing—Idaho—Guidebooks. |
    Kayaking—Idaho—Guidebooks. | Idaho—Guidebooks.
Classification: LCC GV776.I2 (print) | LCC GV776.I2 S83 2016 (ebook) | DDC
    797.12209796—dc23
LC record available at http://lccn.loc.gov/2016009280

Printed in India

Contents

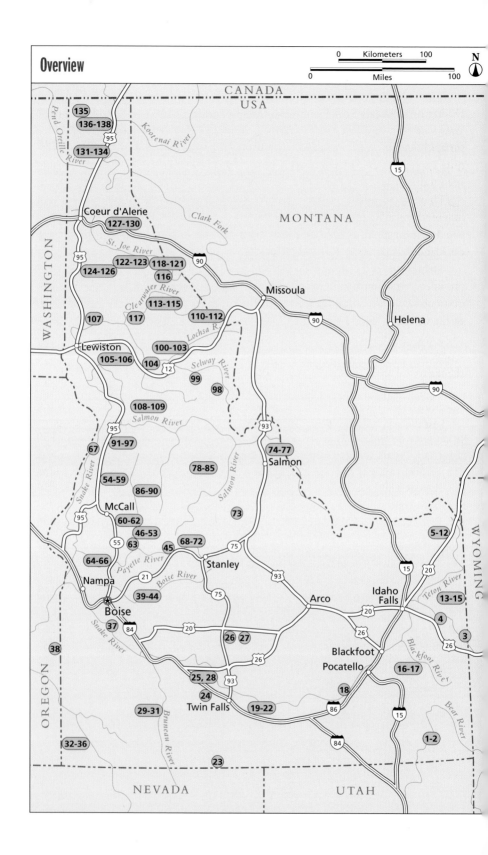

Overview

0 Kilometers 100
0 Miles 100

N

CANADA
USA

135
136-138
95
131-134

Pend Oreille River

Kootenai River

MONTANA

Coeur d'Alene
127-130

Clark Fork

St. Joe River

95

122-123 118-121
124-126 116

WASHINGTON

113-115

107 117 110-112

Clearwater River

Missoula

Helena

Lochsa R.

Lewiston
105-106
104 12
99
98

Selway River

100-103

90

108-109
95
Salmon River

74-77
Salmon

93

67 91-97

54-59
86-90

78-85

Snake River

McCall
60-62
46-53
55 63
64-66 45 68-72
Stanley
75

73

75

93

5-12

15 20

WYOMING

Payette River
21 Boise River
Nampa
39-44
37 84 20
38 26 27
26
Boise

Snake River

Arco
20 26

Idaho
Falls

Teton River

13-15

4

3

26

Blackfoot
Pocatello
16-17

Blackfoot River

Bear River

25, 28
93
24
Twin Falls 19-22
29-31

18

86

15

OREGON

Bruneau River

84

1-2

23

NEVADA

UTAH

Acknowledgments

Doling out thank-yous for help with a big project is always a challenge. There are always more owed than it's possible to give. With Paddling Idaho several rise to the surface. Thank you to my parents for introducing me to rivers when I was a kid. The time I spent on the rivers and lakes of central Pennsylvania helped mold the person I am today.

There have been dozens of paddling friends over the years to whom I'm deeply indebted, but I've probably explored the most with Sean Flynn, Sam Parker, and the late Andrew Post. Thank you for your friendship and the hours, days, and weeks spent on Idaho's unparalleled rivers and creeks.

Thanks are also due to the paddling friends and acquaintances who have both provided write-ups for this book and reviewed various parts of it. Todd Hoffman in particular helped make sure that north Idaho whitewater is fairly represented. More of his work is available online at northidahorivers.com. Also thanks to Mike Copeland, whose adventurous spirit revived a modern-day classic kayak run at Succor Creek State Park. The description of that run in this book is his. Also, importantly, thanks to the authors of Idaho's existing guidebooks. You have been my guides.

Further thanks to Mark Lindemer and David Olson for reviewing various parts of this book—and sharing some river miles with me.

Last but not least, thanks to my wife, Wendy, for joining me on numerous adventures, as well as for putting up with the hundreds of hours when I vanished to pore over maps and punch at the keyboard to compile this book.

Introduction

Paddling is a way of life in Idaho. The state oozes with huge, unspoiled watersheds full of gentle headwaters streams and challenging, roiling whitewater. Rafts, kayaks, and canoes are as common on or behind the cars coursing Idaho's highways as camp trailers and roof-top carriers. Increasingly there are touring kayaks and stand-up paddleboards plying Idaho's waterways and lakes—and highways—as well.

"With apologies to the potato," writes Boise journalist and whitewater kayaker Joe Carberry, "Idaho is arguably most famous for its rivers."

Idaho has more than 100,000 miles of rivers and streams, with more than 3,100 miles of whitewater suitable for rafting, kayaking, and canoeing. Idaho also has four of the original eight rivers protected in 1968 with passage of the Wild and Scenic Rivers Act. Nearly forty years later those four rivers—and other Idaho rivers that have been designated since—are still some of the best and most prized Wild and Scenic Rivers in the nation.

Idaho is blessed with 35 million acres of public land, which is more than 65 percent of the state's 53 million total acres. It has 4.8 million acres of congressionally designated wilderness areas where motorized and mechanized travel is not allowed. Several of Idaho's largest watersheds are almost completely within designated wilderness areas, meaning paddlers traveling to and through these places are experiencing some of the most remote and pristine country in the lower forty-eight United States.

It's easy to get away from roads, trails, and people on the rivers of Idaho, where there are 35 million acres of public land. The South Fork of the Boise is one of the rivers where you can get away from it all as a day trip.

All of this uniquely wild whitewater and wilderness has forged a unique pedestal for Idaho among the nation's paddling destinations. Idaho has wild rivers, but it also has very big, steep rivers. At the apex of spring runoff many can be very challenging. These rivers have forged high-level paddlers who have embarked upon successful expeditions and first descents around the globe. In the paddling world, Idaho isn't just on the map; in many ways it's at the center of the map.

The legendary Middle Fork of the Salmon, Selway, and Main Salmon Rivers are among the most sought-after wilderness river trips in the nation—exceeded only by a trip on the Colorado River through the Grand Canyon. The North Fork of the Payette's 15 miles of Class V is one of the country's most popular and demanding expert-level runs. And the scenic glacial lakes of the Sawtooth Valley of central Idaho draw visitors seeking reflective calm and staggering mountain views. And that's really just a tiny smattering of what Idaho has to offer.

Idaho's official moniker is The Gem State, but it could just as easily be The River State, The Paddling State or, as a prior guidebook coined it, The Whitewater State. It is unmatched in its quality and quantity of big, beautiful rivers and scenic mountain lakes that are waiting for paddlers of all abilities to dip a paddle, take a stroke, and start exploring.

Safety

For all the adventure, camaraderie, and unique experiences that rivers and lakes provide, none of us belong there if we aren't prepared. Safety is the number-one consideration for any paddler, and paddlers need to take responsibility to ensure the safety of themselves and those with whom they're paddling.

Canoeing, kayaking, rafting, and other paddle sports have inherent dangers. Rivers are dynamic environments where conditions can change, and rapidly. Weather, water levels, and rivers and lakes themselves may change. Fundamentals include checking the weather forecast, wearing proper paddling gear, taking along safety and first-aid equipment, and setting an estimated takeout time and letting someone know where you'll be. All paddlers should know basic first aid. All paddlers should know—and practice—whitewater rescue techniques. Better yet, take a river rescue course.

Additionally, paddlers assume responsibility for their knowledge about a particular river or

The Snake River is the primary artery into which the majority of Idaho's rivers flow. Auger Falls is an infrequently paddled whitewater section downstream from Perrine Bridge in Twin Falls.

Rental gear dries at picturesque Redfish Lake, near the headwaters of the Salmon River.

lake. This guide will help with that, but it cannot offer all of the information there is to know about a particular stream, rapid, or lake. As just one example, the summer of 2015 was a hot, dry year in Idaho, and wildfires consumed tens of thousands of acres of Idaho's forests. The denuded mountainsides will likely give way when fall and winter precipitation come and could form new rapids where before there were none.

In the words of kayaking instructor Gordon Grant in the foreword of *River Rescue* (third edition): "We can't entirely eliminate risk from the sport of running whitewater rivers and streams. But we can intelligently manage the risks we take, and the focus of that risk management means a sharpening of perceptions that brings greater awareness, pleasure, and—yes—safety to our experiences out there."

Proper preparation and making smart decisions will prevent most accidents, but paddlers must be prepared to deal with accidents if they do occur. Following is a basic safety checklist for all paddlers to follow:

When the surf's up in southern Idaho, it's time to hike to the Bliss wave.

- Be prepared for the weather: Know what is forecast for the day or week of your paddle.

- Water levels: Check the water level of your intended run before putting on, and be sure the current level is within the recommended flow range.

- Bring proper clothing and equipment: Always wear a properly fitted personal flotation device and wear appropriate clothing layers to stay warm in wet and cold conditions. At least one first-aid kit is recommended within each group.

- Paddle with partners: There is safety in numbers. Do your best to never paddle alone.

- Let others know your plan: Relay the day's paddling plan to others outside the paddling group who will know when and where to look for you if you don't arrive when expected.

- Be prepared: Prepare for the worst by taking extra clothing, a first-aid kit, and obtaining river rescue training.

- Know your capabilities: Be honest about your skill level, and always paddle within your abilities.

- Know and understand river difficulty ratings: Many rivers increase in difficulty as flows increase, and some of Idaho's rivers have enormous windows in which they're runnable. Know how increased flows affect the particular run you're attempting before you put on the water. Following are the standard river difficulty ratings, which are referenced extensively in this book:

    - Class I: Easy. Flat water or moving water with easy, small waves, if any. Little to no maneuvering required. No obstructions.

    - Class II: Medium. Easy rapids with a few small obstructions that are easily avoidable. Increased water speed. Clear routes downstream.

    - Class III: Difficult. Numerous rapids with larger irregular waves requiring more precise maneuvering between obstacles. Increased water speed. More obstructed routes may require scouting.

    - Class IV: Very difficult. Longer more powerful rapids with large waves between large rocks and other obstacles. Very obstructed route. High skill level with scouting is highly recommended.

    - Class V: Extremely difficult. Long, violent rapids that drop steeply with extremely fast current. Complex route-finding required between potentially hazardous features. Extensive experience and skill recommended. Scouting is mandatory.

    - Class VI: Unrunnable.

Flows

Each river run outlined in this guide has a recommended flow range coupled with the river difficulty rating. In some cases multiple ranges are offered. Sections of rivers can be paddled outside recommended flow ranges, but you risk a lower-quality paddle if the water is too low or one that's more difficult—and potentially dangerous—if the water level is higher than the recommended flow. Just one example is the Lower Salmon, Canyons run. At recommended flows it is a relatively mellow Class II and III whitewater run, but at high water it forms a very big Class V rapid.

In order to stay within a section of river that matches your difficulty level, check the flow of the section as close as possible to the time and day you are planning to paddle. Use the water level resources provided in the guide to check the most current flows. Then reference the current flow with the recommended flow range for the section you are planning to paddle. This will give you an informed idea as to what to expect regarding the character and difficulty of that section prior to putting in. Doing your homework before paddling is an important part of ensuring a safe and enjoyable trip on the water.

There is a distinct season to most of the paddling in Idaho. Generally many of Idaho's rivers tend to increase in flow in April and May, peaking within a week or so of Memorial Day, and drop to low flows by mid-summer. The obvious exceptions to this are north Idaho and southwest Idaho runs, which tend to peak earlier.

Also note that many of the rivers outlined in this guide are controlled by dams and do not follow the natural seasonal runoff cycle. It's important to verify your

The South Fork of the Clearwater is raucous at high water. This is the South Fork at 6,000 cfs.

Staircase on the South Fork Payette at 12,000 cfs

actual dam releases and flows if you intend to paddle these rivers. The operations of dams will ultimately determine the true season of the river's run, as well as the true flow range from low to high years.

Regulations

Idaho's huge diversity of rivers flows through lands that are also diversely managed. More than 65 percent of Idaho consists of publicly owned land administered primarily by the USDA Forest Service and Bureau of Land Management, and in many locations those agencies require permits to access and camp on a given river. Other areas are managed by the State of Idaho.

Specific regulations vary. For example, to paddle the Bruneau River in southwest Idaho, a self-issue permit is required and administered by the Bureau of Land Management. To paddle the Selway, Snake, Salmon, or Middle Fork of the Salmon River, paddlers must enter a forest service lottery, called the Four Rivers Lottery. Only those who win the lottery are issued permits, and each river has different specific regulations that relate to its permit season. Check recreation.gov or call (877) 444-6777 for more information about the Four Rivers Lottery, but mark your calendars for the months of December and January, when paddlers must apply.

Many of Idaho's rivers also flow through areas of abundant private property. While the State of Idaho, which manages rivers and water resources, does not restrict paddling on navigable rivers through private land, it is incumbent on paddlers to respect private property rights. Areas below the mean high water mark are open to public

When considering where to paddle, make sure to choose runs that are within your ability.

access. That means scouting and portaging is okay; walking across a lawn to put on or take off a river or lake is not.

Finally, in 2009 the Idaho Legislature passed a law requiring all motorized and nonmotorized boats in Idaho to carry a state-issued invasive species sticker. Proceeds from the stickers go to help prevent the introduction of zebra and quagga mussels, invasive species that can be transferred by motorboats, paddlers, and anglers. The annual stickers for nonmotorized vessels can be purchased at sporting goods stores throughout the state, as well as by contacting the Idaho Department of Parks and Recreation at (800) 247-6332 or parksandrecreation.idaho.gov.

How to Use This Guide

Paddling Idaho is organized by river basin. Paddlers planning to travel to a particular part of Idaho can reference this guide based on region and determine what paddling opportunities are in the area. Each region includes a range of runs of varying difficulty, from flatwater lakes to Class V whitewater. Make sure to choose runs that are within your ability.

Nearly all of Idaho's rivers are tributaries of the Snake River, which is the largest of the Columbia River's tributaries. This book starts at the top of the Snake River

Weather can be chilly any time of year, and paddlers must prepare accordingly. This image was taken on Memorial Day weekend.

Basin on the Idaho-Wyoming border and works downstream. Where a major tributary enters, that sub-basin is then described from its top down. This means that this guide flows much as Idaho's rivers do, but it also roughly translates into a southeast to northwest migration of descriptions.

Each region is introduced with an overview of paddling, history, geology, and additional information about the area. Ensuing sub-basins also include overviews. Then each river segment or lake includes the following basic data:

Section map: A general map is included with each river description, or combination of river descriptions, to help paddlers get oriented in finding access points, as well as nearby landmarks and shuttle routes. Numbers on the overview map at the beginning of this book correspond to paddle numbers.

Section description: This describes a section's location and geographic location, its characteristics and paddling quality, and highlights the overall route. This description also may point out idiosyncrasies with flows and gauges, and additional information that doesn't easily fit into the quick reference materials.

Distance: A fairly accurate measurement of the section to be paddled, measured in miles.

Difficulty: The ideal skill level recommended for the section.

Craft: The recommended type of watercraft for the section.

Approximate paddling time: A range of time measured in hours it should take to paddle a section.

Flows: A range of flows at which the section can be paddled, measured in cubic feet per second (cfs). Many of Idaho's rivers fluctuate dramatically during the spring season. Unless otherwise specified, difficulty ratings have been selected to reflect rivers at high flows, when they're more difficult. In general, expect a Class IV to paddle more like a Class IV- or Class III+ later in the season. Dam-controlled sections are also noted, providing paddlers with a heads-up that dam operations will ultimately determine flows.

Gauge: The recommended online gauge used to measure a run's flows. Visual gauges, when applicable, are described in section descriptions.

Season: A recommended time frame for the best paddling flows on the section. For certain basins in Idaho, seasons have been getting earlier than in the past due to warmer winters. That is reflected here.

Put-in: A recommended launch access to begin the described section.

Takeout: A recommended exit point to finish paddling the described section.

Shuttle: Detailed route descriptions for driving and completing the shuttle to access the takeout and put-in for the described trip.

Additional information: Additional paddling options and other information are sometimes mentioned. This may include a higher or lower access point or a means of conducting further research.

Depending on the popularity of your chosen run, put-ins and takeouts might be well developed or extremely primitive. This is the rather primitive put-in for Canyon Creek in east Idaho.

Giving Back

Some of Idaho's most prized rivers have been preserved because paddlers cared enough to get involved. In 1991 a ragtag group of kayakers and rafters came together to successfully defend the world-famous expert whitewater on the North Fork of the Payette from a hydroelectric developer. In 2004 paddlers organized in southeast Idaho and secured scheduled whitewater releases on the dam-controlled Black Canyon of the Bear River. More recently, in 2009, paddlers helped secure Wild and Scenic River designations for the Bruneau, Jarbidge, and Owyhee Rivers in southwest Idaho—the most recent additions to the Wild and Scenic Rivers System in Idaho. These are only three examples of many in which paddlers made a tangible and immediate difference for Idaho's rivers.

Idaho's rivers and glacial lakes are incredibly special places cherished by people the world over, but their health is the result of hard work by many over the course of decades. While he's not solely responsible, the late Senator Frank Church, a native Idahoan, was one of the key elected leaders who ushered through passage of the Wilderness Act in 1964. He was also the key architect and sponsor of the Wild and Scenic Rivers Act, which was signed into law in 1968 while simultaneously protecting four of Idaho's most prized wild rivers.

After construction of three dams in Hells Canyon on the Snake River wiped out anadromous fish, Church conceived the bill for the specific purpose of protecting Salmon River salmon from the impacts of dams that hadn't yet been built. His

Riley Creek, near the town of Hagerman, has a small waterfall that plunges into the Snake River.

original Salmon River Preservation Bill failed to gather political support in 1959 and 1960. In March 1965 he changed tack and introduced the National Wild Rivers Bill, which would become the Wild and Scenic Rivers Act.

"If we fail to give these rivers, which are assets of unique and incomparable value, statutory protection now, while there is still time, we shall have only ourselves to blame later, when time has run out," he told Congress.

Idaho's wild salmon are still in peril because of dams located outside of Idaho downstream, but Church's efforts succeeded at protecting the Salmon, Middle Fork of the Salmon, Selway, Lochsa, Snake, St. Joe, and other rivers. These Wild and Scenic Rivers are some of the most beautiful and popular paddling rivers in the United States.

Church was one of Idaho's most prominent river conservationists, but he was far from the first or last. Over the years a number of local and national groups have been formed to protect Idaho's cherished river resources and wealth of public lands. While some rivers and lakes popular with paddlers have been protected or restored, many others remain in peril. Please consult the list in the back of this book to get involved.

Map Legend

Symbol	Description	Symbol	Description
90	Interstate Highway	✕	Airport
93	US Highway	≋	Boat Ramp
21	State Highway	⏝	Bridge
	Forest/Local Road	■	Building/Point of Interest
524	Unpaved Road	▲	Campground
	Railroad	✪	Capital
	International Border	•—•	Gate
	State Border	▬	Lodging
	Small River/Creek	▲	Mountain Peak
	Body of Water	✿	Overlook/Viewpoint
	Waterfall	①	Paddle
	State Park	🏠	Ranger Station/Headquarters
	Access	○	Town/City

Bear River Basin

The Bear is the only river in Idaho that's not a tributary of the Columbia River and, ultimately, the Pacific Ocean. It flows north out of Utah, then west and south again, creating a giant horseshoe on a map. It flows back into Utah and the Great Salt Lake near Brigham City.

The Bear River is also the site of continued debate over a large water storage project that would completely inundate one of the river's most beautiful and popular canyons. Since the early 2000s a local irrigation company has been proposing to build a new dam at Oneida Narrows. If constructed, this new dam would flood the canyon and its popular floating and fishing opportunities.

The Bear River has a number of floatable sections, but the two most popular are the Black Canyon whitewater run and the more mellow Oneida Narrows.

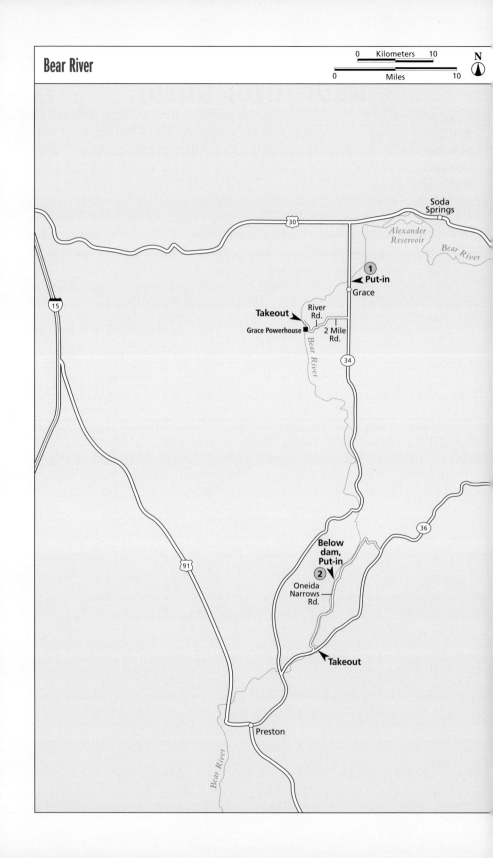

Bear River

0 Kilometers 10
0 Miles 10

N

Soda Springs

30

Alexander Reservoir

Bear River

15

Put-in 1

Grace

Takeout
River Rd.

Grace Powerhouse

2 Mile Rd.

Bear River

34

36

Below dam, Put-in 2

Oneida Narrows Rd.

Takeout

91

Preston

Bear River

1 Bear River, Black Canyon

Distance: 9.3 miles
Difficulty: Class IV–V
Craft: Kayak, raft
Approximate paddling time: 3–5 hours
Flows: 750–1,500 cfs (**Gauge:** Check pacificorp.com or call (800) 574-1501 for the utility's flow line.)
Season: Apr, May, June (dependent on dam releases)
Put-in: North Main Street, Grace, Idaho (42.585590, -111.729898)
Takeout: Grace Powerhouse (42.5436585, -111.7974035)

Shuttle: To reach the takeout from Grace, drive south on ID 34 (Main Street in Grace) for 2 miles and turn west onto 2 Mile Road. Go 1.5 miles and turn south on River Road. Take River Road 1.2 miles and turn right (west) onto Grace Power Plant Road. Go 1 mile to the power plant and turn right to go upriver 0.5 mile to the takeout. To reach the put-in, return to the city of Grace. The put-in is at the north end of town on the upstream side of the ID 34 bridge.

The Bear River cuts through a scenic basalt canyon below Grace Dam. Barring huge spring runoff that pressures dam managers into releasing lots of water, this challenging Class IV–V stretch generally runs at up to 1,500 cfs. Flows are completely controlled by Grace Dam, but spring releases are scheduled each year from April through June and run from 10 a.m. to 4 p.m. Check pacificorp.com for flow information. Generally releases are 900 cfs.

After putting on the river in the town of Grace, a mile of mellow floating leads to two Class III drops and then Grace Falls, a Class IV–V. Grace Falls consists of three ledges, the last dropping about 10 feet.

At about mile 4.5 some houses come into view on the river-right canyon rim as the river turns hard to the left. This signifies the start of Boo-Boo Rapid, a long Class V. It starts with a short Class III drop, so don't be lulled into complacence by the easy rapids above. From Boo-Boo to the takeout it's easy floating with some fun play opportunities.

2 Bear River, Oneida Narrows

Distance: 6.3 miles
Difficulty: Class II
Craft: Canoe, kayak, raft
Approximate paddling time: 3-5 hours
Flows: 500–1,800 cfs (**Gauge:** Check pacificorp.com or call (800) 574-1501 for the utility's flow line.)
Season: Apr, May, June (dependent on dam releases)
Put-in: Below Oneida Narrows Dam (42.263907, -111.752428)

Takeout: ID 36 bridge at Mink Creek (42.193175, -111.778349)
Shuttle: From Preston take ID 34/36 north 4.7 miles and turn east, staying on ID 36. Go 3.4 miles to the Bear River bridge. There's a dirt pulloff on the south side of the highway near Mink Creek. To get to the put-in, return on ID 36 0.5 mile to the west and turn north on the Oneida Narrows Bear River Road. Go 6.1 miles and turn into the dirt parking area just upstream of the bridge.

Oneida Narrows is a beautiful canyon and one of the most popular sections of the Bear River for a variety of recreational pursuits. The river is mellow, the scenery worthwhile, and the trout fishing excellent.

From the put-in it's mostly a combination of swift and calm water for a few miles. The bridge at mile 2.7 signifies the start of a mile of swift Class II water. There's a clearly defined Class II rapid created by an irrigation diversion at mile 4.5 and another at mile 5.6 beneath the irrigation pipe suspended above the river. The takeout is on river-left at Mink Creek above or below the ID 36 bridge. Please be respectful of private property in this area.

Oneida Narrows would be completely inundated by a reservoir if current plans to build the Oneida Narrows Dam come to fruition.

Oneida Narrows is easily visible from the nearby hills. PHOTO BY KEVIN LEWIS

Upper Snake River Basin, Eastern Idaho

At 1,038 miles, the Snake River is the longest and largest of the Columbia River's tributaries and threads a diverse landscape including three states, two national parks, several mountain resorts, agricultural communities, blue-collar cities, huge basalt canyons, and the Palouse hills of eastern Washington. It also boasts excellent whitewater and flatwater paddling.

The Snake originates in Yellowstone National Park at 9,500 feet and meanders south past the picturesque Tetons and through Jackson, Wyoming, before wending west into the basalt canyons of southern Idaho.

The upper Snake River Basin, which for the purposes of this guide ends at Lake Walcott near the southern Idaho town of Burley, drains southern and western portions of Yellowstone National Park and all of the Grand Tetons. In addition to its excellent paddling, the upper Snake basin boasts some of the West's most prolific fly fishing. The upper Snake's collection basin drains more than 13,500 square miles.

The upper Snake has several key tributaries, but most notable in Idaho is the Henry's Fork of the Snake, which is fed by several additional outstanding rivers with high-quality fishing and paddling opportunities.

The Snake is a big, roiling river that carries considerable runoff from the mountains of northwest Wyoming and eastern Idaho. Its natural cycles in the upper basin have been tamed by dams, but it still generally boasts flows in the upper basin of between 2,000 and 20,000 cfs, with peak flows approaching 40,000 cfs, depending on runoff and irrigation cycles.

3 | Snake River, Alpine Canyon

Distance: 7.4 miles
Difficulty: Class III (IV above 12,000 cfs)
Craft: Kayak, raft
Approximate paddling time: 3 hours
Flows: 1,000–20,000 cfs (**Gauge:** USGS, Snake River near Alpine)
Season: Mar–Nov
Put-in: West Table (43.204673, -110.821309)

Takeout: Sheep Gulch (43.185971, -110.955001)
Shuttle: To reach the takeout from Alpine, a town on the Idaho-Wyoming border, drive 3.3 miles upriver (east) on US 26 to Sheep Gulch. To reach the put-in, return to US 26 and drive 7.5 miles upriver to Sheep Gulch. The Sheep Gulch put-in is also 25 miles south/southwest from Jackson on US 26.

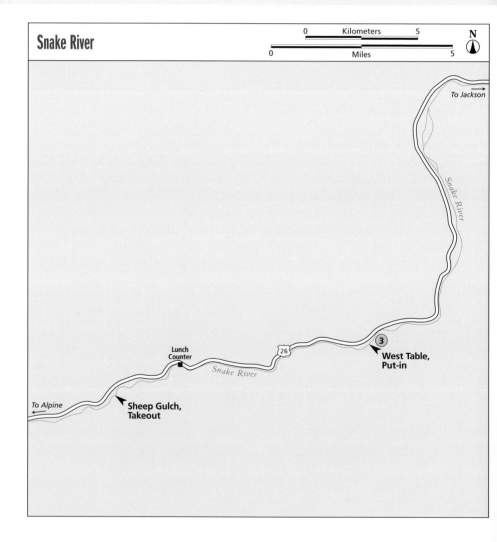

Alpine Canyon is on the Wyoming side of the Idaho-Wyoming border, but it's an extremely popular stretch of classic western whitewater. With fun, straightforward rapids and outstanding play boating in a conifer-enshrouded gorge, Alpine Canyon's sterling reputation is well earned among western boaters.

In the spring at flows above 10,000 cfs, the run takes on Class IV character, but in the summer the run provides consistent and enjoyable Class III paddling. Notable Class III rapids are Double D at mile 1.8, Big Kahuna at mile 5.1, Lunch Counter at mile 5.2, Rope at mile 5.7, Champaign at mile 6.3, and Cottonwood at mile 6.8. At levels over 12,000 cfs a dangerous hole, Three Oar Deal, forms at mile 2.7. Stay right to avoid it.

There are a number of well-known surf waves in Alpine Canyon, but the big wave at the top of Lunch Counter is widely revered as one of the best surf spots in the region. It's in at levels ranging from 6,000 to 13,000 cfs.

4 Snake River, South Fork of the Snake Canyon

Distance: 24 miles
Difficulty: Class II
Craft: Kayak, raft, canoe, drift boat
Approximate paddling time: 2 days
Flows: 1,500–20,000 cfs (**Gauge:** USGS, Snake River near Irwin)
Season: Mar–Nov
Put-in: Connant Boat Ramp (43.463506, -111.427311)
Takeout: Byington Boat Ramp (43.622362, -111.665442)

Shuttle: To reach the takeout turn north on 175 E off of US 26 and drive 1.1 miles. Then turn right (east) on Ririe Highway and follow it 1 mile to Byington Boat Ramp. To reach the put-in, return to US 26 and turn left (east). Drive 17.4 miles to South Fork Lodge. Turn left and pass the lodge, and the boat ramp will be visible straight ahead.

For more information, and in particular to plan different trip options, go to blm.gov and type "South Fork of the Snake" in the search box.

The South Fork of the Snake boasts extremely scenic flatwater paddling and legendary tailwater fly fishing. For the 64 miles below Palisades Dam until the Snake merges with the Henry's Fork, the river boasts 4,000 fish per mile, making it one of the most productive fisheries in the country.

Since 1985 the South Fork of the Snake has been eligible for inclusion in the nation's Wild and Scenic Rivers System. It features the largest riparian cottonwood forest in the West and is home to 126 bird species, including twenty-one raptors, earning it a "National Important Bird Area" designation.

Paddlers and anglers have divided the South Fork into four sections, each accessible via developed boat ramps. The third, a 24-mile stretch beginning at Conant Boat Ramp, is called the Canyon and boasts sixteen Bureau of Land Management and national forest campgrounds, making this run an excellent option for paddlers organizing an overnight float. Campsites are free via self-issued permits and are first-come, first-served. Fire pans and human waste disposal are required. The takeout at Byington includes waste disposal facilities.

The South Fork Canyon has spectacular conifer-speckled walls that loom hundreds of feet straight above the river and feels remote despite being only a few hundred feet below nearby cultivated fields. The river is calm, but its powerful currents can be deceptive.

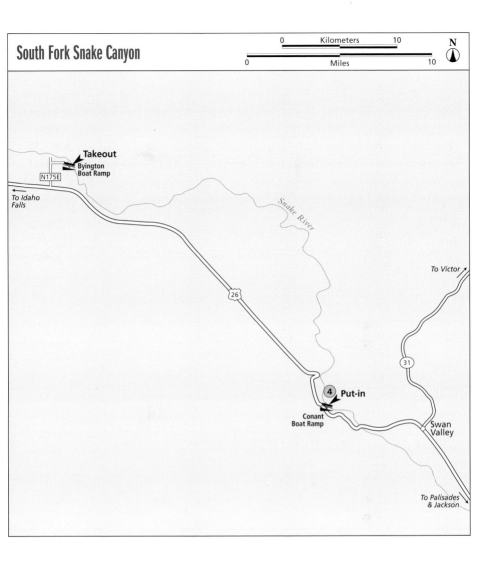

South Fork Snake Canyon

0 Kilometers 10

0 Miles 10

N

Takeout
Byington
Boat Ramp

N175E

To Idaho
Falls

Snake River

26

To Victor

31

4 Put-in

Conant
Boat Ramp

Swan
Valley

To Palisades
& Jackson

Henry's Fork of the Snake

The 127-mile Henry's Fork descends from the Continental Divide near the intersection of the Idaho, Wyoming, and Montana borders, an area that's also the northwest corner of Yellowstone National Park. The upper reaches of the Henry's Fork emerge from springs on the edge of the Island Park Caldera, which stretches east into the center of Yellowstone. In other words, the upper Henry's Fork is very similar to Yellowstone geologically, biologically, and hydrologically. Boaters and campers need to be prepared for potential encounters with elk, moose, black bears, and grizzly bears.

There are at least a dozen paddling options in the Island Park area, ranging from placid streams flowing through enchanted woodlands to hair-raising Class V in the gorge below the caldera's rim.

The Henry's Fork originates at Big Springs, which discharges 120 million gallons into the river each day, making it one of the largest freshwater springs in the country. The river then works south across a high plateau and passes through Island Park Reservoir before descending through a small gorge.

The river emerges from the gorge at Last Chance and meanders across a broad, flat, stunningly beautiful meadow, then picks up steam as it plummets over the edge

The Henry's Fork of the Snake is a picture postcard with a diversity of paddling options.

of the Island Park Caldera, roaring through increasingly difficult rapids and then over 114-foot Upper Mesa Falls and 65-foot Lower Mesa Falls. The two-tiered river-left line at Lower Mesa Falls is a popular park-and-huck kayaking spot. If such expert fare is your cup of tea, you won't need this guide to figure it out.

The Henry's Fork emerges on the Snake River Plain near Ashton and flows south to join the Snake River near Rexburg. Named for Andrew Henry, a fur trapper who built Fort Henry near what is now St. Anthony, Idaho, the Henry's Fork is renowned for its blue-ribbon trout fishery, spectacular waterfalls, and truly incredible flatwater paddling.

The upper Henry's Fork is part of the Greater Yellowstone ecosystem. Paddlers need to be on the lookout for black and grizzly bears and moose.

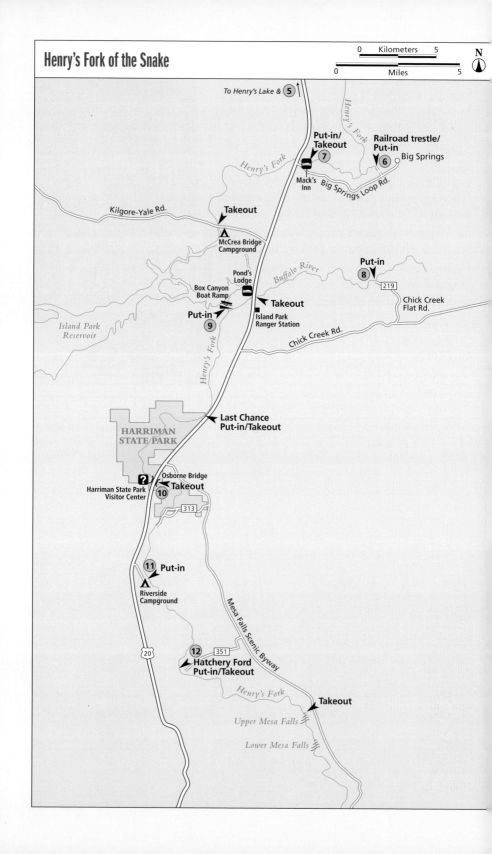

Henry's Fork of the Snake

5 Henry's Lake

Distance: 1–8 miles
Difficulty: Flat water
Craft: Canoe, kayak
Approximate paddling time: 1–5 hours
Season: May, June, July, Aug, Sept, Oct
Launch site: Henry's Lake State Park boat ramp (44.619928, -111.373816)

Access: From West Yellowstone drive 14.5 miles east-southeast on US 20. Turn right (west) onto Henry's Lake State Park Road and drive 1 mile to the park boundary and 2 miles to the boat ramp.

Additional information: parksandrecreation .idaho.gov/parks/henrys-lake

Henry's Lake is nestled in the northeast corner of southern Idaho, on the borders of Wyoming and Montana. With abundant rainbow, cutthroat, brook, and cut-bow hybrid trout, the lake is considered one of the finest trout fisheries in the West. It's estimated that Henry's Lake has more than a million big, catchable trout.

While it's at the headwaters of an incredibly beautiful river, Henry's Lake in and of itself isn't all that stunning. It's in a wide, broad valley and surrounded by high-desert vegetation. It's also known to produce significant whitecaps when the wind picks up, which can happen quickly.

Flatwater paddlers can launch from one of the lake's four boat ramps, but access at the 585-acre Henry's Lake State Park may help offer protection from the wind if it picks up.

Henry's Lake is in a wide-open valley where afternoon winds can whip the water into whitecaps.

From the state park boat ramp, try paddling the shoreline clockwise, which will take you around a prominent point and into Henry's Lake Outlet, where you can avoid the open water of the main lake and still enjoy views of 10,237-foot Black Mountain to the north. Henry's Lake is shallow, about 25 feet at its deepest, so it can become overrun with moss and reeds during summer months.

Paddling is popular at Henry's Lake, particularly among anglers.

6 Henry's Fork, Big Springs National Water Trail

Distance: 3.6 miles
Difficulty: Class I
Craft: Canoe, kayak, raft
Approximate paddling time: 1.5–3 hours
Flows: 186–300 cfs (the spring emits an estimated 186 cfs)
Season: May–Oct
Put-in: Water Trail put-in at old trestle (44.497026, -111.271468)
Takeout: Water Trail takeout (44.500816, -111.325954)

Shuttle: To reach the takeout from Mack's Inn, drive north across the bridge and take the first right. Drive 0.4 mile to a pullout and dirt boat ramp on the right. It's labeled "Day Use Area." To reach the put-in return to Mack's Inn and go south on US 20 for a few hundred feet. Take Big Springs Loop Road east for 3.9 miles and turn north, following signs for the Big Springs Water Trail Launch Site. The old Yellowstone Branch Line trestle, Water Trail parking, and a small wood dock are 2,000 feet ahead.

The Big Springs National Water Trail may be the most popular flatwater day trip in eastern Idaho. The run is scenic and accessible, and has consistent flows with a year-round water temperature of 52°F. For open canoeists and recreational kayakers, it's a beautiful, accessible, and gentle float.

The well-developed access to the Big Springs National Water Trail starts at an old railroad trestle.

Canoeing is popular along the upper Henry's Fork.

From the put-in at the old railroad trestle the river meanders gently among a beautiful conifer forest. Elk, moose, deer, bald eagles, and other wildlife are common. The spring's glassy-clear water and cobbled riverbed also make this section ideal for rearing big trout. Leave your fishing pole at home, though. No fishing is allowed between the spring and Henry's Lake Outlet. The forest opens into a meadow toward the takeout, and homes begin to crowd the riverbank.

As of this writing, Mack's Inn near the takeout offers canoe and kayak rentals, as well as a shuttle. Call (208) 558-7272 for details. There's also a forest service campground at Big Springs.

7 Henry's Fork, Coffee Pot

Distance: 6 miles
Difficulty: Class III
Craft: Kayak, whitewater canoe, raft
Approximate paddling time: 2–4 hours
Flows: 500–1,000 cfs (**Gauge:** USGS, Henry's Fork below Coffee Pot Rapids)
Season: May, June, July

Put-in: Mack's Inn (44.500669, -111.336485)
Takeout: McCrea Bridge Campground (44.4621036, -111.4020694)
Shuttle: To reach the takeout from Mack's Inn, go 3.5 miles south on US 20 to Kilgore-Yale Road. Then go west 2 miles to the McCrea Bridge Campground.

For 6 miles below Mack's Inn, the Henry's Fork is secluded and, for the most part, flat water. The exception is Coffee Pot Rapid at mile 3.2. Coffee Pot is 0.5 mile of pool-drop Class III whitewater in a scenic gorge. Keep your eyes peeled for logs.

After the rapid it's another 2.5 miles to the takeout on river-left, where there's a boat ramp at the McCrea Bridge Campground.

An extra word of caution needs to be issued here. Because of the popularity of flatwater paddling on Big Springs upstream, this run can seem inviting to recreational paddlers who want to extend their trips or who are looking for an additional challenge. It is not suitable for either of these purposes and has been the location of several unfortunate and unnecessary fatalities.

Recreational boaters who want to pursue more difficult water in the area should visit the Harriman State Park or Box Canyon runs farther downstream.

8 Buffalo River

Distance: 6.2 miles
Difficulty: Class I
Craft: Canoe, kayak
Approximate paddling time: 3-5 hours
Flows: 200-300 cfs (**Gauge:** None)
Season: June-Sept (wait for high water to recede)
Put-in: FR 219 (44.432832, -111.273743)
Takeout: US 20 bridge (44.422433, -111.371174)

Shuttle: The takeout is on the north side of the Buffalo River bridge, which is just north of the Island Park Ranger Station and south of Pond's Lodge on US 20. To reach the put-in, drive south on US 20 2.1 miles and turn left on Chick Creek Road. Drive 6.7 miles east to the intersection with Chick Creek Flat Road (FR 292). Turn left (north) and go 1.3 miles to FR 219. Follow FR 219 on a deeply rutted road (high-clearance vehicle needed) about a mile to a small dirt parking area and the put-in.

Buffalo River may be the best canoe trip in Idaho—or anywhere, for that matter. The paddle starts on a small creek you can almost jump across. Only 100 feet downstream it picks up another spring and grows slightly. By the takeout at US 20 it's a 100-foot-wide, glassy-calm river.

Buffalo River begins as a spring-fed creek you can practically jump across.

The water is mellow and crystal clear, and the river flows through an enchanting and secluded forest for the first two-thirds of the trip. Though it's easy floating, there's a constant danger of river-wide logs. There's also a barbwire fence you'll have to deal with about halfway through the trip. The water is calm and shallow, so getting out of your boat to pass it under the fence is easy and safe. The fence is just downstream from the old Yellowstone Branch Line railroad bridge.

Buffalo River gradually expands into a beautiful, wide spring-fed river.

9 | Henry's Fork, Box Canyon

Distance: 4 miles
Difficulty: Class II
Craft: Kayak, canoe, raft
Approximate paddling time: 2–4 hours
Flows: 1,000–2,000 cfs (**Gauge:** USGS, Henry's Fork near Island Park)
Season: May, June, July, Aug
Put-in: Box Canyon Boat Ramp below Island Park Dam (44.416281, -111.395060)
Takeout: Last Chance Boat Ramp (44.371029, -111.402584)

Shuttle: The takeout is in Last Chance, 22.5 miles from Ashton via US 20 and 10 miles south of Mack's Inn in Island Park. Get on Old Highway 191 and drive 0.4 mile upriver to a dirt parking area and small boat ramp. To reach the put-in take US 20 toward Island Park 4.5 miles and turn left (west) after passing Pond's Lodge. After a mile, turn left on the raised roadbed and travel another 0.5 mile to the dam. Descend a steep and winding S-curve road to the base of the dam and the put-in on river-left.

Box Canyon is a short, scenic, and playful float that's probably better known for its trout fishing than its whitewater. From the put-in below Island Park Dam, the river winds through a picturesque mini-gorge before rejoining the highway at Last Chance.

This run is a good choice for an array of craft including canoes, kayaks, drift boats, and rafts. The swift current and its riffles are continuous, yet pose little danger or difficulty.

The swift current and continuous riffles of Box Canyon on the Henry's Fork are a good choice for a variety of paddlers.

10 Henry's Fork, Harriman State Park

Distance: 6.5 miles
Difficulty: Class II-
Craft: Kayak, canoe, raft, drift boat
Approximate paddling time: 3–5 hours
Flows: 500–2,000 cfs (**Gauge:** USGS, Henry's Fork near Island Park)
Season: May–Oct
Put-in: Last Chance Boat Ramp (44.371029, -111.402584)
Takeout: Osborne Bridge (44.321700, -111.449563)
Alternate takeout: Wood Road (44.306051, -111.441902)

Shuttle: The takeout at Osborne Bridge is just off US 20, 3.7 miles south of Last Chance. The alternate takeout is off the Mesa Falls Scenic Byway. From the intersection with US 20, take the byway 2.5 miles and turn right, immediately after the second cattle guard. Go 1.6 miles to a large dirt parking and staging area beside the Henry's Fork. To reach the put-in return to US 20 and go 3.7 miles to Last Chance. The put-in is 0.4 mile up Old Highway 191, which serves as a frontage road along the river.

From Last Chance to Osborne Bridge below Harriman State Park, the Henry's Fork winds through a big, broad, beautiful meadow with views of timber-covered mountains and ample opportunities to see wildlife including numerous bird species.

The Henry's Fork in this stretch is very calm except for two Class II rapids, one beneath an old bridge about 4 miles from the start and the second 0.25 mile before the takeout. This is also the most popular trout fishing reach in the area, so bring your fly rod and otherwise be courteous to anglers by giving them wide berth.

Harriman State Park is a prolific wildlife refuge where moose, elk, sandhill cranes, and trumpeter swans all thrive. The park, which is named for the family of Union Pacific Railroad tycoon Averell Harriman, was deeded to the State of Idaho by railroad investors in 1977. In its heyday as a ranch, guests included John Muir, who spent ten days there in 1923.

To add 2.5 to 3 miles of perfectly calm Class I flat water to this trip, continue downstream to Wood Road. There's good access and a dirt boat ramp 2.5 miles below Osborne Bridge on river-left. Wood Road also parallels the river for another 0.5 mile if you haven't yet had enough.

11 Henry's Fork, Riverside to Hatchery Ford

Distance: 4.7 miles
Difficulty: Class III
Craft: Kayak, raft, canoe
Approximate paddling time: 2-4 hours
Flows: 1,000-3,000 cfs (**Gauge:** USGS, Henry's Fork near Ashton)
Season: June-Sept
Put-in: Riverside Campground (44.266295, -111.455195)
Takeout: Hatchery Ford (44.216912, -111.431526)

Shuttle: The takeout at Hatchery Ford is well signed from the Mesa Falls Scenic Byway (ID 47). The turn is 4.7 miles upstream from Upper Mesa Falls and 8.2 miles downstream from US 20. After 1,500 feet the road bears left, then after another 2,000 feet turn right. Follow the dirt road another 3 miles to the river. To get to the put-in, go back to ID 47 and head upstream. At US 20 turn left and go 4.1 miles. Turn left and descend to the river, where there's a parking area for boat access in the campground.

This is where the Henry's Fork starts to get down to business, and paddlers who haven't honed their skills on tougher water need to be cautious. "You're at the oars, working the whole way," remarked a local drift boat guide.

From Riverside Campground to Hatchery Ford, the Henry's Fork is continuous Class II and III whitewater best suited to rafts, kayaks, and whitewater canoes. It can be done in an open canoe, but should be attempted only by very accomplished canoeists. To keep things interesting, there are also a number of logs pinned to mid-river rocks in this reach.

Don't continue past Hatchery Ford unless you're in a hard-shell kayak and know what you're doing in it. The river below here is experts-only fare. (Read Sheep Falls description on page 23 for more information.)

12 Henry's Fork, Sheep Falls

Distance: 6.9 miles
Difficulty: Class V
Craft: Kayak
Approximate paddling time: 3–5 hours
Flows: 1,000–3,000 cfs (**Gauge:** USGS, Henry's Fork near Ashton)
Season: May, June, July, Aug
Put-in: Hatchery Ford (44.216912, -111.431526)
Takeout: Upper Mesa Falls (44.187852, -111.329322)

Shuttle: To reach the takeout from Ashton take the Mesa Falls Scenic Byway, ID 47, for 14.7 miles to Upper Mesa Falls, a fee area. Please scout the takeout before continuing to the put-in. To get to the put-in, continue on ID 47 toward Island Park for 4.7 miles. Turn left when you see a sign for Hatchery Ford. After 1,500 feet the road bears left, then after another 2,000 feet turn right. Follow the dirt road another 3 miles to the river. You'll know you're in the right spot when you see a sign warning of dangerous downstream waterfalls.

Though scenic and accessible, the Sheep Falls run needs to be taken seriously. There are three distinct Class V rapids, and the takeout is right at the lip of 114-foot Upper Mesa Falls. Miss the takeout, and it might be the last mistake you make.

With the hazards clear, it should be said that the Sheep Falls run goes through a beautiful canyon and mostly consists of Class II and III whitewater. The Class V rapids can also be portaged with relative ease.

Notable Class Vs are Sheep Falls at mile 2.7, a second rapid immediately below Sheep Falls at mile 2.8, and a third at mile 5. There's also a sticky Class IV ledge at mile 6.3 that can be run anywhere with a strong bow-up paddle stroke (or "boof") but is safest on river-left. The first and second Class V rapids can be scouted and portaged on the right. The third is easiest to scout from the left and is probably easier to portage on the right. Note that at low water of about 1,600 cfs and below, the hydraulic at the second Class V gets super sticky, and the rapid is usually portaged. At high water the third rapid feeds into an undercut on river-left.

Because the takeout is immediately atop Upper Mesa Falls, it is imperative that you scout it while setting up your shuttle. The final 200 or so feet before the falls are swift with scarce eddies; this is not the place to save a few footsteps. Your goal is to get out of the river upstream of the boardwalk near the falls and walk a primitive path downstream to the boardwalk, where tourists will no doubt want to take your picture.

Teton River Basin

The Teton River is home to one of Idaho's biggest blunders. On June 5, 1976, the US Bureau of Reclamation's 305-foot-tall Teton Dam failed as it was filling for the first time, resulting in a catastrophic flood that killed eleven people and 13,000 head of cattle. The remnants of the $40 million dam still stand today and serve as a cautionary tale.

The Teton River begins as a trickle near the town of Victor but quickly picks up flow as tributaries join from the Grand Tetons to the east and the Big Hole Mountains to the west. The upper reaches meander among potato fields and pastures. It's a beautiful spring creek with excellent fly fishing.

The lower Teton, called the Narrows, starts at Harrop Bridge on ID 33 and descends rapidly into a stunning gorge with expert-level whitewater. Below the confluence with Bitch Creek, rapids on the Teton were created by landslides that sloughed off the saturated canyon walls following Teton Dam's failure.

While a few of the Teton's tributaries can be paddled, the most notable are the Teton River itself and the tributary called Bitch Creek. Well-prepared groups of experts can also explore Canyon Creek by putting in at the ID 33 bridge and taking out at the old dam site on the Teton River, but it's a tight, swift, all-day expedition with ample wood, steep drops, and blind corners that can contain river-wide logs.

Packing up after a day on the water at what remains of Teton Dam

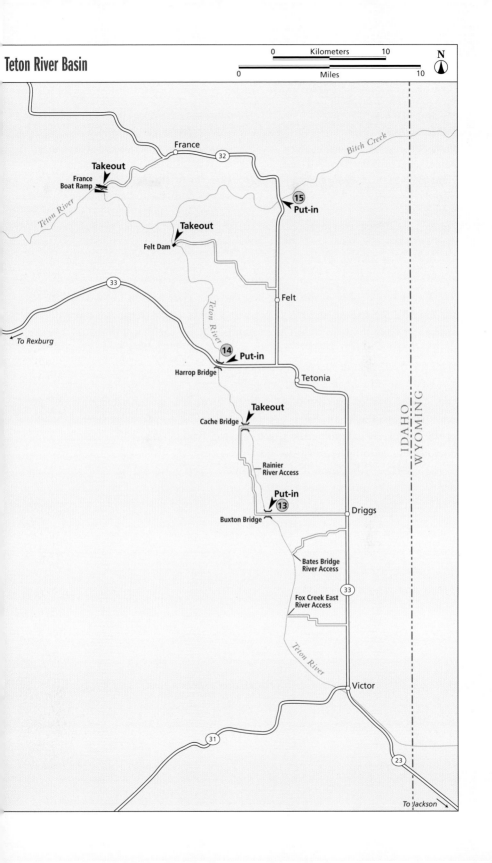

Teton River Basin

Kilometers
0   10

0   Miles   10

N

France

Bitch Creek

32

Takeout

France
Boat Ramp

Teton River

15 Put-in

Takeout

Felt Dam

Felt

33

Teton River

To Rexburg

14 Put-in

Harrop Bridge

Tetonia

Takeout

Cache Bridge

IDAHO WYOMING

Rainier
River Access

Put-in
13

Driggs

Buxton Bridge

Bates Bridge
River Access

33

Fox Creek East
River Access

Teton River

Victor

31

23

To Jackson

13 Teton River, Upper

Distance: 6.9 miles
Difficulty: Class I
Craft: Canoe, kayak, raft, drift boat
Approximate paddling time: 3-6 hours
Flows: 300-1,000 cfs (**Gauge:** Teton River near Driggs)
Season: July-Oct
Put-in: Buxton Bridge (43.723608, -111.187394)

Takeout: Cache Bridge (43.781304, -111.210049)
Shuttle: To get to the takeout drive north on ID 33 from Driggs for 4 miles and turn left (west) on Packsaddle Road. The river is 4.9 miles ahead. Access is on the south side of the bridge. (To locate the ID 33 bridge, please see the Teton River, ID 33 to Felt Power Plant put-in description.)

The upper Teton River is one of the best flatwater river trips in the West. It's an outstanding fishing stream, and has unparalleled views of the Teton Mountain Range. Every section of the Teton River, from its headwaters near Victor to the ID 33 bridge near Tetonia—a distance of 20.5 miles—is navigable Class I, and a number of roads cross the river, making access a breeze.

There are more than a half-dozen public access points on the upper Teton, so the river can be divided into five or six different floats. This stretch, from Buxton Bridge near Driggs to Cache Bridge, is 6.9 miles and affords some of the river's best views of the Tetons. By extending the trip to Harrop Bridge on ID 33, another 6.5 miles could be added to make an all-day float.

Below ID 33, the Teton River drops into a steep gorge and its character changes dramatically. Do not continue past ID 33 unless you're prepared for a Class V whitewater adventure.

14 Teton River, ID 33 to Felt Power Plant

Distance: 8.2 miles
Difficulty: Class IV–V
Craft: Kayak
Approximate paddling time: 4–6 hours
Flows: 500–2,000 cfs, optimal around 1,000 cfs (**Gauge:** USGS, Teton River near St. Anthony)
Season: Apr, May, June, July
Put-in: Harrop Bridge on ID 33 (43.825190, -111.232987)
Takeout: Felt Power Plant (43.907725, -111.284813)

Shuttle: To reach the takeout from Tetonia, follow ID 33 north for 5.5 miles and turn right on ID 32, heading toward Ashton. In 3 miles the highway crosses Badger Creek. A short distance farther is Power Plant Road. Turn left and follow the gravel road past several barns and houses until you arrive at the Felt Power Plant. To get to the put-in, return to ID 33 via ID 32 and turn right (east) at the T intersection. The bridge is 2.6 miles farther.

The Teton River gives boaters a great glimpse into the erosive power of rivers. It starts as a meandering stream in a broad meadow and gradually drops into a tight, constricted gorge with consistent, challenging whitewater.

The canyon walls start closing in at mile 1, and the whitewater starts at mile 4 with a Class II rock garden that leads into a Class IV–V jumble of rocks.

At most flows the river offers technical Class IV whitewater with one distinct Class V at Boulder Dam, mile 6.4. This difficult, rocky drop is easy to spot and can be scouted or portaged on river-left.

At high flows the Teton is a wild river with the ever-present danger of logjams. Things completely flatten out near Felt Power Plant, the suggested takeout. Get out river-right and hike up the trail to your car.

For a longer float you can continue to France Boat Ramp (see Bitch Creek takeout), but a long portage of the entire power plant diversion is recommended. This adds another 6 miles to the trip.

15 Bitch Creek, Canyon, ID 32 Bridge to France Boat Ramp

Distance: 13 miles
Difficulty: Class IV/V
Craft: Kayak
Approximate paddling time: 6–8 hours
Flows: 600–1,500 cfs (**Gauge:** None)
Season: May–July
Put-in: ID 32 bridge (43.936218, -111.178154)
Takeout: France Boat Ramp (43.947180, -111.351162)
Shuttle: To reach the takeout from Tetonia, follow ID 33 north and then west 1.6 miles, turn right on ID 32, and head toward Ashton 15.2 miles. Shortly after passing a Pillsbury grain silo, the road begins to curve right and go up a hill. Turn left on the gravel road before the hill. Drive west until the road forks. Stay left. Follow this fork into the canyon and over the crumbling boat ramp that serviced the short-lived reservoir. Follow the two-track road down to the river. To reach the put-in, return to ID 32. Park on the south side of the Bitch Creek bridge.

Bitch Creek flows through a secluded and beautiful canyon nestled amid rolling farmland on the west slope of the Tetons. At medium flows, it's mostly a swift run of Class IV eddy-hopping, blind corners, and the ever-present danger of logjams. At high water, above 800 cfs, it's a fast-paced Class V affair.

Bitch Creek is a steep, fun, continuous paddle.

Bitch Creek has two distinct Class V rapids: Driscoll's Drop a couple miles into the run and Roscoe's Rock about halfway through. Both are easy to scout or portage.

After the confluence with the Teton River at mile 8, the canyon yawns open a bit, and there are five more pool-drop rapids until the takeout at France Boat Ramp on river-right. The run is not recommended at low water.

Tricky currents form at the base of a Bitch Creek pour-over.

Blackfoot River Basin

The Blackfoot River flows northwest through a remote basalt canyon from its headwaters in the Caribou-Targhee National Forest. It courses 135 miles until it meets the Snake River in the town of Blackfoot.

The Blackfoot's spring runoff is captured by Blackfoot Reservoir, but summer irrigation releases keep it flowing long into the summer and early fall most years. While Blackfoot Reservoir can be paddled by canoe and other flatwater craft, it's not particularly scenic. The canyons downstream, conversely, are stunning examples of southern Idaho's array of incised basalt desert geology.

There is no online source for flow information, but you can call Blackfoot Water Users at (208) 238-0586 for the latest about dam releases.

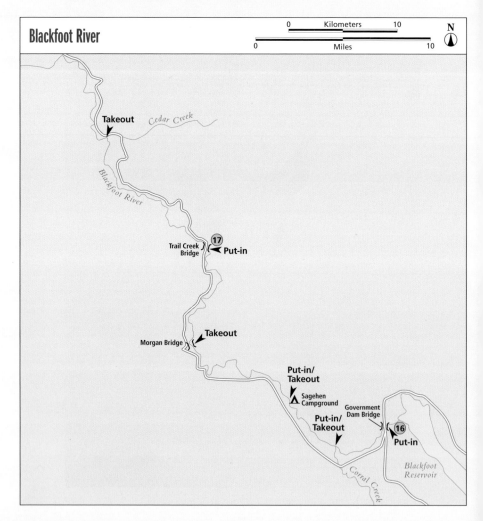

16 Blackfoot River, Upper

Distance: 15.6 miles
Difficulty: Class I–II
Craft: Canoe, kayak, raft
Approximate paddling time: 6–8 hours
Flows: 500–900 cfs (**Gauge:** Blackfoot Water Users, 208-238-0586)
Season: May, June, July, Aug, Sept (dam release dependent)
Put-in: Upper bridge on Government Dam Road (43.000999, -111.729683)
Takeout: Morgan Bridge (43.059755, -111.927173)
Shuttle: To reach the takeout from Blackfoot, take the Yellowstone Highway (US 91) 9.5 miles northeast and turn right (east) on Wolverine Road. Follow Wolverine Road 10.5 miles and turn right (south) on Blackfoot River Road. After 14 miles you'll hit Trail Creek Bridge where the road turns into Trail Creek Road, which you'll take 6.5 more miles to Paradise Road. Turn left on Paradise to find the takeout at Morgan Bridge. You can also access this area by taking exit 80 on I-15 and heading east. (Please consult a map.) To reach the put-in from Morgan Bridge, head upriver on Blackfoot Reservoir Road, which becomes Corral Creek Road, for 15 miles until you reach a T intersection. Turn left; the put-in is a little less than 0.5 mile ahead.

The upper Blackfoot has several floatable sections below Blackfoot Dam ranging from Class I to Class III. For the most part, they're mellow floats through a mildly scenic desert canyon with excellent odds of seeing wildlife.

Between Blackfoot Dam and Trail Creek Bridge, a distance of 23 miles, there are three good put-in and takeout options. This description covers the upper 15 miles of the run, which consists of Class I and II rapids.

The final section between Morgan Bridge and Trail Creek Bridge is a little tougher, with a 2-mile stretch of Class II–III rapids. If you're after mellow water, please don't float past Trail Creek Bridge. There's very challenging whitewater in a secluded canyon below (see Wolverine Canyon description).

17 Blackfoot River, Wolverine Canyon

Distance: 9.8 miles
Difficulty: Class V (VI)
Craft: Kayak
Approximate paddling time: 6–8 hours
Flows: 300–600 cfs (**Gauge:** Blackfoot Water Users, 208-238-0586)
Season: July, Aug, Sept (dam release dependent)
Put-in: Trail Creek Road Bridge (43.129324, -111.911043)
Takeout: Cedar Creek (plus 0.5-mile hike out of canyon) (43.210862, -112.002797)

Shuttle: To reach the takeout from Blackfoot, take the Yellowstone Highway (US 91) 9.5 miles northeast and turn right (east) on Wolverine Road. Follow Wolverine Road 10.5 miles and turn right (south) on Blackfoot River Road. Go 4.3 miles to Cedar Creek. The river won't be in sight, but this is where you'll reunite with your car after hiking out of the canyon via Cedar Creek. To reach the put-in, continue on Blackfoot River Road, staying right at intersections, for 9.7 miles to Trail Creek Road Bridge.

This run isn't for the faint of heart. It's steep, hazardous, and the riverbanks are almost completely encased in poison ivy. The secluded canyon also boasts abundant rattlesnakes with which you'll have to contend, because it can't be done without at least one portage and a healthy 0.5-mile, 200-vertical-foot hike out at the end of the day.

Teller Tube rapid is the first serious test paddlers face in Wolverine Canyon.
PHOTO COURTESY DAVID OLSON

Difficult rapids continue nonstop for a little more than 2 miles in Wolverine Canyon.
Photo courtesy David Olson

If you haven't been scared off yet, maybe Wolverine Canyon is the next adventure on your Idaho paddling bucket list. If that's the case, you're in for a treat. The Blackfoot is fed by summer releases from Blackfoot Reservoir, and its continuous Class IV and V rapids are a worthwhile challenge for well-prepared groups of expert boaters.

From the put-in at the bridge on Trail Creek Road, it's gentle floating for about 3 miles. Sit back, relax, and collect yourself while you watch the canyon walls close in. At about mile 3 a series of ledge drops give paddlers a small taste of what's to come. At about mile 4 the whitewater picks up and becomes fairly continuous. At mile 5 a huge horizon appears. This is your indication that it's time to get out and scout Teller Tube rapid on river-right. This is an important scout, as there is often wood and a must-make eddy midway through. At least two boaters have died here.

From Teller Tube downstream about 2 miles the river is fast, furious, and continuous Class IV with a few Class Vs. During typical summer releases of about 500 cfs, the riverbed is rocky and has ample pin-and-broach potential. The final large rapid of the run, at about mile 7.3, is a mandatory portage. Get out and carry through the boulders on river-right.

After another 2.3 miles, the river makes a hard left bend just before Cedar Creek at mile 9.8, where you'll get out river-right and shoulder your boat for a 0.5-mile hike out of the canyon.

Mid Snake River Basin, Magic Valley

The Snake River in the Magic Valley of southern Idaho is characterized by the Earth's volcanic architecture. With steep rapids, massive waterfalls, and gentle canyon floats, there's something for any level of paddler to enjoy.

Near the town of Burley, the Snake is placid and calm, working lazily between reservoirs. About 12 miles west, at Milner, the river drops abruptly into a dramatic canyon carved by the world's second most powerful deluge: the Bonneville Flood.

When the Great Salt Lake poured over Red Rock Pass into what is now Idaho, it found a chink in the desert's basalt armor at Milner. The Bonneville Flood scoured the canyon for six weeks 15,000 years ago, moving house-size boulders and digging the canyon 100 to 200 feet deeper than it was. All told, 1,128 cubic miles of water crashed through southern Idaho, carving out the Snake River Canyon, Twin Falls, and Shoshone Falls—a thunderous cascade taller than Niagara.

The canyon was a serious impediment to early European travelers. Washington Irving recounted the canyon's early exploration in "Astoria or Anecdotes of an Enterprise Beyond the Rocky Mountains." He describes five explorers aboard canoes discovering the rapids of the Snake River Canyon for the first time in September 1811.

"The wreck struck the rock with one end, and, swinging round, flung poor Clappine off into the raging stream, which swept him away, and he perished. His comrades succeeded in getting upon the rock, from whence they were afterward taken off.

"This disastrous event brought the whole squadron to a halt, and struck a chill into every bosom. Indeed, they had arrived at a terrific strait that forbade all further progress in the canoes, and dismayed the most experienced voyageur."

That was the end of river travel for the Astor Expedition, which completed its voyage to the Columbia River on foot. Though the rapids of the Snake River Canyon are now tamed by dams, there are still several unrunnable waterfalls and a number of challenging rapids.

While the middle Snake River has its fair share of difficult whitewater, it is also very navigable using modern river craft. Between runs with abundant rapids, there are also excellent flatwater floating opportunities set in the stunning backdrop of southern Idaho's dramatic desert canyons.

Mid Snake River

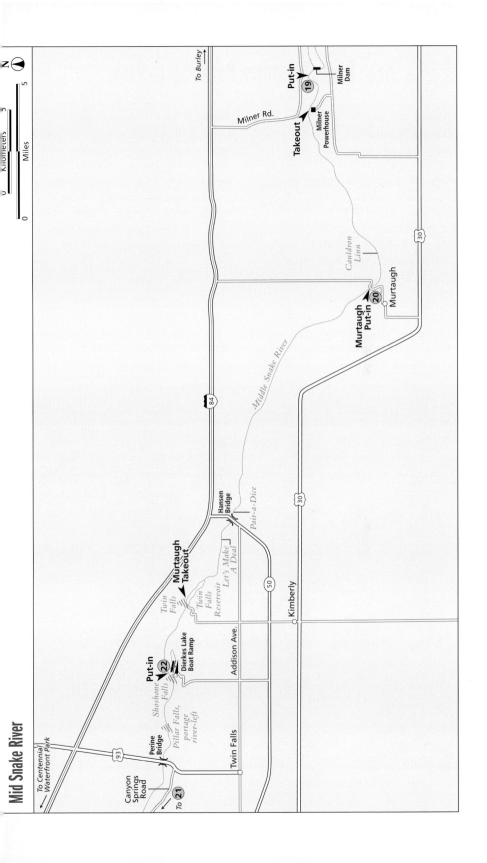

18 Snake River, Massacre Rocks State Park

Distance: 11.5 miles
Difficulty: Class II–III
Craft: Kayak, raft, canoe
Approximate paddling time: 3–5 hours
Flows: 6,000–20,000 cfs (**Gauge:** USGS, Snake River at Neeley)
Season: Year-round
Put-in: Sportsman's Landing at American Falls Dam (42.773872, -112.874175)
Takeout: Massacre Rocks State Park boat ramp (42.661490, -113.004380)

Shuttle: To reach the takeout, get off I-84 at exit 28. Drive north-northwest to Park Lane and travel upriver 0.75 mile to Massacre Rocks State Park. The boat ramp is at the downriver end of the park. To reach the put-in, return to I-84 and travel east 8 miles to exit 36. After exiting, take Rock Creek Road north a short distance to Eagle Rock Road and follow signs for Sportsman's Landing.

Below American Falls dam the Snake River leaves the highway and cuts through a small gorge. If you're traveling the long miles across southern Idaho and need a few hours of splashy river time, this accessible stretch is a good option.

The Snake River at Massacre Rocks State Park works through a small and scenic gorge.

The river is mellow in this reach but includes Class II ledges at miles 6 and 7.5, as well as a Class III rapid, Angel Falls, at mile 7, where the river wraps around an island.

Those seeking flatwater paddling can start and end their trips at the takeout, where the river is extremely calm. Simply paddle upstream into the canyon as far as you like and then return via the same route to your car.

Massacre Rocks State Park at the takeout has several great hiking options, as well as a Frisbee golf course. The park features a configuration of boulders that western emigrants named Massacre Rocks for fear of being ambushed while passing. Remnants of Oregon Trail wagon-wheel ruts can still be viewed at Massacre Rocks today.

At high water when American Falls dam is releasing significant water, this reach has powerful currents. In May 2011 the Power County Sheriff's Office closed boating access in the area when the river was flowing at 25,700 cfs.

19 Snake River, Milner Mile

Distance: 1.2 miles
Difficulty: Class V+
Craft: Kayak
Approximate paddling time: 15 minutes
Flows: 12,000–15,000 cfs (**Gauge:** USGS, Snake River at Milner)
Season: Mar, Apr, May, June (depending on dam releases)
Put-in: Milner Dam (42.528741, -114.017198)
Takeout: Milner powerhouse (42.527524, -114.038137)

Shuttle: Take exit 194 from I-84 and turn onto the South Frontage Road, heading east 1 mile. Turn right onto Milner Road and go 4.3 miles to a public access on the north side of the Snake River. This is the put-in. The entire run can be scouted and shuttled on foot via the southern canyon rim from here. To drive to the takeout, cross the bridge and continue 0.5 mile to a road on the right that parallels a canal. Drive 1 mile to the Milner powerhouse and a set of metal stairs descending to the river.

In the first mile below Milner Dam, the Snake River constricts and drops at close to 100 feet per mile, producing a true Class V experience fit for focused expert kayakers only. It could be the biggest whitewater on offer in a state renowned for its huge rivers and big rapids.

Dry most of the year because of irrigation and power diversions, the Milner Mile should only be attempted at high flows of about 10,000 to 15,000 cfs. Somewhere around 8,000 cfs and below, a river-wide hole forms about a third of the way through and must be portaged. The entire length of the Milner Mile can and should be scouted by hiking the south canyon rim.

Settled within its basalt canyon walls, the Snake River works past the Milner Mile takeout a few miles toward the ominous horizon of Cauldron Linn, also called Star Falls. This dangerous waterfall has been run at low water, but it's a stunt. This 30-foot drop should be avoided.

20 Snake River, Murtaugh

Distance: 13 miles
Difficulty: Class IV–V
Craft: Kayak, raft (rafts should avoid levels below approximately 4,000 cfs)
Approximate paddling time: 3–6 hours (all day at low flows)
Flows: 500–20,000 cfs (**Gauge:** USGS, Snake River at Milner)
Season: Apr, May, June, July, Aug (dependent on dam releases)
Put-in: Murtaugh Bridge (42.499273, -114.152674)
Takeout: Twin Falls Reservoir boat ramp (42.587959, -114.352504)
Shuttle: The Murtaugh shuttle includes a number of twists and turns amidst flat farmland and can be difficult. To get to the takeout, exit I-84 at Twin Falls and take US 93 south across Perrine Bridge. You'll turn left (east) 2.5 miles after the bridge onto Addison Avenue E and go 8.5 miles following signs for the Twin Falls Reservoir boat ramp and park. Turn left (north) on N 3500 E and go 2.6 miles into the canyon, through the park and to the boat ramp. To get to the put-in, take N 3500 E back out of the canyon and go straight at Addison Avenue E, traveling a total of 4.5 miles to downtown Kimberly. Turn left (east) on US 30 and travel 12.3 miles to N 4500 E. Turn left (north) and go 1.25 miles to Archer Street. Turn right and go into the town of Murtaugh, turning left on 4525 East Road. Cross the railroad tracks and go a short distance before turning right on E 3425 N. Travel another mile (bearing left at the T intersection to pick up Murtaugh Road) to the put-in.

When it's flowing big the Murtaugh is world-class whitewater. When it's flowing medium or low, it's still really great paddling with tons of play boating for kayakers.

The Murtaugh has the rare combination of steep gradient, breathtaking scenery, and lots of water—when it has water at all. Since 1905 irrigation diversions have largely dried the Snake below Milner Dam from April through October. But in good water years or when dam managers are passing water from upper basin to lower basin

Pair-a-Dice rapid looks mean at 17,000 cfs.

reservoirs, the Murtaugh comes in. Though it can be run at a wide variety of levels with vastly different personalities at each, it's best between 8,000 and 20,000 cfs, when its big-water character shines.

Things start fast under the bridge just below the put-in with a long Class III rapid (watch for a play wave at low water). There are no immediate hazards, but at high water the size of the waves and power of the river are indications of what's to come. At big water, with two notable exceptions, the rapids blend into one another, and the river moves fast. At medium and low flows the river's inner gorge and basalt ledges produce a dozen or more steep rapids with sticky hydraulics. At the lowest runnable flows of around 1,000 cfs, rapids are more characteristic of a steep creek than a big western river, and paddling the flats between drops is a slow, arduous endeavor.

Notable Class IVs on the run are Maybelline at mile 2.5, Misty at mile 6.9, Pair-a-Dice at mile 9.3, Hooker at mile 9.8, Let's Make a Deal at mile 10.4, Redshanks at mile 10.5, and Duck Blind at mile 11.

Pair-a-Dice is one of the run's two stand-out rapids. You'll know you're there when you see Hansen Bridge suspended above the canyon and arrive at a big basalt island on river-left. There's a distinct notch on the upstream side of the island. Pull into the notch, get out and scout, or carry across the island to portage. Be careful not to float into the river-right channel, where a very powerful and dangerous hydraulic would be unavoidable. The standard line is down the tongue in the center channel. It's a big hit, but it flushes. If you're nuts enough to be in the canyon at flows of 30,000 cfs or more, be careful. The island at Pair-a-Dice may be covered. If you've never floated the Murtaugh before, this rapid can and should be scouted from Hansen Bridge while you're setting up shuttle.

About a mile below Pair-a-Dice is Let's Make a Deal, easily recognizable by three columns of rock protruding 50 feet from the riverbed. The columns produce five doors that are all in at high flows. They get progressively harder from left to right: Door 1 through Door 5. At low water, Door 5 may be your only option, but Doors 2 and 3 are considered the safest. Doors 4 and 5 get easier as the water comes down.

At high water, the last rapid, Duck Blind, isn't much more than a wave train, but at medium flows, around 3,000 to 6,000 cfs, it's a challenging drop that's made swimmers out of more than one accomplished boater.

Below Duck Blind is the Idaho Connection surf wave on river-left. This wave became popular in the days of long, fast kayaks. It's really good when the river's flowing between 7,000 and 12,000 cfs.

From the Idaho Connection it's a 1.5-mile paddle across the lake to the takeout.

Though it may not feel remote, you are largely on your own while paddling the Murtaugh. The canyon walls are steep, and the riverbanks are lined with poison ivy and rattlesnakes. There are a few trails that lead into and out of the canyon, but they're difficult to locate if you're not familiar with them.

21 Snake River, Shoshone Falls

Distance: 7 miles round-trip
Difficulty: Class I
Craft: Canoe, kayak
Approximate paddling time: 5–6 hours
Flows: 1,000–3,500 cfs (**Gauge:** USGS, Snake River at Milner)
Season: Year-round (dependent on dam releases)
Put-in and takeout: Centennial Waterfront Park boat ramp (42.601131, -114.469362)

Shuttle: From I-84 take the Twin Falls exit and turn south on US 93. Go 2.7 miles and cross Perrine Bridge. After another 0.5 mile, you'll turn right on N 3000 E Road and pass some shopping complexes. Follow signs to Centennial Park, which will lead you to Canyon Springs Road. Turn right at the bottom switchback to go to the park boat ramp.

Don't let the name of this run intimidate you. The dramatic 212-foot Shoshone Falls is for scenery only and is the upstream destination for this beautiful and easy paddle through the heart of the dramatic Snake River Canyon.

From Centennial Waterfront Park below Perrine Bridge in Twin Falls, it's an upstream 2-mile paddle across placid water to Pillar Falls, where you portage river-left

If it's not flowing big, you can paddle close to the bottom of 212-foot-tall Shoshone Falls.
Photo by Lisa Hackett

Shoshone Falls and the Snake River Canyon were formed by a massive flood 15,000 years ago. The falls are the upstream destination for this scenic paddle.

(the right side of the river going upstream) and go another 1.5 miles to the base of Shoshone Falls, a waterfall taller than Niagara.

This trip can be done at an array of levels, but the easiest portage at Pillar Falls—the far river-left channel—comes in at levels below about 3,500 cfs. If the channel is full of water, Pillar Falls is the end of your trip. If it's dry, carry your boat up and continue to Shoshone Falls. Be careful here on your return journey. It would be a shame to turn an otherwise easy day of paddling into an expert-level whitewater misadventure.

Hitting this stretch when the water's just right could be the hardest part. Too low, and Shoshone Falls won't be flowing. Too high, and the currents and portage will be too challenging.

With the exception of a portage around Pillar Falls, the paddle upstream to and downstream from Shoshone Falls is mellow and scenic. PHOTO BY LISA HACKETT

22 Dierke's Lake

Distance: 1–2 miles
Difficulty: Flat water
Launch site: Dierkes Lake Park boat ramp
(42.594419, -114.391890)
Craft: Canoe, kayak, stand-up paddleboard
Approximate paddling time: 1–2 hours
Season: Year-round, unless frozen

Access: From Twin Falls head east on Falls Avenue and turn left on 3300 E. It's another 1.2 miles to the park. There's an access fee. After entering the park, turn right on Dierke's Road. This will lead you to a large parking lot. A primitive boat ramp is at the northwest end of the lot.

Dierke's is a small lake on the south rim of the Snake River Canyon near dramatic Shoshone Falls. Though Dierke's Lake Park is better known for its rock climbing and public swimming area, it's a safe, accessible, and picturesque place to paddle flat water and practice your boating skills. At 0.5 mile long and 0.25 mile wide, it's not big, but it's set among scenic basalt cliffs.

23 Salmon Falls Creek

Distance: 11.7 miles
Difficulty: Class I (one portage)
Craft: Canoe, recreational kayak
Approximate paddling time: 6–8 hours (best as an overnight)
Flows: 300–600 cfs (**Gauge:** USGS, Salmon Falls Creek near San Jacinto, Nevada)
Season: Apr, May, June
Put-in: US 93 river access (41.943423, -114.687488)
Takeout: Upper Salmon Falls access (42.029710, -114.728732)

Shuttle: To reach the takeout from Twin Falls, take US 93 south toward Jackpot, Nevada. Check your odometer at Rogerson and go 10.4 miles before turning right (west) on a small dirt road. Go 3 more miles and turn left. Follow this road 2.5 miles to the river. To get to the put-in, return to US 93 and head 7.7 miles to Jackpot. Drive another 3 miles south from Jackpot, and there's a small parking lot and river access on the south side of the bridge.

Salmon Falls Creek is a small, gentle river that flows north through a beautiful canyon before joining the Snake River near Hagerman. This 11-mile run in the upper basin, best as an overnight, starts near Jackpot, Nevada, and ends at Salmon Falls Creek Reservoir in Idaho.

Once on the river, you quickly enter a secluded canyon and leave civilization behind. The creek meanders considerably and forms handsome sand beaches on outside corners. There's a dam at mile 3.2 that must be portaged. The dam creates a long pool, so there's plenty of time to see it coming and no danger. When the water pools, paddle along the river-right bank, where you'll find a well-trod path around the dam.

The Salmon Falls drainage basin, spread across approximately 2,100 miles, is small, and empties the east side of the Jarbidge Mountains and northern portions of the Gollahar Mountains. As a whole, the watershed is very arid and receives less than 10 inches of rain annually. The window to float Salmon Falls Creek is correspondingly small.

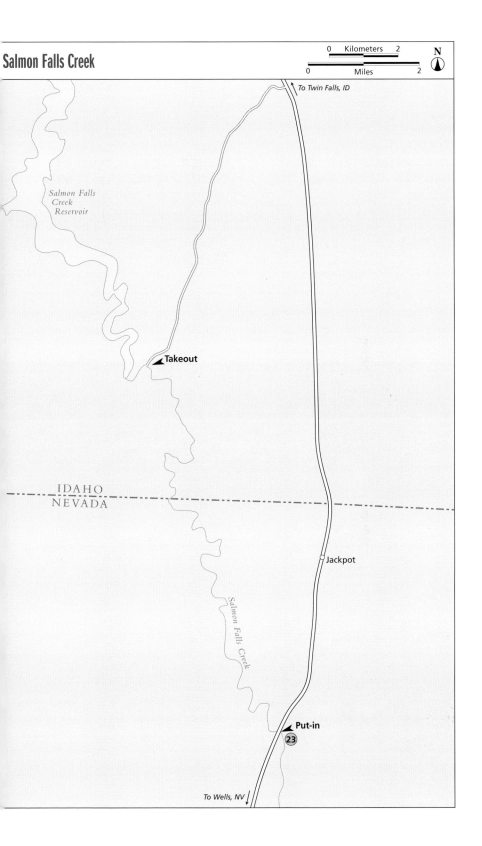

Salmon Falls Creek

24 Snake River, Thousand Springs

Distance: 4.5 miles
Difficulty: Class I
Craft: Canoe, recreational kayak, raft
Approximate paddling time: 2–4 hours
Flows: 5,000–20,000 cfs (**Gauge:** USGS, Snake River at Murphy)
Season: Year-round
Put-in: Banbury Hot Springs (42.690549, -114.826157)

Takeout: 1000 Springs Resort (42.741918, -114.847851)
Shuttle: To reach the takeout from Hagerman, take US 30 southeast (upriver) for 6.3 miles. Thousand Springs Resort is on the left. To get to the put-in, return to US 30 and continue southeast 2.1 miles, turning left on River Road. Take River Road 2.6 miles and turn left on Banbury Road. Banbury Hot Springs is 0.25 mile ahead.

The Thousand Springs portion of the Snake River reveals one of the largest ground-water systems in the world. The Snake River Plain Aquifer underlies almost the

With abundant springs and riparian areas, the Hagerman Valley of southwest Idaho is a haven for a variety of birds.

entirety of the Snake River Plain, an area stretching from Yellowstone National Park to southwest Idaho, and discharges 5,800 cubic feet per second at freshwater springs along the Snake River's canyon walls and a few of its tributaries near Hagerman.

A highlight of this run is the Thousand Springs waterfall, which gushes from the canyon wall and is easily visible while paddling. At Blueheart Springs, 1.5 miles from the put-in on river-right, the aquifer bubbles up into a beautiful and clear turquoise pool. It's the thirteenth largest natural spring in the nation. Box Canyon, which joins the Snake just upstream of Bluehart Springs, is the eleventh largest.

There is an abundance of private property along the Snake River in this area. Please be respectful. The put-in and takeout are private businesses, and fees are required to use their ramps, docks, parking, and facilities.

25 Snake River, Bliss

Distance: 5.6 miles
Difficulty: Class II-III
Craft: Kayak, raft, canoe, drift boat
Approximate paddling time: 2-4 hours
Flows: 5,000-20,000 cfs (**Gauge:** Idaho Power: Snake River below Lower Salmon Falls)
Season: Year-round
Put-in: Malad River confluence (42.861823, -114.904590)
Takeout: Shoestring Road Bridge (42.915984, -114.967975)
Shuttle: To get to the takeout, get off I-84 at exit 141, one of two Bliss exits. Go west on US 30, through Bliss, for 0.75 mile and turn left (south) on River Road, which will wind down a steep grade into the canyon. After 1.1 miles,

make a hard, sharp right on Bliss Grade Road and go 1 mile to a large boater access area on the north side of the river, just downstream of the bridge. To reach the put-in, return via Bliss Grade Road to River Road and turn right. This will keep you in the river canyon en route to the put-in. Take River Road 4.2 miles to US 30, turn right, and cross the bridge and turn right again immediately after the bridge onto a dirt road. Take another immediate right where the dirt road splits, and follow the road 0.75 mile to the large boater access area and primitive boat ramp near the confluence of the Malad and Snake Rivers.

*Please see map of the Bliss and Malad Rivers for Route 25 put-in location.

The Bliss has been the proving ground for many of southern Idaho's novice and intermediate whitewater boaters. It's a relatively big-volume stretch with powerful eddies and currents, but its Class II+ rapids are easily navigable by kayak or raft. The run also includes one of the best year-round surf waves in Idaho.

The first rapid comes about 0.5 mile below the put-in and is recognizable by an old stone pier sticking out of the riverbed. About a mile below the put-in is the surf wave. When the river funnels toward some rocks on river-left, aim for the eddy behind the rocks. The powerful eddy line is ferocious, but the surfing is worth the effort.

Less than 0.5 mile of flat water later is the run's biggest rapid, which appears after a hard right bend. From there it's almost all flat water, with the exception of a final rapid immediately above the bridge near the takeout.

A big, fast surf wave is the destination for many kayakers heading to paddle the Snake River near Bliss.

Malad and Wood River Basin

The Big Wood River emerges at a spring near 8,701-foot Galena Summit, the divide between this southern Idaho trout stream and Idaho's famed Salmon River. After descending from the mountains and flowing through America's first ski resort, Sun Valley, the Big Wood continues south and west across the Snake River Plain before joining its sibling, the Little Wood River, to form the Malad, which then enters a tight gorge and plummets over a 60-foot waterfall. The Malad joins the Snake River near Hagerman.

The Big Wood, Little Wood, and Malad Rivers don't have an abundance of paddling opportunities. The Big Wood through the towns of Ketchum, Hailey, and Bellevue has been floated by experienced boaters looking to get wet, but because of the amount of deadfall in the river it's generally considered a Class II float with Class V consequences.

The mountainous headwaters of the Wood River Basin give rise to relatively small rivers with limited paddling opportunities.

26 Camas Creek

Distance: 10 miles
Difficulty: Class III
Craft: Canoe, kayak, raft
Approximate paddling time: 3–5 hours
Flows: 500–3,000 cfs (**Gauge:** Camas Creek near Blaine)
Season: Mar, Apr, May
Put-in: Macon Flat Road (43.337078, -114.599422)
Takeout: Moonstone Landing (43.335121, -114.432661)

Shuttle: The takeout at Moonstone Landing is 18.16 miles east of Fairfield on US 20. It is 7.7 miles east on US 20 from the intersection with ID 75. Follow the signs for Moonstone Landing and drive 1,000 feet to the Moonstone Landing boat ramp. To reach the put-in, return to US 20 and drive 8.6 miles west to Macon Flat Road. Drive south 0.5 mile to the bridge crossing at Camas Creek. There are pullouts on both sides of the bridge.

Take a look at Camas Creek in July or August and you'll be surprised it can be paddled at all. This small desert stream shrivels up completely by June most years. In early spring, however, Camas Creek picks up considerable flow from the Bennett Hills to

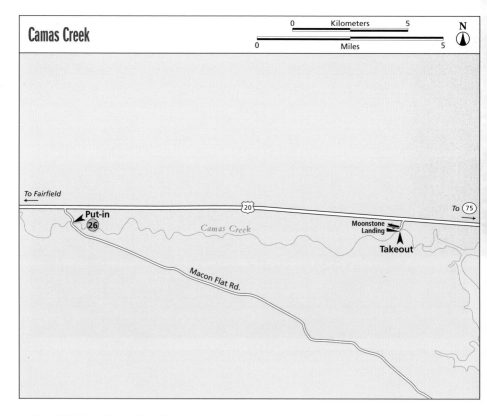

the south and Soldier Mountains to the north and can run at several thousand cfs in a good year. It's a beautiful, accessible, and fun stretch of river that probably doesn't get the attention it deserves because of its short runnable window.

At 500 cfs and over, the run consists of roughly a half-dozen pool-drop Class II and III rapids in a secluded basalt gorge. Somewhere below 500 cfs several of the rapids become too shallow and end in boulder sieves, so be careful at low water.

Camas Creek originates on the Camas Prairie, an area renowned for its spring wildflower displays and diversity of avian species.

27 Silver Creek

Distance: 2.9 miles
Difficulty: Class I
Craft: Canoe, recreational kayak
Approximate paddling time: 1–2 hours
Flows: 80–120 cfs (**Gauge:** Silver Creek at Sportsman Access near Picabo)
Season: Year-round
Put-in: Stalker Creek Bridge (43.314413, -114.135721)
Takeout: Kilpatrick Bridge (43.311092, -114.169009)

Shuttle: To get to the takeout from the Sun Valley area, drive south on ID 75 to the intersection with US 20. Turn left (east) and go 7.3 miles to a sign indicating Silver Creek Preserve. Turn right (south) and go 0.75 mile to Kilpatrick Bridge. To get to the put-in, continue on to the Silver Creek Preserve Visitor's Center to sign in and then drive another mile to Stalker Creek Bridge.

The only difficulty with paddling postcard-perfect Silver Creek is figuring out how not to disturb the dozens of anglers sure to be crowding this world-class fly-fishing destination.

Silver Creek is a crystal-clear, spring-fed, high-desert stream that meanders along the base of the Picabo Hills before joining the Little Wood River. The creek's unique aquatic ecosystem features one of the highest densities of stream insects in North America, which supports the world-class fishery. The Nature Conservancy owns 851 acres along Silver Creek and has protected more than 12,600 additional acres

Silver Creek's sinewy ribbons are entirely fed by springs. PHOTO BY JENNIFER STAHL

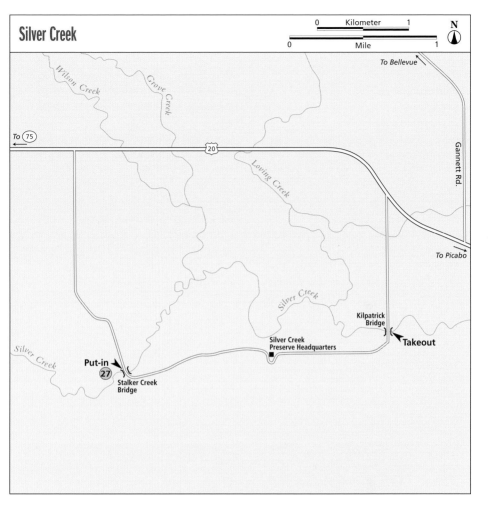

through conservation easements, making Silver Creek one of the most successful private stream conservation efforts ever undertaken for public benefit.

There are several floatable sections of Silver Creek, but this uppermost paddle between Stalker Creek Bridge and Kilpatrick Bridge goes through the heart of the preserve. There's one portage at a low wood bridge, but the water is extremely calm. The portage doesn't pose any threat.

If you're looking for more paddling, you can also paddle the 4-mile section of Silver Creek between the US 20 bridge and Picabo Bridge farther downstream.

To avoid conflicts with anglers, try paddling Silver Creek before fishing season opens on Memorial Day weekend or go during the heat of the day, when fishing pressure slacks off a bit. Also, The Nature Conservancy requests that all river users stop at preserve headquarters to sign in. Donations are also encouraged and benefit upkeep of the facilities.

28 Malad River

Distance: 1.8 miles
Difficulty: Class IV
Craft: Kayak
Approximate paddling time: 1 hour
Flows: 500–1,500 cfs (**Gauge:** Idaho Power: Lower Malad near Bliss)
Season: Upper—year-round. Lower—hydro diversion dependent
Put-in: End of Malad access road at locked gate (42.864699, -114.875214)
Takeout: Snake River confluence (42.861785, -114.904820)
Shuttle: Get off I-84 at exit 141, one of two Bliss exits. Just 1,000 feet west of the interstate, turn south on US 30 toward Hagerman.

Drive 5 miles, crossing a high bridge that spans the Malad River, and take the first left after the bridge, heading north. Drive 1.2 miles to a locked gate. Either put in here or shoulder your boat a bit farther for some additional eddy hopping and a few small drops. To get to the upper section takeout, return to the diversion dam, which is also the put-in for the lower section. To reach the takeout for the lower section, drive back to US 30, cross the highway, and pick up another dirt road. Take an immediate right and follow the road 0.75 mile to the boat ramp near the confluence of the Malad and Snake Rivers.

The Malad has two sections, a very short 0.8-mile upper that is always running and a longer 1-mile bottom section that generally only comes in when the stream's hydro diversions are undergoing maintenance. The Malad's beautiful spring-fed water is clear and a constant 55°F. The upper is an accessible section of Class III–IV creeking that can be paddled year-round.

This rocky and fun Class IV rapid is on the part of the Malad that can be paddled year-round.
Photo by Sean Flynn

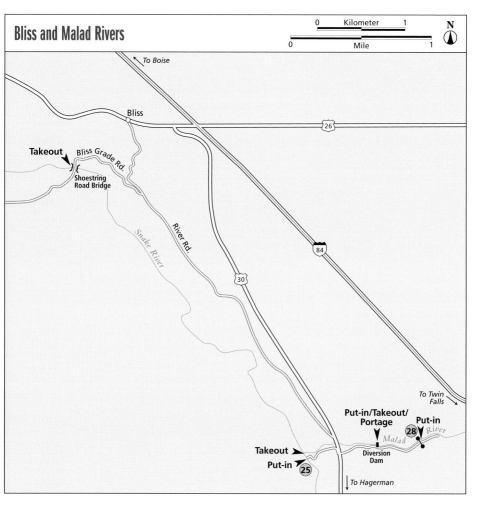

Bliss and Malad Rivers

On the upper section, things start with very shallow water, some eddy hopping, and small boofs over shallow rocks. After a short pool, rapids are continuous and get progressively harder as you paddle toward the diversion dam. The final 0.25 mile is great Class IV creeking, and the final rapid (easily scouted from the road on your way to the put-in) consists of a series of ledges and fast water that ends at the dam. Get out to portage or hike back to the put-in on the left.

When the diversions and hydro facilities are undergoing maintenance, which sometimes happens for a month or more at a time, the lower Malad is runnable. This continuous whitewater section starts hard and gets progressively easier as you approach the confluence with the Snake. At normal dam-controlled flows, the Malad is very rocky. Pin-and-broach potential is constant. During high-water events, which are rare, both sections are extremely continuous and considerably more difficult.

Southwest Idaho

The huge swath of desert centered on the intersection of Nevada, Oregon, and southwest Idaho is one of the most remote parts of the contiguous United States. Called the Owyhee Plateau, this area is arid, rugged, and beautiful country with wide-open skies, snowcapped mountains, rolling sagebrush plateaus, and deeply incised canyons with dramatic vertical cliff walls.

For decades, the canyon country of southwest Idaho was starkly divided between those seeking protections for the area's natural wonders and the hard-working ranchers making a living from the land. A glimmer of resolution was achieved in 2009 when a bill was signed into law that included wilderness and Wild and Scenic River protections for large portions of the landscape while simultaneously preserving the pastoral way of life for ranchers whose ancestors homesteaded the area. The result of an eight-year collaborative convened by Senator Mike Crapo, R-Idaho, the legislation established 517,000 acres of wilderness and designated 325 miles of Wild and Scenic Rivers.

The rivers of southwest Idaho are the primary engineers of the area's stunning scenery. Fed by snowmelt in the Owyhee and Jarbidge Mountains, they cut deep canyons into the basalt and rhyolite layers of the Owyhee Plateau before joining the Snake River. Snow in the arid mountain ranges typically begins melting earlier than

The snowcapped mountains of southwest Idaho give rise to rivers that have cut deep canyons across the desert.

in other parts of Idaho, and the window to float the Bruneau, Jarbidge, Owyhee, and their tributaries is typically early and usually small. By early June in most years, when central Idaho's rivers are pumping near peak, the desert streams of southwest Idaho have all but withered.

This is remote country, and access is not easy. Many of the runs require four-wheel-drive vehicles with ample clearance, as well as beefy spare tires. A spare can of gas and a high-lift jack aren't bad ideas, either, and don't expect your cell phone to work. For those willing to embrace the adventure, though, the rivers of the Owyhee Plateau are some of the finest wild rivers in the nation.

Bruneau and Jarbidge Basin

The Bruneau River flows north from the Jarbidge Mountains of northern Nevada on its deeply incised course to the Snake River. It has two key tributary canyons: the Jarbidge and West Fork Bruneau Rivers. The Jarbidge carries the majority of the system's flow and becomes the Bruneau River where the West Fork empties into the Jarbidge, about 24 miles north of the Nevada border. Adventurous Class V kayakers have also explored and safely descended Sheep Creek, a tributary that enters the Bruneau from the southwest. It's a very challenging and committing trip.

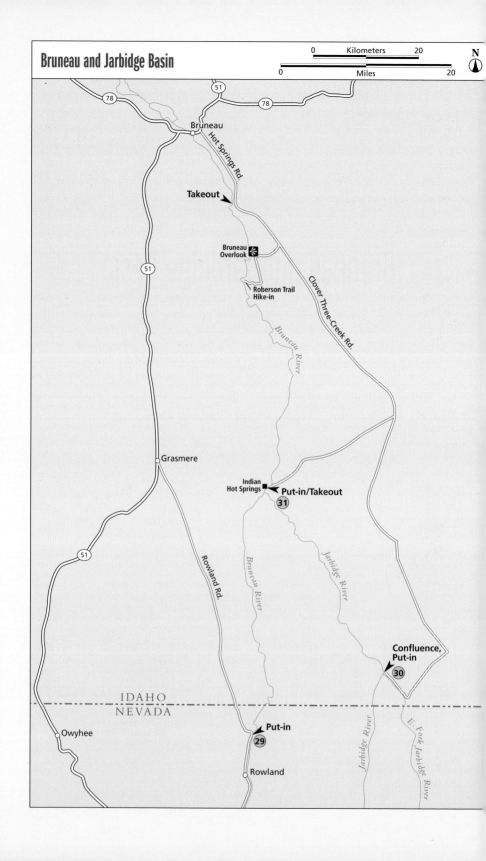

0   Kilometers   20

0   Miles   20

N

78

51

78

Bruneau

Hot Springs Rd

Takeout

Bruneau
Overlook

Roberson Trail
Hike-in

51

Clover Three-Creek Rd.

Bruneau River

Grasmere

Indian
Hot Springs   Put-in/Takeout

31

51

Rowland Rd.

Bruneau River

Jarbidge River

Confluence,
Put-in

30

IDAHO
NEVADA

Owyhee

Put-in

29

Rowland

Jarbidge River

E. Fork Jarbidge River

29 West Fork of the Bruneau

Distance: 34 miles
Difficulty: Class V
Craft: Kayak
Approximate paddling time: 2–3 days on the West Fork plus 2 days on the Bruneau
Flows: 250–500 cfs (**Gauge:** USGS, Bruneau River at Rowland, Nevada)
Season: Apr, May
Put-in: Rowland, Nevada (41.950734, -115.676927)
Takeout: Indian Hot Springs (42.338692, -115.647385)
Alternative takeout: Bruneau River Takeout (42.775333, -115.718652)
Shuttle: To get to the takeout from the town of Bruneau, go 8.2 miles south on Hot Springs Road and turn right onto an unmarked dirt road. Go another mile and bear right toward the river. The takeout is above the first of two irrigation dams that shouldn't be run. Scout beforehand to get your bearings. To get to the put-in, return to Bruneau and go west on ID 78 for 2 miles. Bear to the left at the Y intersection onto ID 51. Take ID 51 south for 37.7 miles and turn left in Grasmere onto a dirt road called Rowland Road. Continue 36 miles to Rowland and park in one of the pullouts along the road.

Additional information: The Bureau of Land Management has excellent resources online, as well as at their offices. Call (208) 373-4000 or log onto blm.gov/id.

This is an experts-only multiday kayak run and the most remote of the Bruneau basin's remote wilderness rivers. Plan on two to three days to paddle the West Fork, plus another two days to paddle out on the Bruneau.

The West Fork of the Bruneau is a remote multiday challenge for expert kayakers.

The West Fork's canyon isn't as stunning at the Bruneau River downstream, and its whitewater is more challenging than the Jarbidge River, one canyon to the west. It's also a lower-elevation watershed that has an earlier snowmelt than the Jarbidge. It's runnable with around 300 cfs or more on the Rowland USGS gauge on the Idaho-Nevada border.

The West Fork has numerous unnamed Class III and IV rapids, as well as three challenging Class Vs. The first, Pin Toe, comes 4 miles into the trip and is just on the Idaho side of the Nevada-Idaho border. The second, Al Beam Falls, is a short boulder sieve and comes at mile 17. The third and toughest, Julie Wilson Falls, is at mile 19. You may want to portage one or all three of these rapids.

Julie Wilson Falls gained notoriety in 1974 when Atlanta boater Julie Wilson drowned there. Her grave is above the river on the left. Be careful entering this part of the canyon; Julie Wilson Falls creeps up on you after a long stretch of Class II–III water.

It should go without saying for a run of this nature, but basic survival gear, including spare paddles and water filters, is essential.

30 Jarbidge

Distance: 30 miles
Difficulty: Class IV (V+, VI)
Craft: Kayak
Approximate paddling time: 1-2 days
Flows: 600-2,500 cfs (**Gauge:** USGS, Bruneau River near Hot Springs and Jarbidge near Jarbidge, Nevada)
Season: Apr, May, June
Put-in: Confluence of Jarbidge and East Fork Jarbidge Rivers (42.049835, -115.390479)
Takeout: Indian Hot Springs (42.338692, -115.647385)
Shuttle: To get to the takeout, refer to the Bruneau River put-in description. Note that it is a very serious four-wheel-drive put-in and cannot be underestimated. To get to the Jarbidge put-in, return to Clover Three-Creek Road and go 27 miles. Turn right (west) at the T intersection onto 3 Creek Road and go 6.3 miles to the Murphy Hot Springs airstrip. Continue into the canyon 4.8 miles to the confluence of the east and west forks of the Jarbidge, where there's camping, boat ramps, and an outhouse. The Jarbidge put-in is suitable for two-wheel-drive vehicles. Because of the difficulty of the takeout, many boaters choose to paddle a couple days on the Jarbidge plus two or three more on the Bruneau.
Additional information: The Bureau of Land Management has excellent resources online, as well as at their offices. Call (208) 373-4000 or log onto blm.gov/id.

Fed by snowmelt from the north flank of the Jarbidge Mountains in northern Nevada, the Jarbidge is a narrow and technical river with constant whitewater, including a couple of Class V drops that should probably be portaged. Moreover, portaging is an arduous process that makes this run difficult for anything but kayaks. The river is runnable in small rafts, but requires constant maneuvering in constricted spaces. Boats over 14 feet aren't recommended, and because of the portages are in fact discouraged.

From the put-in, there are several miles of Class II to III whitewater in a scenic broad valley. The canyon walls start to take shape about 1.5 to 2 miles in. The canyon starts to get really tight and deep after about 5 miles.

There's a Class IV rapid about 10 miles into the run, but the first major drop comes at mile 17.9, where a huge landslide swept into the Jarbidge from river-right in 2009. The resulting pool inundated the old Sevy Falls and created a new Class V+ called Castle Grayskull. From there it's more continuous Class II and III in one of the most stunning canyons in southern Idaho until mile 21.3 and Wally's Wallow, a tight Class IV. From Wally's Wallow downstream for 7 miles it's very continuous Class II and IV whitewater. This stretch also includes Jarbidge Falls at mile 22. It's a Class V+ and another recommended portage.

Additional hazards on the Jarbidge are the ever-changing logjams. Be cautious of blind corners and constricted areas where logs can stick on rocks and trees lean in from the banks. Due to rising and falling flows, the locations and severity of logjams can be different from one day to the next.

Flows generally peak mid- to late-May. As a rough indicator, watch for the Bruneau gauge to read over 1,000 cfs. The gauge on the Jarbidge in Nevada represents roughly a third to half of the river's flow at the put-in.

31 Bruneau

Distance: 40 miles
Difficulty: Class IV
Craft: Canoe, kayak, raft
Approximate paddling time: 2-3 days
Flows: 500-2,500 cfs (**Gauge:** USGS, Bruneau River near Hot Springs)
Season: Apr, May, June
Put-in: Indian Hot Springs (42.338692, -115.647385)
Day trip put-in: Roberson Trail (42.652171, -115.697265)
Takeout: Bruneau River Takeout (42.775333, -115.718652)
Shuttle: To get to the takeout from the town of Bruneau, go 8.2 miles south on Hot Springs Road and turn right onto an unmarked dirt road. Go another mile and bear right toward the river. The takeout is above the first of two irrigation dams that shouldn't be run. Scout beforehand to get your bearings. To get to Roberson Trail, the day trip put-in accessible via a tough hike, return to Hot Springs Road, which becomes Clover Three-Creek Road and go southeast for 7.5 miles and turn right. Go 2.3 miles and turn left. Go another 2.7 miles and turn right. The Roberson Trail is not a straightforward place to find, so consult a map and take it with you. To get to Indian Hot Springs, first make sure you've got a high-clearance vehicle, a high-lift jack, and a spare tire. From the Bruneau River takeout, go south on Clover Three-Creek Road for 32 miles. About 1.4 miles after crossing Clover Creek turn right. Indian Hot Springs is about 20 miles of dirt roads ahead. There are numerous dirt roads weaving through the desert in this area, and most don't lead anywhere, so travel cautiously and be prepared.

Additional information: The Bureau of Land Management has excellent resources online, as well as at their offices. Call (208) 373-4000 or log onto blm.gov/id.

The Bruneau River flows through a stunning desert canyon and provides a high-quality wilderness experience. There are more than twenty Class III and IV rapids in

The Bruneau Overlook offers a bird's-eye view of some of the Bruneau's toughest rapids.
PHOTO BY JENNIFER STAHL

Once inside the Bruneau River canyon, paddlers will discover an enchanting world far removed from the day-to-day hustle. PHOTO BY KEVIN LEWIS

the Bruneau's 40 miles. Depending on where you camp, there are about a dozen Class III rapids during the first day on the river.

The most difficult whitewater begins downstream, at about mile 30, with Bonyard, a Class IV. The ensuing 5 miles, collectively called Five Mile, is a blur of Class IV whitewater that becomes Class IV+ at high water. From Five Mile downstream there are a few additional Class III rapids, with a final Class IV standout called Wild Burrow, a hard left corner with powerful currents, about 4 miles before the takeout. Be cautious not to paddle over the diversion dam below the takeout.

Kayaks can scrape down the Bruneau as low as 500 cfs, but rafts should consider 1,000 cfs a good starting point. Above 2,500 cfs the river gets very pushy with long and continuous whitewater, with few eddies. The BLM discourages launches above this level.

Owyhee Basin

At 11,000 miles, the Owyhee River basin is large but receives scant precipitation. It's a desert basin with stunning, secluded canyon geography and a paddling season that's earlier than most of Idaho's.

The Owyhee originates from the Bull and Jarbidge Mountains in northern Nevada. It flows north through the Duck Valley Indian Reservation and the town of Owyhee, Nevada, before working across the southwest corner of Idaho, where it picks up the flow from several key tributaries. It then flows into Oregon and north to meet the Snake River west of Boise.

The Owyhee and its tributaries are extremely remote and flow through deep, secluded canyons where rescue would be next to impossible. The land is both beautiful and inhospitable, and nearly all Owyhee expeditions are multiday paddles that require planning, wilderness survival skills, and plenty of gear. Flows in the main stem of the Owyhee can fluctuate widely during the runoff season, between 1,000 and 50,000 cfs, but by mid-summer the river generally tops out at 200 cfs. That means the upper tributaries may consist of nothing more than puddles.

The Owyhee River basin contains some of the most stunning desert rivers in America.
PHOTO BY JAY KRAJIC

There are relatively few gauges in the Owyhee system. There's a gauge near the town of Rome, Oregon, that historically has served as a rough barometer for the entire system. Particularly for some of the upper tributaries, this gauge may not accurately reflect what is happening on the water. Generally, the Owyhee's various upper-basin runs are good when the gauge at Rome is between 1,000 and 6,000 cfs. The lower run below Rome is good up to 10,000 cfs.

In 1984 Congress designated 120 miles of the Owyhee River in Oregon as a Wild and Scenic River. In 2009 rivers throughout southwest Idaho were added to the Wild and Scenic Rivers System, including twelve in the Owyhee basin. The Owyhee's canyons were also protected as designated wilderness. In other words, almost the entirety of this magical and special place is protected, and paddlers are required to fill out and carry self-issued permits. This guide covers five segments of the Owyhee, including two of its upper tributaries. If you're looking for even more options, ask the Bureau of Land Management about Deep Creek, a Class I tributary of the East Fork Owyhee, or the North Fork Owyhee, a Class IV tributary that joins the Owyhee River at Three Forks.

This is extremely remote, inhospitable country with dangerous, steep cliffs, hazardous whitewater amidst otherwise calm reaches of river, and ample rattlesnakes. Weather and water levels can change drastically, and fast, during the typical early-spring boating season. You're on your own when you're out there, so prepare for anything, paddle responsibly, and enjoy southern Idaho's stunning desert scenery and seclusion.

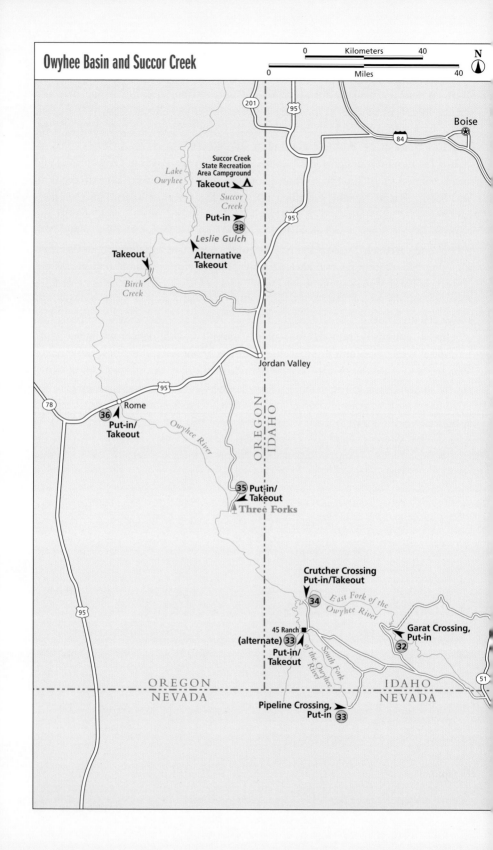

32 East Fork of the Owyhee

Distance: 42 miles
Difficulty: Class III (IV, VI)
Craft: Canoe, kayak
Approximate paddling time: 2–3 days
Flows: 500–1,000 cfs (**Gauge:** USGS East Fork Owyhee at Crutcher Crossing)*
Season: Late Mar–early June
Put-in: Garat Crossing (42.185986, -116.505636)
Takeout: Crutcher Crossing (42.260757, -116.870727)
Shuttle: First, call the Bureau of Land Management to get the latest on road conditions and make sure you've got the latest BLM maps. Also consider hiring a shuttle driver;

check shuttlequest.com for the latest listings. To get there take ID 51 south through Bruneau and Grassmere into the Duck Valley Indian Reservation. After passing the Idaho-Nevada state line, take your first right (west) and go 2.6 miles and bear to the right. Continue north and west through some turns for 3 miles and turn left. If you don't have your map out yet, pull over to consult it. This is your surest way to navigate the complex of dirt roads that lies ahead.

*The gauge on East Fork is relatively new. As a rough guide, watch for flows of 1,000 to 6,000 cfs on the Owyhee River at Rome gauge. Call the BLM to confirm its level.

This 42-mile paddle on the East Fork of the Owyhee is the most challenging of the upper Owyhee's paddling options. It might be the most scenic as well.

Because of the arduous portages that are required, the run is recommended only for whitewater kayaks, pack rafts, and whitewater canoes that can handle rough, steep rapids and/or easily be carried. With that said, most of the run is fairly flat and manageable.

Just 4.5 miles downstream from the Garat Crossing put-in, the canyon opens up and reveals a rock formation called The Tules, one of the most photographed locations in the basin.

At mile 23 Deep Creek enters from river-right. Just a mile later you'll arrive at Boulder Jam, a Class III rapid. Another 3.5 miles lead to

Paddling the East Fork Owyhee requires several arduous portages. PHOTO BY JAY KRAJIC

Paddling the East Fork Owyhee includes rapids and portages, but most of the run is fairly flat.
Photo by Jay Krajic

Owyhee Falls, a Class VI that should be portaged river-left. After another mile is Thread the Needle, a Class IV. A series of Class III rapids will then take you through the ensuing mile or two. Crutcher Crossing is at mile 42. Take out river-left.

With permission from officials at the Duck Valley Indian Reservation, paddlers can also start 20 miles farther upstream. This adds some very tough whitewater, and probably some additional portages. Floating is not recommended on the East Fork unless the river is bank-full or higher at the reservation.

33 South Fork Owyhee

Distance: 38 miles, plus 2 upstream miles on the East Fork
Difficulty: Class II–III
Craft: Canoe, kayak, raft
Approximate paddling time: 2-3 days
Flows: 200-1,000 cfs* (**Gauge:** USGS, Owyhee River at Rome, Oregon)
Season: Late Mar-early June
Put-in: YP Ranch (41.805025, -116.473528)
Put-in: Pipeline Crossing (41.952720, -116.685061)
Alternative put-in/takeout: 45 Ranch (42.167413, -116.871120)
Takeout: Crutcher Crossing (42.260350, -116.866949)
Shuttle: First, call the Bureau of Land Management to get the latest on road conditions and make sure you've got the latest BLM maps.

Also consider hiring a shuttle driver; check shuttlequest.com for the latest listings. The takeout at Crutcher Crossing is on the East Fork of the Owyhee, 2 miles upstream of the confluence with the South Fork. To get there take ID 51 south through Bruneau and Grassmere into the Duck Valley Indian Reservation. After passing the Idaho-Nevada state line, take your first right (west) and go 2.6 miles and bear to the right. Continue north and west through some turns for 3 miles and turn left. If you don't have your map out yet, pull over to consult it. This is your surest way to navigate the complex of dirt roads that lies ahead.

*There is no gauge on the South Fork. As a rough guide, aim for 1,000 to 6,000 cfs on the Owyhee at Rome gauge.

In 40 miles the South Fork of the Owyhee has fewer than twenty Class II and III rapids and lots of miles of calm, reflective water in one of the most beautiful and remote canyons in the country. What's more, most of the rapids are concentrated in a 5-mile section starting just a mile into the trip. When the series ends, you'll have crossed the border from Nevada and be in Idaho.

Shortly after crossing into Idaho, you'll pass Bull Camp on river-right. This is where poacher Claude Dallas killed two Idaho Department of Fish and Game officers in 1981 before fleeing into Nevada and evading capture for more than a year.

Another landmark to watch for is Coyote Hole, 16 miles into your trip, where there's good springwater and a homesteader ruin on river-right. The 45 Ranch at mile 25 is another put-in option, and could probably be used to create a South Fork day trip by taking out at Crutcher Crossing.

At about 250 cfs the South Fork is easily accessible to amateurs paddling just about any craft. At high flows most of the rapids wash out, but the river moves quickly. Open canoeists may have to scout, line, or portage a few of the rapids at certain levels. As a rough guide, watch for 1,000 to 6,000 cfs on the Owyhee gauge at Rome.

There's another put-in option 20 miles farther upstream at the YP Ranch in Nevada. It's on private property, however, and permission is required to use it.

When you reach the confluence with the East Fork, it's time to turn upstream for a 2-mile slog to Crutchers Crossing. At low to medium flows this shouldn't be a problem, but it'll require more effort than you had to expend on the South Fork. Your alternative is to continue downstream another 36 miles to Three Forks, but that will require running and/or portaging some tougher whitewater (see Owyhee River, Crutcher Crossing to Three Forks description on page 71).

The Owyhee cuts increasingly deep canyons as it works downstream. PHOTO BY JAY KRAJIC

34 Owyhee River, Crutcher Crossing to Three Forks

Distance: 36 miles
Difficulty: Class II (IV, IV)
Craft: Canoe, kayak, small raft
Approximate paddling time: 2–3 days
Flows: 1,000–6,000 cfs (**Gauge:** USGS, Owyhee River at Rome)
Season: Late Mar–early June
Put-in: Crutchers Crossing (42.260757, -116.870727)
Takeout: Three Forks (42.544393, -117.168915)
Shuttle: This one's a long shuttle. You could try to cut it short by taking back roads, but that would be inviting disaster. To get to the takeout, travel via US 95 toward Rome, Oregon. After passing through Jordan Valley, look for Three Forks Road on the left. It's 15.8 miles west of Jordan Valley. Take Three Forks Road 32 miles to Three Forks. Use a high-clearance vehicle. To get to the put-in, return to Marsing, Idaho, via US 95 and turn south on ID 78. Go 76 miles and turn right (south) on ID 51. Take ID 51 south through Grassmere into the Duck Valley Indian Reservation. After passing the Idaho-Nevada state line, take your first right (west) and go 2.6 miles and bear to the right. Continue north and west through some turns for 3 miles and turn left. Now get out your BLM map and find your way to Crutcher Crossing, which is on the East Fork of the Owyhee, just a few miles upstream of its confluence with the South Fork.

Sometimes called the Upper Owyhee, this 36-mile paddle has a 250-mile shuttle. The paddling takes two to three days; the shuttle may take close to a day. Hire a shuttle driver if you can.

The launch is at Crutcher Crossing on the East Fork of the Owyhee. After 2.5 miles the South Fork joins to form the main stem of the Owyhee River, and you'll hit a few Class III rapids pretty quickly.

This upper run from the confluence of the East and South Forks to the confluence with the North Fork is mostly mellow Class I and II water with a few Class IIIs, but like a lot of the Owyhee basin's rivers it has an additional pair of tougher rapids to keep you on your toes. Cabin Rapid, named for Stateline Cabin, which comes 15 miles into the trip, is Class IV and almost 0.5 mile long. Cabin is followed in short order by Cable, another Class IV. Depending on your abilities and the water level, one or both of these can be portaged, but they're arduous portages.

35   Owyhee River, Three Forks to Rome

Distance: 38 miles
Difficulty: Class IV (V+)
Craft: Canoe, kayak, raft
Approximate paddling time: 2–4 days
Flows: 1,500–3,000 cfs
Season: Apr–early June
Put-in: Three Forks (42.544393, -117.168915)

Takeout: Rome, Oregon (42.836389, -117.621627)
Shuttle: The takeout is in Rome, Oregon, just off US 95. It's on the river-right side upstream of the bridge. To get to the put-in, go 16.7 miles east on US 95 and turn right (south) on Three Forks Road. Continue 32 miles to Three Forks. Use a high-clearance vehicle to get to the put-in.

This is the Owyhee's standard expert run. The 38 miles from Three Forks to Rome has a pool-drop character with long sections of flat water interspersed with numerous Class III and IV rapids, including a big V+. The trip can be done in two to four days and should only be undertaken by accomplished boaters.

The whitewater starts at Ledge, a Class IV, about 1.5 miles below the put-in. Rapids then unfold quickly. The toughest rapid, Widowmaker, is 20 miles into the trip and can be scouted or portaged on the right. It's an arduous portage.

The Owyhee can peak at very high flows, particularly with a mid-winter or early-spring rain-on-snow event. The drive to the put-in, however, is hazardous if it's wet, and potentially closed. It's best to aim for this one post-peak, when flows are more predictable and the shuttle road has a higher probability of being open.

36 Lower Owyhee, Rome to Birch Creek

Distance: 48 miles
Difficulty: Class III
Craft: Canoe, kayak, raft
Approximate paddling time: 4–6 days
Flows: 800–10,000 cfs
Season: Late Mar–early June
Put-in: Rome, Oregon (42.836389, -117.621627)
Takeout: Birch Creek (43.225531, -117.496088)
Shuttle: First, call the Bureau of Land Management to get the latest on road conditions and good maps. Then consider getting a shuttle driver. Log on to shuttlequest.com to get the latest listings for this and other Idaho runs. If you're determined to find the takeout on your own, know that the Leslie Gulch option is easier and better maintained. From Rome take US 95 west to Jordan Valley and then north for a total of 58 miles. Turn left (west) on McBride Creek Road and go 8.7 miles to Succor Creek Road. Turn right and take Succor Creek Road 1.8 miles. Turn left on Leslie Gulch Road. Go 14 miles to the boat ramp in Leslie Gulch. Leslie Gulch is well signed and relatively easy to find from the highway. To get to Birch Creek there are multiple options, all between 40 and 60 miles and all requiring multiple dirt roads. This is the route the BLM suggests. From Rome, go east to Jordan Valley. From Jordan Valley go north on US 95 for 8 miles and turn left (west) onto Jordan Craters Road. Continue to Birch Creek Road and descend into the canyon.

The four- to six-day float on the lower Owyhee below Rome is the river's most popular section. With pool-drop character, most rapids are relatively short and the scenery stunning.

While the whitewater is fun, the lower Owyhee is more of a camping and hiking trip suitable for a range of watercraft. The river is excellent between 6,000 and 10,000 cfs, and an early spring temperature spike can provide good paddling opportunities. In a normal snow year, the window is late March through early June, with late May probably the best combination of predictable water and nice weather.

The river starts by meandering between farms to the west and the Cliffs of Rome to the east before dropping into Sweetwater Canyon at about mile 6. From here down to the takeout at Birch Creek, the river rears back for dozens of Class II and III rapids.

Like nearly all of the Owyhee's access points, the road to Birch Creek is steep and has tight turns and water crossings that are prone to washing out. The road may be impassable, or closed, during periods of heavy rain, and four-wheel-drive vehicles are recommended. If you can't take out at Birch Creek, the alternative is to take out at Leslie Gulch, but you'll have to paddle an additional 17 miles, most of which is across the Owyhee Reservoir.

Mid Snake River, Birds of Prey

The Snake is a big lazy river as it curves north toward Idaho's border west of Boise. It travels through a mix of dry desert canyons and farmland and is held back by a handful of relatively small dams. It isn't frequently paddled in these reaches with the exception of the miles below Swan Falls Dam, where there's a stunning density and diversity of raptors.

37 Mid Snake River, Birds of Prey

Distance: 15.8 miles
Difficulty: Class II
Craft: Canoe, drift boat, raft, kayak
Approximate paddling time: 8 hours
Flows: 10,000–20,000 cfs (Snake River at Murphey)
Season: Year-round
Put-in: Swan Falls Dam Boat Ramp (43.245391, -116.378760)
Takeout: Walter's Ferry Bridge Boat Ramp (43.341624, -116.603366)
Shuttle: From Nampa, go south on ID 45 to Walter's Ferry. A large parking area and boat ramp are on the south side of the river. From Walter's Ferry to Swan Falls Dam, it's a lot of turns on farm roads. Return north across the bridge on ID 45 and turn left onto Ferry Road. Go 2 miles and turn right (south) on Hill Road, which will turn into Warren Spur Road. Follow Warren Spur Road for 5.8 miles and turn right on McDermott. Go 1 mile and turn left on Victory Road. Go 3 miles to South Swan Falls Road and turn right (south). Follow South Swan Falls Road 6.5 miles to a hairpin turn on the canyon rim, and then another 1.5 miles into the canyon. Once at the bottom of the grade, bear left, and you'll arrive at the boat ramp and a large parking area.

The Snake River Canyon opens up a bit in southwest Idaho, and the river's gradient relaxes as it turns north through the Snake River Birds of Prey National Conservation Area. The 485,000-acre reserve was established in 1993 and includes North

The put-in for the Birds of Prey paddle is below Swan Falls Dam, the first hydroelectric project on the Snake River. PHOTO BY JENNIFER STAHL

The cliffs along the Snake River above Swan Falls Dam are a great habitat for raptors, which the area has in abundance. PHOTO BY JENNIFER STAHL

America's highest density of nesting raptors. The river can be paddled year-round, but the best time to see the canyon's abundant prairie falcons, golden eagles, bald eagles, red-tailed hawks, peregrine falcons, and at least eight other species is mid-March through the end of June.

The float includes some Class II riffles, mostly concentrated near the top of the run, but open canoes are well suited to the float. It's a big river and has swirly eddies and a few waves, but there's little hazard.

The run can also be shortened by taking out on river-right at Celebration Park, an archaeological park with a small museum where visitors can learn about southern Idaho's Native American heritage and view petroglyphs on boulders. Celebration Park is 10 miles below Swan Falls Dam.

Built in 1901, Swan Falls Dam was the first hydroelectric project on the Snake River and the first dam on the Snake to block migrating salmon, which once made it as far upstream as Shoshone Falls. Water levels on the Birds of Prey stretch can fluctuate widely from hour to hour based on electricity demand and corresponding releases at the dam, so either tie your boat up securely or drag it far up the bank if you get out to hike or eat lunch.

Succor Creek

At about 70 miles long, Succor Creek is a small desert stream that starts and ends in Idaho, while flowing for about 40 miles thorugh Oregon. It is a tributary of the Snake River. The rock formations found at Succor Creek State Recreation Area and nearby Leslie Gulch are unique and attract hikers and campers.

38 Succor Creek

Distance: 6.2 miles
Difficulty: Class V
Craft: Kayak
Approximate paddling time: 5–8 hours
Flows: 180–260 cfs (**Gauge:** National Weather Service: Succor Creek near Homedale)
Season: Mar, Apr, May (dependent on rain events)
Put-in: Succor Creek Road (43.380049, -117.119029)
Takeout: Succor Creek State Recreation Area campground (43.453800, -117.119622)
Shuttle: The takeout is at a bridge adjacent to the Succor Creek State Recreation Area campground. To get there take US 95 west toward Jordan Valley and turn right (west) onto McBride Creek Road. Go 8.7 miles to Succor Creek Road and turn right (north). Go 11.3 miles to a bridge crossing the creek next to a campground in Succor Creek State Recreation Area. To get to the put-in, return upriver (generally south) 7.2 miles until Succor Creek Road meets Succor Creek near a ranch. There's a small dirt road near the Pole Creek confluence. Park along Succor Creek Road and walk your boat to Succor Creek. Be respectful of private property in this area, and ask the landowner for permission to access the creek.

The Succor Creek whitewater run is in Oregon, but this tiny creek's headwaters in the Owyhee Mountains and confluence with the Snake River at Homedale are both in Idaho. Among the region's abundant whitewater kayaking opportunities, Succor Creek is unique and possibly the best creeking near Boise.

There are dozens of distinct Class IV and V rapids on this creek. The whitewater starts about 0.25 mile below the put-in with Rattlesnake. If this rapid is outside your comfort zone, it's probably best to hike your boat back to your car, because things only get more challenging downstream when you encounter rapids with names like Swisher Sweets, Italian Pinch, Vietnam, Scary Falls, Lost and Found, Dbag, Skatepark, Barfight, and many others. The most dramatic series of rapids is in Scary Canyon, where five or six unique drops culminate in Scary Falls. The entire canyon can be scouted on the left from a cow trail. There is one rapid that has not been run on Succor Creek. It is just below Scary Canyon. Scout and portage on the left.

This tiny creek is steep and tight and depends almost entirely on rain-on-snow events or a very good winter snowpack for optimal flows. It consists of a dozen or more Class IV and V drops, some extremely tight, and is only navigable via whitewater kayak. It's set in a stunning and secluded desert canyon.

Succor Creek has been run as low as 60 cfs with a number of portages, but the minimum recommended flow is 140 cfs, and it's best between 180 and 260 cfs. As the creek approaches 300 cfs, things start to get rowdy.

With such a small window for optimal flows, figuring out when to go is one of the biggest challenges. There's a gauge in Homedale below the run, but it runs about 12 hours behind what's happening on the whitewater run upstream. There's also a gauge at Jordan Valley above the run, but it only represents a portion of what's going on in the canyon downstream and is only a reliable gauge when the water is coming from snowmelt later in the season.

The rapids in Succor Creek are created by large round polished rhyolite boulders and ledges, which aren't as sticky as the basalt features you find on other runs in southwest Idaho and southeast Oregon. All of the rapids are easily scouted and portaged. Although dirt and gravel, the road is generally in good shape, even during rain events.

—Mike Copeland

Boise River Basin

With its headwaters at 10,000 feet in the Sawtooth Mountains, the Boise River flows west for 200 miles before emptying into the Snake River near the pastoral town of Parma. The upper Boise and its tributaries work through basalt and granite canyons before spilling into the Treasure Valley, where the river meanders gently through the city of Boise and farther west through the Treasure Valley's agricultural communities.

The Boise River basin offers diverse paddling opportunities. This is the put-in for the canyon section of the Boise's South Fork.

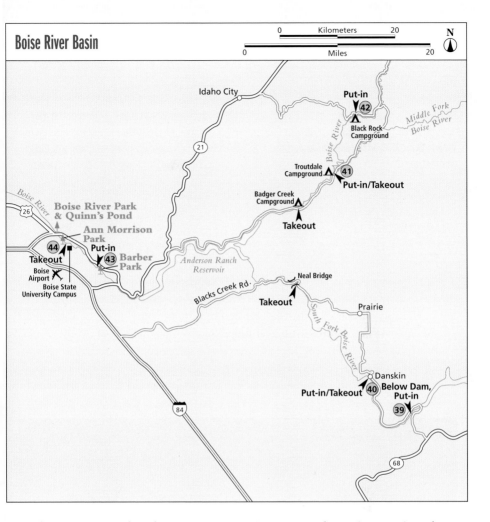

The Boise River has three major reservoirs, two on the main stem just above the city of Boise and another on the South Fork of the Boise. These dams provide irrigation and drinking water for Treasure Valley farmers and residents, but they also create reliable summer flows for several of the Boise River's floatable sections.

Once the second most polluted river in Idaho, the Boise River is now one of the state's most popular natural assets. During a three-month period in the summer, more than 100,000 people float a gentle section through the city of Boise, and the city boasts one of the best river greenbelts and system of riverside parks anywhere in the country.

39 South Fork of the Boise, Dam to Danskin Bridge

Distance: 11 miles
Difficulty: Class II
Craft: Canoe, kayak, raft, drift boat
Approximate paddling time: 4–6 hours
Flows: 600–2,000 cfs (**Gauge:** Anderson Ranch Dam)
Season: May–Sept (dependent on dam releases)
Put-in: Anderson Ranch Dam (43.354740, -115.454659)

Takeout: Danskin Bridge Boat Ramp (43.403692, -115.562414)
Shuttle: From US 20 turn north onto FR 134 (20.7 miles east of I-84 near Mountain Home). From there it's only 5 miles to Anderson Ranch Dam, the put-in, and another 10 miles downstream to the takeout at the boat ramp above Danskin Bridge.

This roadside run used to be a great deal easier, but landslides in 2013 and 2014 raised the stakes a bit. It's still a good run for intermediate kayakers, rafters, and drift boaters, but open canoeists should either be prepared to portage some rapids or adjust their put-ins and takeouts to miss the bigger drops.

As of this writing, there still hasn't been a large spring runoff. When that happens, some of the new rapids could ease in difficulty as the river's erosive power goes to work. The water in the South Fork drainage is clear and very, very cold. Prepare accordingly.

The rapids on the upper South Fork of the Boise are fairly straightforward, but open canoeists might want to portage.

40 South Fork of the Boise, Canyon

Distance: 16.5 miles
Difficulty: Class IV+
Craft: Canoe, kayak, raft
Approximate paddling time: 4–6 hours
Flows: 600–3,000 cfs (**Gauge:** South Fork Boise at Anderson Ranch Dam)
Season: May–Sept (dependent on dam releases)
Put-in: Danskin Bridge Boat Ramp (43.403692, -115.562414)
Takeout: Neal Bridge (43.550045, -115.721602)
Shuttle: From Boise go 10 miles south on I-84 to exit 64, Blacks Creek Road. Travel 6.3 miles east and turn left (north) to stay on Blacks Creeks Road. Continue 18 miles to a bridge that crosses the South Fork. The takeout is on river-left just above the bridge. The put-in is 20.7 miles away. Cross the bridge and continue on FR 189 11 miles to Prairie. Turn right onto FR 113 (Prairie Road) and follow it 10 miles to the takeout. You can also access the area from US 20 near Mountain Home. The turn onto FR 134 is 20.7 miles east of I-84 near Mountain Home. From there it's only 5 miles to Anderson Ranch Dam, and another 10 miles downstream to the put-in.

The South Fork of the Boise underwent an abrupt transformation in 2013 when a wildfire swept through the area and left the canyon walls covered in charcoaled trees—and less vegetation to hold soil in place. Heavy rains during the summer of 2014 then resulted in huge landslides that plowed into the river and rearranged this classic Idaho whitewater run.

In general, the river is similar to the way it was—with the addition of several new rapids including a big Class IV+. It's very likely that this and other new rapids on the stretch will continue to change as water ebbs and flows from year to year, so don't rely too heavily on this or any other guide, and do some homework before you launch. The fire also caused a large number of very big trees to fall into the river, and they are certain to shift. Be prepared to scout blind horizons.

New rapids in the South Fork Boise River canyon make the run considerably tougher and warrant scouting.

Scenery in the South Fork Boise canyon is stunning.

The run starts gently in a broad and scenic valley. About 4.5 miles from the put-in, an inner basalt gorge takes shape, and this is where the water starts to take on Class II characteristics. In fact, from here to the takeout, it's a very lively float. At about mile 8 granite rock formations start to define the lower canyon walls, as well as the riverbed. The first named rapid, Raspberry, comes at mile 9 and is followed by Devil's Hole at mile 10.5. After this, settle in for a few miles of splashy Class II, and when the river pools and you see pine trees protruding from the depths, get out to scout on the left. This is Buffalo Creek, the biggest of the new rapids, at mile 13.

At 1,800 cfs, a little more than the standard summer release, Buffalo Creek is a solid Class IV+, and it probably becomes Class V as water levels climb higher. As of this writing there were also several logs in the middle of the rapid, making it an even tighter run. It's also long, and paddlers should make sure to scout the bottom, which contains some shallow rocks and at least one big log. The portage is doable but long, and over rough terrain.

The final rapid, mile 15.5, is also new. This Class IV drop is fairly straightforward but has big waves and a couple of sticky holes.

Summer flows on the South Fork Boise are released from the bottom of Anderson Ranch Dam, and the water is very cold. This makes for great fishing, but it also means paddlers must be prepared with proper gear.

41 Middle Fork of the Boise, Twin Springs

Distance: 10.5 miles
Difficulty: Class II–III
Craft: Canoe, kayak, raft
Approximate paddling time: 2–4 hours
Flows: 500–3,000 cfs (**Gauge:** Boise River at Twin Springs)
Season: May, June, July
Put-in: Troutdale Campground (43.713026, -115.634450)

Takeout: Badger Creek Campground (43.662054, -115.711733)
Shuttle: From Boise take ID 21 east past Lucky Peak Dam. Go about 6 miles past the dam and turn right onto Lucky Peak Road, which passes Spring Shores Marina. Stay on the road, which changes name a few times, for 21.5 miles to the takeout. To get to the put-in, continue another 10 miles upstream. Troutdale Campground will be on your left.

The Middle Fork of the Boise through Twin Springs is a mellow stretch of swift water suitable for beginning kayakers, rafters, and ambitious open canoeists. During summer flows the river is swift but straightforward, but it picks up steam during runoff with big breaking waves and powerful eddies.

Because the entire run is roadside, put-ins and takeouts are somewhat arbitrary. The entire float can be scouted while setting up shuttle.

42 North Fork of the Boise

Distance: 10.2 miles
Difficulty: Class IV
Craft: Canoe, kayak, raft
Approximate paddling time: 3–5 hours
Flows: 1,500–5,000 cfs (**Gauge:** None. Approximately 40 percent of the Boise River at Twin Springs.)
Season: May, June, early July
Put-in: Black Rock Campground (43.795458, -115.589249)
Takeout: Troutdale Campground (43.713026, -115.634450)

Shuttle: To get to the put-in from Idaho City, go 2.1 miles northeast on ID 21 and turn right on FR 327. Continue over the divide and down along Rabbit Creek for 18 miles until you reach the North Fork and, shortly after, Black Rock Campground. To get to the takeout, continue upstream 3.7 miles and turn right onto FR 376. Cross the river and drive over the mountain, 5 miles to FR 82, Middle Fork of the Boise River Road. Turn right, downstream, and go 8.8 miles to Troutdale Campground.

The North Fork of the Boise is a fantastic and beautiful Class IV whitewater run for rafts, kayaks, and whitewater canoes. While the float through the North Fork's roadless granite canyon is worth the effort, the 20-mile shuttle is long and climbs over a 1,000-foot divide that can be snowed in early in the season. This is truck country, where even four-by-four cars may struggle.

Paddlers collect themselves before starting the North Fork Boise's continuous whitewater.

The 12 miles of whitewater begin at Black Rock Campground, the put-in, and within a mile or two of scenic, easy floating the road vanishes. After a few more bends in the river, a gray granite wall slants over the river's northwest bank. This is where things get interesting.

The river begins to drop at close to 200 feet per mile, and the mile-long rapid is a blur of crashing waves and holes. It's manageable whitewater for Class IV boaters, but the wilderness setting and length of the rapid raise the stakes.

Several steep rapids follow in the miles after this exhilarating initiation to the North Fork, but they ease in difficulty as the river descends. The lower canyon changes character, with sagebrush hills studded with the gold blooms of arrowleaf balsamroot sloping to the water's edge in spring.

43 Boise River, Barber Park

Distance: 5.8 miles
Difficulty: Class II
Craft: Canoe, kayak, raft
Approximate paddling time: 2–4 hours
Flows: 500–1,500 cfs (**Gauge:** Boise River at Glenwood Bridge)
Season: June, July, Aug, Sept
Put-in: Barber Park (43.566244, -116.133528)
Takeout: Ann Morrison Park (43.611894, -116.217283)
Shuttle: There are numerous put-in and take-out options along the Boise River. This standard float, however, ends in Ann Morrison Park. From 9th Street turn west onto Royal Boulevard and go about 0.5 mile into the park, where there's street-side parallel parking and a few paved lots within a short walk of the river and the takeout near a pedestrian bridge. There are a number of fairly efficient ways to get to the put-in from Ann Morrison Park. One is to return to 9th Street, which quickly becomes Capitol Boulevard, and head south, bearing left onto Federal Way. Take Federal Way 3.8 miles and turn left onto Amity Road. After 1.8 miles Amity Road will bear left and become Healey Road. Healey Road will then become Eckert Road. The turn into Barber Park is on the south side of the bridge spanning the Boise River.

This mellow cruise through the heart of downtown Boise is one of the most popular paddles in America, with more than 100,000 people floating the river during a typical summer season. On a hot sunny afternoon, hundreds of canoeists, rafters, inner tubers, and pool-toy floaters can be seen bobbing down the Boise River's swift and very chilly currents.

The section has a great combination of consistent water flowing through a beautiful greenbelt with incredibly easy access. There are three diversions at normal summer flows that create straightforward and short Class II rapids. There are also a few powerful eddy lines and some corners where the current attempts to push paddlers into low-hanging trees. It can be a challenge in an open canoe. To beat the crowds, try floating this one in the morning. Also, don't miss the takeout on river-left at Ann Morrison Park; there's a low-head dam a few hundred yards downstream.

The section has some very good playboating opportunities for kayakers when water

The Boise River flows through the heart of downtown Boise.

A huge, nearly river-wide wave forms below Barber Park at high water.

is high. At 5,000 to 8,000 cfs (generally in April and May, if at all), there's an incredible river-wide wave that forms at an irrigation diversion about a mile below the Barber Park put-in. Another mile downstream at a diversion boaters call The Weir is a shallow surf wave that's in at about 1,000 to 3,000 cfs.

For those seeking additional swift and brushy floating opportunities, the Boise River has several floatable sections downstream of the Barber Park run. Try putting in below the low-head dam at Ann Morrison Park near Americana Boulevard and floating to Glenwood Bridge 5 miles downstream. This section includes the first phase of Boise's new whitewater park, which so far consists of an outstanding surf wave for kayakers and surfboarders. (See Boise River Park on page 89.) Another option is to put on at Glenwood Bridge and float to Star Road via the south channel at Eagle Island. Both runs are brushy and include several irrigation diversions.

44 Boise River, Boise River Park and Quinn's Pond

Difficulty: Class I-II
Craft: Canoe, kayak, raft, surfboard, stand-up paddleboard
Flows: 500-3,000 cfs (**Gauge:** Boise River at Glenwood Bridge)
Season: Year-round
Access: Boise River Park (43.625468, -116.234289)

Shuttle: The Boise River Park is off of Whitewater Boulevard in Boise. Access could change slightly with construction of Phase 2, but it is near Idaho River Sports, an excellent local paddling shop that offers rentals.
Additional information: boiseriverpark.com

In 2012 the city of Boise unveiled the first phase of a multi-million-dollar river park on the Boise River near Quinn's Pond. The $3.6 million first phase involved installing two state-of-the-art pneumatically operated air bladders that elevate stainless steel flashboards beneath the river's surface. What this means is the city can adjust the resulting waves and shape them to work at varying water levels and to meet desired

Quinn's Pond is an excellent, family-friendly location to paddle right in the heart of Boise.

The first phase of Boise River Park includes waves that are excellent for surfing and kayaking.

surfing conditions. The devices, called Wave Shapers, were designed by Denver-based McLaughlin Whitewater Design Group, and the cool part is that they work.

During normal summer flows, the adjustable Wave Shapers create two waves—one about 20 feet wide, the other about 25 feet wide—and there's fantastic eddy service for both waves. Since the Wave Shapers' installation the park has become extremely popular with kayakers, surfboarders, boogie boarders, and crowds of onlookers. Idaho's land-locked surfboarders, in particular, have blossomed in number, and the features are shaped to meet surfers' need for greener waves every other day.

The new surf waves are adjacent to Quinn's Pond, an excellent location for stand-up paddleboards, canoes, and recreational watercraft of any kind. The $7.3 million second phase of the Boise River Park commenced in 2015 with plans to expand the downriver portion of the park for 0.5 mile. The second phase, when complete, will also include rehabilitation of two additional ponds within 55-acre Esther Simplot Park, an area that was once an unsightly concrete plant. Paddlers should be able to float down the Boise River and return upstream via the ponds and a system of canals with only short walks across pedestrian and bicycle paths.

Payette River Basin

The Payette River system is sometimes called Idaho's "University of Whitewater." The North and South Forks of the Payette benefit from dams and irrigation releases that keep water flowing all summer on outstanding runs of every level of difficulty. For this reason and more, the Payette basin is perhaps the most popular and well-known whitewater drainage in Idaho, with an incredible diversity of runnable rivers.

The Payette was named for a French-Canadian explorer and fur trapper, Francois Payette, whose exploits have been preserved in regional nomenclature, including the river and a west Idaho town. With its headwaters at over 10,000 feet in the Sawtooth and Salmon River Mountains, the Payette has a 3,240-square-mile drainage basin that benefits from heavy winter snowfall and resulting spring runoff.

Camping at USDA Forest Service campgrounds throughout the basin is excellent, and services include restaurants, gas stations, grocery stores, and lodging in a number of small towns.

The Payette River Basin is chock-full of diverse, revered paddling opportunities. This is Steepness on the Payette's North Fork.

The primary tributaries of the Payette are the North and South Forks, which feature some of the state's most popular whitewater. The North Fork starts in the mountains northeast of McCall and meanders south across a broad and scenic prairie before dropping into a 16-mile canyon that's widely considered one of the most challenging whitewater runs in America. The predominantly Class IV South Fork starts high in the Sawtooth Mountains and flows swiftly west through ponderosa pine forests and canyons before joining the North Fork at Banks to form the Main Payette, a Class II and III standout.

Less than an hour from Boise, the village of Banks is the hub of the basin's whitewater activity and lies at the confluence of the North and South Forks. Don't let the Payette's reputation as a world-class whitewater destination keep you away if you're a flatwater paddler. There are amazing mountain lakes, gently meandering streams, and standout beauty at every turn.

South Fork of the Payette

The South Fork of the Payette starts high in the Sawtooth Mountains, central Idaho's backbone and the headwaters of four major river basins. It flows clear and cold among a ponderosa pine forest for more than 70 miles before merging with the North Fork at Banks. At high water boaters have been known to run the entire length of the river in a day, but it's a very big and challenging day.

The uppermost reaches of the South Fork are within the Sawtooth Wilderness Area and can be accessed only on foot. Paddling opportunities start at Grandjean, an outpost named for Danish forester Emile Grandjean, who in the early 1900s was among the most educated forest rangers in the country and the second supervisor of the Boise National Forest.

From Grandjean downstream, the South Fork gradually grows from a swift mountain stream to a large and powerful river. It's primarily an advanced whitewater river with three sections of outstanding Class IV. There are also two good mellow floats, a Class II whitewater run, and a flatwater canoe trip on the South Fork itself, and a Class I canoe trip on the Middle Fork of the Payette, which joins the South Fork in Garden Valley.

The Deadwood River meets the South Fork below Lowman and feeds it with dam-released irrigation flows through the entire summer, long after spring snowmelt has ebbed. The only paddle that doesn't benefit from the Deadwood's summer-long boost of water is the uppermost section that starts at Grandjean.

Camping at forest service campgrounds along the entire length of the South Fork is outstanding, and there are a number of excellent hot springs as well.

45 South Fork Payette, Grandjean

Distance: 28 miles
Difficulty: Class III–IV
Craft: Kayak, raft, canoe
Approximate paddling time: 8 hours
Flows: 500–3,000 cfs (**Gauge:** USGS, South Fork Payette at Lowman)
Season: May, June
Put-in: Wapiti Creek Road bridge in Grandjean (44.162265, -115.188760)
Alternate put-in/takeout: Helende Campground (44.093754, -115.469560)

Takeout: Mountain View Campground (44.078121, -115.603733)
Shuttle: From Banks, take the Banks Lowman Road 33.3 miles to a T intersection with ID 21. Turn left, heading east on ID 21, and go 0.6 mile to Mountain View Campground on the right. To reach the put-in, return to ID 21 and continue east for 20.4 miles. Turn right on Grandjean Road and go 4.7 miles to Wapiti Creek Road and the bridge. Helende Creek Campground is 8.2 miles east on ID 21 from Mountain View Campground.

From Grandjean to Lowman, the South Fork tumbles through a narrow, steep-walled valley next to ID 21. The riverbed is, for the most part, cobbled and nondescript, but there are a handful of good Class III and IV rapids that vary in character.

At the top of the run, the river is small, swift, and prone to collecting wood, but it quickly picks up the flows from a number of tributary streams. Canyon Creek Rapid, a Class IV, comes at mile 3.6 and can be scouted from Grandjean Road while you're setting up shuttle. There's a series of Class III waves at mile 7.5 near Warm Springs Creek, and another good Class IV below Chapman Creek, mile 8.6. River access is difficult for about 9 miles below Chapman Creek, particularly for rafters. For this reason many paddlers choose to start their trips at Helende Campground, another 5 miles downstream.

Rapids pick up again 3.7 miles below Helende Campground and culminate at Kirkham Gorge. The hot springs in the gorge are outstanding, but they're also popular. Don't expect a secluded soak. Kayakers can take out here, but rafters should continue another 3 miles to Mountain View Campground, 9.1 miles below Helende.

There's an abundance of public land surrounding the upper South Fork, and put-ins and takeouts are somewhat arbitrary, particularly for kayakers.

South Fork Payette River

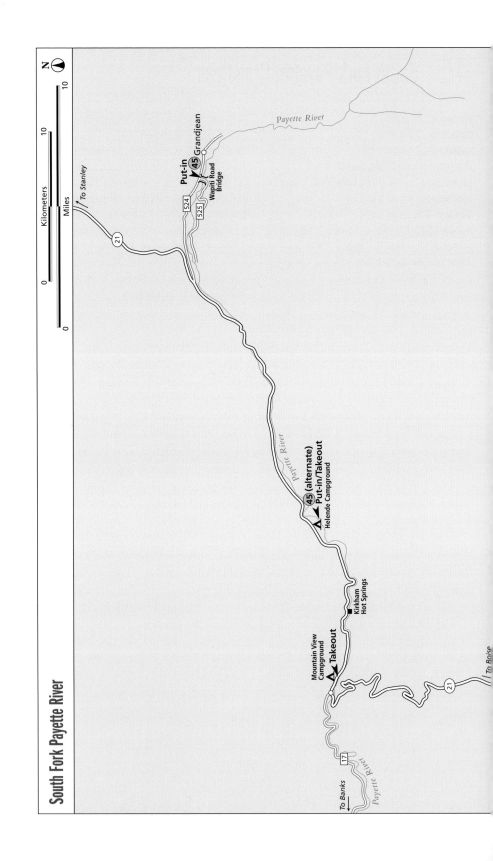

N

0   Kilometers   10

0   Miles   10

To Stanley

21

524

525

45   Put-in

Grandjean

Wapiti Road Bridge

Payette River

Payette River

45 (alternate)
Put-in/Takeout

Helende Campground

Kirkham Hot Springs

Mountain View Campground

Takeout

21

To Boise

17

To Banks

Payette River

Payette River

46 Deadwood Reservoir

Distance: 1–12 miles
Difficulty: Flat water
Launch site: Cozy Cove Campground (44.291817, -115.653154)
Craft: Canoe, kayak, stand-up paddleboard
Approximate paddling time: 1–8 hours
Season: June–Oct
Access: Deadwood Reservoir can be accessed via dirt roads from Cascade, Stanley, and Garden Valley. The directions here are from Garden Valley and the South Fork of the Payette. From Garden Valley drive 13.1 miles east on Banks Lowman Road and turn left on Scott Mountain Road (there's a sign for Deadwood Reservoir). Go 9.8 miles on Scott Mountain Road and turn right to stay on Scott Mountain Road, continuing 14.3 miles. Cozy Cove Campground and Deadwood Reservoir will be on your left.

At 2 miles across and 3 miles long and just over a mile above sea level, Deadwood Reservoir is a decent-size body of water that's far off the beaten path for flatwater paddlers. There may be some anglers motoring around, but you can almost count on seclusion and solitude.

Built in 1931 by the US Bureau of Reclamation, Deadwood Dam is a concrete arch dam that's 165 feet tall and provides regulated flows for irrigation and power production far downstream below Horseshoe Bend. The reservoir fills each spring and gradually empties through the summer, so try to visit early in the season.

47 Deadwood River

Distance: 22.9 miles
Difficulty: Class V
Craft: Kayak
Approximate paddling time: 1 day
Flows: 500-1,500 cfs (**Gauge:** USGS, Deadwood River below Deadwood Reservoir near Lowman)
Season: June, July, Aug (dependent on dam releases)
Put-in: Deadwood Dam (42.263907, -111.752428)
Takeout: South Fork Payette Confluence (44.080750, -115.657801)

Shuttle: From Banks, take the Banks Lowman Road 30 miles upriver to Deadwood Campground at the confluence of the Deadwood River with the South Fork. Getting to the put-in is an ordeal. Return to the Banks Lowman Road, heading downriver, for 6.8 miles and turn right on Scott Mountain Road (there's a sign for Deadwood Reservoir). Go 9.8 miles on Scott Mountain Road and turn right to stay on Scott Mountain Road, continuing 14.5 miles. There's parking at the bridge below Deadwood Dam.

The Deadwood is a beautiful and secluded river that's full of difficult rapids and dangerous logjams. This is a challenging all-day paddle that includes numerous portages. The Deadwood's flows are supplied by releases from the bottom of Deadwood Reservoir, and the water is very cold. Paddlers must dress warm.

The Deadwood used to be divided into a difficult 14-mile upper section and a more manageable 8-mile lower. The road to access the lower section washed out more than a decade ago, and the entire 23 miles must now be done as a single trip.

The run is mostly Class III and IV, but there are several more difficult sections that include Class V rapids. The logjams, which shift from year to year, are a significant hazard. Blind corners and horizon lines must always be scouted.

The first series of rapids starts at mile 3.4 on a hard right bend. From there the river is continuous Class IV–V for 1.5 miles. After this initiation to the Deadwood, it's another 5 miles of swift Class II and III before the hardest rapid, 0.5-mile-long drop that is guaranteed to be full of logs. Most boaters at least portage the top half. Another series of difficult rapids starts 2 miles later.

At mile 14.3, you'll pass under a bridge. This used to be the put-in for the lower Deadwood and now marks the end of the white-knuckle part of the run. Logjams, however, are a constant threat on any part of the river, and paddlers cannot let down their guard. It's another 8.6 miles of fairly continuous Class III and IV to the confluence with the South Fork.

South Fork/North Fork/Middle Fork Payette River

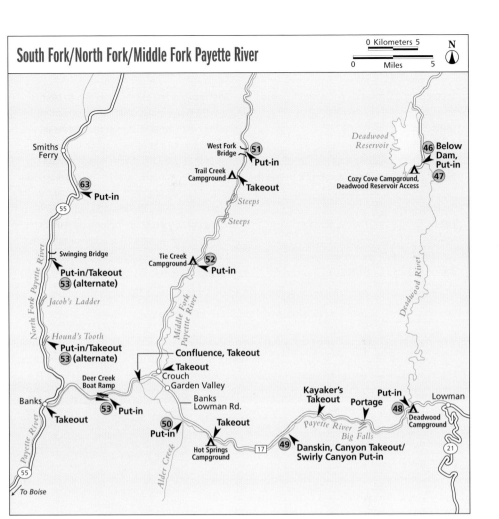

0 Kilometers 5

0 Miles 5

N

Deadwood Reservoir

Smiths Ferry

West Fork Bridge **51** **Put-in**

Trail Creek Campground **Takeout**

46 **Below Dam, Put-in**

Cozy Cove Campground, Deadwood Reservoir Access **47**

63 **Put-in**

55

Steeps

Steeps

Swinging Bridge
Put-in/Takeout
53 **(alternate)**

Tie Creek Campground **52** **Put-in**

Deadwood River

North Fork Payette River

Jacob's Ladder

Middle Fork Payette River

Hound's Tooth
Put-in/Takeout
53 **(alternate)**

Confluence, Takeout

Takeout
Crouch
Garden Valley

Deer Creek Boat Ramp

Kayaker's Takeout

Put-in
Portage **48**

Lowman

Deadwood Campground

Banks
Takeout

53 **Put-in**

Banks Lowman Rd.

50 **Put-in**

Takeout

Payette River
Big Falls

Payette River

Hot Springs Campground

17 **49** **Danskin, Canyon Takeout/ Swirly Canyon Put-in**

21

Alder Creek

55
To Boise

48 South Fork Payette, Canyon

Distance: 11.7 miles (9.1 miles to kayaker takeout)
Difficulty: Class IV (V+/VI)
Craft: Kayak, raft, canoe
Approximate paddling time: 4-6 hours
Flows: 500-3,000 cfs (**Gauge:** USGS, South Fork Payette at Lowman plus Deadwood flow)
Season: Apr–Aug
Put-in: Deadwood River confluence (44.080750, -115.657801)
Takeout: Danskin Station Boat Ramp (44.062114, -115.812910)

Shuttle: To reach the takeout from Banks, take Banks Lowman Road 20 miles upriver to the east. Danskin Station Boat Ramp, a fee area, is on the right. To get to the kayaker takeout, continue 2.3 miles farther to highway mile 21.9. It's a large and fairly distinctive dirt pullout but is unmarked. To reach the put-in, continue upriver to Deadwood Campground at the confluence of the Deadwood River. There's boater access via a large paved pullout and boat ramp across the highway from the campground. Both the put-in at Deadwood and takeout at Danskin are fee areas.

The competition is stiff, but this could be Idaho's best Class IV day trip. With towering canyon walls, ample seclusion, challenging rapids, and reliable summer flows, the Canyon has a lot going for it.

From the put-in through most of the run, the road climbs far above the river and gives it wilderness character. The canyon walls are steep, the water swift and very cold, even during the hottest parts of the year.

The first rapid, Oxbow, offers a nice warm-up and comes after a little less than a mile. Pine Flat Hot Springs, mile 3.6, is early in the paddle but worth a stop. From Pine Flat it's a short paddle to Gateway, a Class III+ and the first challenging rapid of the run. The slots on the left can be paddled in a kayak, but the standard line is on the right. S-Turn, a long Class IV, comes at mile 5.2 and is recognizable by a sharp left bend around a cliff. The rapids start right after the bend.

About 0.5 mile below S-Turn, boaters need to be on the lookout for Big Falls, a Class V+/VI rapid that's a standard and recommended portage. This huge rapid has been run intentionally (and unintentionally), but boaters who choose to test their mettle here are very selective about flows.

Seal launching after the portage at Big Falls

The water leading into Big Falls consists of Class II riffles, and eddies along the river-left bank where you'll exit are small. This isn't a tough move, but it's not a place to fall asleep either. The portage is also fairly technical. Kayakers should be prepared to climb down a rocky, slippery trail to a 5-foot seal launch. Rafters don't have it so easy and must carry around the falls and then line their boats through the short gorge that follows.

Below Big Falls, the rapids become more difficult and more frequent. At high water, the river is very continuous, but at standard summer flows there's plenty of time to recover between drops.

First up is Blackadar, named for the pioneering Idaho kayaker, Dr. Walt Blackadar, who died in the rapid when he pinned on a log. The line is down the center to center-right, but even if you hit it perfectly you're going to take a big hit. Lower Blackadar, a boulder garden, follows in short order.

The next major rapid, Lone Pine, comes 1.5 miles later, after the road rejoins the river. You'll know you're almost there when you see

The unique hot spring waterfall at Pine Flat is popular.

a large pine tree growing high on the river-right bank. The rapid is divided by a dike in the middle of the river. The standard line is right of the rock.

About 0.5 mile below Lone Pine is Little Falls, a river-wide ledge that's got a sticky and dangerous reversal in the center. At flows between 1,000 and 2,000 cfs, kayakers usually boof the far river-left ledge. As the water gets higher, it's wise to run this one on the right.

After Little Falls the river descends into a small gorge and the run's final standout rapid, Surprise. Enter right, exit left. A huge hole forms near the end of this rapid right of center.

Kayakers can take out shortly after Surprise on the right, just after a small island. A primitive trail ascends to a large, unmarked pullout along the highway. For rafters and others who want a little more time on the river, it's another 2 miles to the Danskin Station Boat Ramp.

Note that the gauge on the South Fork at Lowman does not include flow from the Deadwood River, which is fed by summer irrigation releases.

49 South Fork Payette, Swirly Canyon

Distance: 5.8 miles
Difficulty: Class II–III
Craft: Canoe, kayak, raft
Approximate paddling time: 2–4 hours
Flows: 500–2,000 cfs (**Gauge:** USGS, South Fork Payette at Lowman plus Deadwood flow)
Season: May–Oct
Put-in: Danskin Station Boat Ramp (44.062114, -115.812910)

Takeout: Hot Springs Campground (44.053953, -115.907921)
Shuttle: To get to the takeout from Banks, drive 13.9 miles east on Banks Lowman Road. Hot Springs Campground is on the left (north) side of the highway, and there's a large, paved parking area on the right. To reach the put-in at Danskin Station, return to Banks Lowman Road and drive 5.6 miles east. A large paved parking area, toilets, and boat ramp are on the right.

This is a scenic and usually overlooked stretch that starts where the Canyon paddle ends. The river works through a beautiful gorge with sheer 150-foot walls and a number of rock ledges. True to the run's name, there are also a number of great eddies that create abundant swirly water.

Near the end of the run is an old dam, long since removed, that can create a decent surf wave. As the water comes down in the fall, this is an excellent Class II open canoe run.

50 South Fork Payette, Garden Valley

Distance: 4 miles
Difficulty: Class II
Craft: Canoe, kayak, raft
Approximate paddling time: 1–3 hours
Flows: 500–2,000 cfs (**Gauge:** USGS, South Fork Payette at Lowman plus Deadwood flow)
Season: Apr–Oct
Put-in: Alder Creek Bridge (44.070680, -115.945756)
Takeout: Middle Fork Payette confluence (44.104033, -116.001020)

Shuttle: From Banks go 7.3 miles east on Banks Lowman Road to a pullout on the right side of the highway near the confluence of the Middle and South Forks of the Payette. To reach the put-in, continue east on Banks Lowman Road for 4.4 miles and turn right on Alder Creek Road. Go 0.2 mile to the south side of the bridge, where you'll find parking and a rough trail to the riverbank.

Below Alder Creek Bridge the South Fork mellows as it winds through pastoral Garden Valley. It's excellent as an evening canoe float to take in a day's last sun as it sweeps across the nearby mountains.

You can put in at Hot Springs Campground or Alder Creek Bridge. You can take out at the confluence with the Middle Fork of the Payette or at Deer Creek Boat Ramp. Taking out at Deer Creek adds a couple miles of Class I and II riffles.

The river is very large during spring runoff, but by mid-June most years it is merely swift, with no rapids. The water gets even calmer and slower in the fall, when dam releases are turned off.

From Alder Creek Bridge for 4 miles downstream, the South Fork of the Payette is a scenic, mellow river.

51 Middle Fork Payette, Upper

Distance: 1.8 miles
Difficulty: Class IV
Craft: Kayak
Approximate paddling time: 1–3 hours
Flows: 500–1,000 cfs (**Gauge:** USGS, Middle Fork Payette River at Crouch)
Season: June
Put-in: West Fork Bridge at Silver Creek confluence (44.304233, -115.865007)
Takeout: Hot springs upstream of Trail Creek (44.281919, -115.874087)

Shuttle: The takeout for this run is tough to find. From Crouch drive 15.1 miles up the Middle Fork to where the road starts to climb up above the river. There's a small unimproved dirt road that descends to the Middle Fork. It's about 0.25 mile past Trail Creek Campground. To get to the put-in, continue another 2 miles upriver to West Fork Bridge near the Silver Creek confluence.

This is a short, fun whitewater trip that's 17 miles above Crouch on the Middle Fork. It's got several steep drops, including a small waterfall.

It starts as a swift, shallow stream and after a mile drops into a canyon containing a half-dozen Class IV rapids, culminating with the waterfall.

The Middle Fork crests at several thousand cfs every spring and moves logs around considerably, so keep your eyes peeled and scout blind corners and rapids.

If you're interested in more hair-raising paddling, the Middle Fork Steeps are farther downstream. Because of the amount of wood, there's not usually a continuous combination of drops to put together, but the Class V granite boulders, ledges, and waterfalls are obvious from the road. There are two sections, one 12 miles above Crouch and the other 14 miles above Crouch. Each is about a mile long and should be tested at low water levels, 400–600 cfs.

A roadside rapid, the Middle Fork Steeps can and should be scouted top to bottom before putting on. Photo by Andrew Post

52 Middle Fork Payette, Lower

Distance: 9.7 miles
Difficulty: Class I
Craft: Canoe, recreational kayak, stand-up paddleboard
Approximate paddling time: 2–4 hours
Flows: 500–1,000 cfs (**Gauge:** USGS, Middle Fork Payette River at Crouch)
Season: June, July, Aug

Put-in: Tie Creek Campground (44.208504, -115.925166)
Takeout: Old Crouch Road, Crouch (44.113839, -115.970055)
Shuttle: Plant a takeout vehicle near Old Crouch Road bridge in downtown Crouch near the Crouch Merc. From there take Middle Fork Road 8.1 miles north to Tie Creek Campground.

This enjoyable and gentle canoe float starts in the forest but quickly flows into the pastoral outskirts of Crouch, where it meanders considerably and passes numerous cabins and beneath a few bridges. The current can be swift at medium and high flows, but there are no rapids. It's an excellent canoe trip.

53 South Fork Payette, Staircase

Distance: 4.6 miles
Difficulty: Class IV
Craft: Kayak, raft, canoe
Approximate paddling time: 2–3 hours
Flows: 500–8,000 cfs (**Gauge:** USGS, South Fork Payette at Lowman)
Season: Apr–Oct
Put-in: Deer Creek Boat Ramp (44.092632, -116.042961)

Takeout: Banks (44.084375, -116.116365)
Shuttle: The takeout is at Banks, a fee area that's 15 miles north of Horseshoe Bend on ID 55. To reach the put-in, drive 4.5 miles upriver on the Banks-Lowman Road. The Deer Creek Boat Ramp facility, another fee site, includes ample parking and a toilet.

Staircase is graduate school for aspiring Payette paddlers. At high flows its two long Class IV rapids, Staircase and Slalom, offer a small taste of the challenges offered on the North Fork—with emphasis on the word *small*.

There's a warm-up drop just below the put-in, but the real action starts with Bronco Billy, a long Class III+ about 0.5 mile into the run. A couple more tight Class

At 3,000 cfs Staircase Rapid is only mildly pushy and super fun.

III pool-drop rapids lead to the run's toughest and namesake rapid, Staircase, which can be identified from the road and river by the huge highway pullout. At more than 0.25 mile long, Staircase is a lengthy boulder garden full of eddies and holes.

Slalom is last and comes about 1.5 miles after Staircase. The entry down the tongue is straightforward, but the current feeds into a big hole that's reputable enough to have earned a name: Seymour. Level depending, you can move around it on the left or right, but the left line leaves a bigger margin for error. Particularly at high water Seymour is a big, sticky feature and is almost sure to flip rafts lazy enough to hit it.

This run can be paddled at a wide variety of levels and at low water is technical Class III for kayakers. It starts to take on Class IV characteristics, with

The bottom of Staircase Rapid is a long, continuous run-out.

lines opening up for rafts, around 1,000 cfs. The nearest South Fork gauge is far upstream at Lowman and does not include flows from the Deadwood River, which has a summer-long irrigation release, or from the Middle Fork of the Payette. Another way to calculate the flow is to look at the gauge for the Main Payette at Horseshoe Bend and subtract the flow of the North Fork.

North Fork of the Payette

The North Fork of the Payette flows more than a hundred miles from the mountains above McCall to its confluence with the South Fork of the Payette in Banks, about 40 miles north of Boise. The North Fork contains a dozen or so paddling options, more than half of them ranking among Idaho's best trips. Better still, they are diverse. There are mountain lakes, quiet and meandering canoe miles, hair-raising Class V whitewater, and a great whitewater park in the town of Cascade.

The North Fork descends from the Salmon River Mountains and folds into Payette Lake, where the resort town of McCall is situated on the southwest shore. It continues south across Long Valley until it's stilled by Cascade dam and reservoir. While the reservoir can be paddled, it's shallow and relatively unpopular. The reservoir does, however, provide sustained flows through the entire summer season, and part of the fall season, most years. This means that the flatwater and whitewater paddling downstream from Cascade has a very long season.

The North Fork of the Payette has fantastic whitewater and flatwater paddling opportunities. This is Howard's Plunge, the final Class III rapid on the Cabarton section. PHOTO COURTESY JEFF COLE

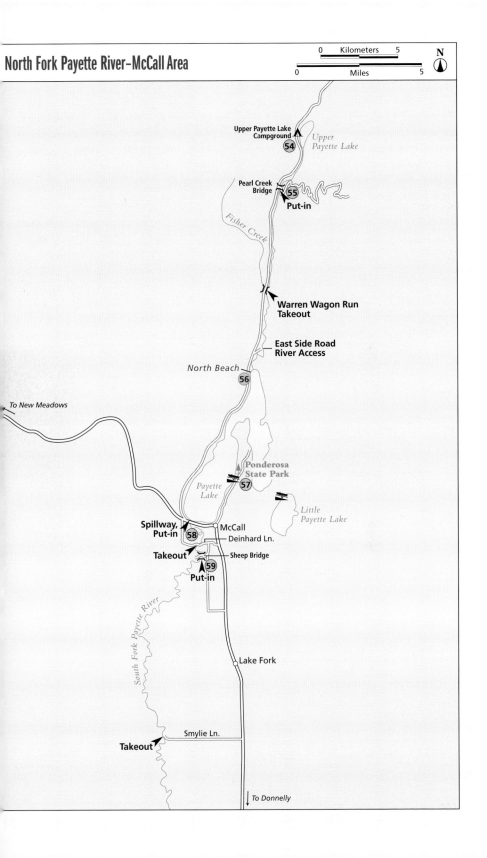

Upper Payette Lake
Campground
54
Upper
Payette Lake

Pearl Creek
Bridge
55
Put-in

Fisher Creek

**Warren Wagon Run
Takeout**

**East Side Road
River Access**

North Beach
56

To New Meadows

**Ponderosa
State Park**
57

Payette
Lake

Little
Payette Lake

**Spillway,
Put-in**
58
McCall
Deinhard Ln.

Takeout
Sheep Bridge
59
Put-in

South Fork Payette River

Lake Fork

Smylie Ln.
Takeout

To Donnelly

54 North Fork Payette, Upper Payette Lake

Distance: 1–4 miles
Difficulty: Flat water
Craft: Canoe, recreational kayak
Approximate paddling time: 1–4 hours
Season: June, July, Aug, Sept
Launch site: Upper Payette Lake Campground
(45.125346, -116.026301)

Access: From downtown McCall take ID 55 1.2 miles and turn right on Warren Wagon Road. Go 15.4 miles and turn left just before the bridge crossing the Upper Payette Lake outlet. The campground is 1 mile ahead on the right.

At 0.5 mile wide and a couple miles long, Upper Payette Lake is small, but it's nestled among white granite mountains and dense stands of Douglas fir near the North Fork of the Payette's headwaters. Paddlers are almost guaranteed to have the place to themselves.

Try going in the early morning or evening twilight, when your odds of seeing deer, elk, moose, and birds of prey are high.

55 North Fork Payette, Warren Wagon Run

Distance: 4.2 miles
Difficulty: Class IV+
Craft: Kayak
Approximate paddling time: 2 hours
Flows: 700–1,500 cfs (**Gauge:** none)
Season: May, June
Put-in: Pearl Creek bridge (45.093686, -116.045414)

Takeout: Fisher Creek bridge (45.037543, -116.057955)
Shuttle: From downtown McCall take ID 55 1.2 miles and turn right on Warren Wagon Road. Go 9.8 miles to Fisher Creek. The put-in at Pearl Creek is another 4 miles up the road.

The upper North Fork of the Payette is nothing like its well-known downstream counterparts. This is a swift, steep, icy runoff stream that's full of boulders. It packs some punch when the water's up.

The top of the run below Upper Payette Lake is the toughest stretch. When the water's low, it's too rocky. When the water's high, it's a frothy nonstop rapid. Because it's roadside, you can put in below this upper section to enjoy the river's predominantly continuous Class IV characteristics without the initial difficulty. The gradient and rapids relax as you approach the takeout.

This is a narrow, shallow, and swift stream, and there are almost always river-wide logs, so scout carefully.

56　North Fork Payette, Meanders

Distance: 1–6 miles
Difficulty: Class I
Craft: Canoe, kayak, stand-up paddleboard
Approximate paddling time: 1–4 hours
Flows: 100–1,500 cfs (**Gauge:** none)
Season: May–Oct

Access: North Beach (44.993246, -116.070793)
Shuttle: From downtown McCall take ID 55 1.2 miles and turn right on Warren Wagon Road. Go 6.6 miles to North Beach, on the right.

For about 3 miles before it folds into the expanse of Payette Lake, the North Fork of the Payette is serene, clear, and completely calm flat water. This run is suitable for any kind of watercraft including canoes, stand-up paddleboards, and recreational kayaks.

As the name of the segment suggests, the river meanders considerably through a tranquil pine forest and is sure to calm overtaxed nerves.

Access is easy and available in a number of places, but the most convenient is at North Beach on Payette Lake. From there you can paddle upriver as far as you want, or until the current pushes back too much. Rentals are available at North Beach for those who haven't dragged gear along.

The Meanders section of the North Fork Payette is a popular, family-friendly section for a diversity of paddlers.

57 Payette Lake

Distance: 1–20 miles
Difficulty: Flat water
Launch site: Ponderosa State Park
(44.925225, -116.090829)
Craft: Canoe, recreational kayak, stand-up paddleboard
Approximate paddling time: 1–8 hours
Season: May–Oct
Launch site: North Beach (44.993246, -116.070793)

Access: To get to North Beach from downtown McCall, take ID 55 1.2 miles and turn right on Warren Wagon Road. Go 6.6 miles to North Beach, on the right. To get to Ponderosa State Park from downtown McCall, turn off ID 55 on Railroad Avenue heading east. Railroad Avenue will bear right and become Pine Street after a few blocks. Go 0.3 mile from the highway and turn left onto Davis Avenue. Go 1 mile to the park entrance. There's a large parking area on the left, just inside the gate.

Payette Lake is the destination for hordes of weekend warriors from Boise and elsewhere during the peak of the summer season. The lake is popular with motorboaters, anglers, paddlers, swimmers, hikers, and bikers, but those willing to get up early or head out midweek are likely to find seclusion and solitude.

Payette Lake can be busy, but when it's not, it is a serene and beautiful place for flatwater paddling. PHOTO BY SCOTT HEADRICK

Formed by a glacier more than 10,000 years ago, Payette Lake has 5,330 acres of surface area and is nearly 400 feet deep. The glacier that formed the lake was more than 1,000 feet high, 2.5 miles wide, and 8 miles long.

The resort town of McCall is on the lake's southwest shore, and public access in town is a breeze. A good portion of the Payette Lake shoreline is also protected as part of the 1,000-acre Ponderosa State Park, which has camping, hiking trails, and an excellent beach area.

One of the best locations for paddlers to access the lake is from North Beach (see North Fork Payette Meanders description), but there are numerous additional access points.

Payette Lake is popular for a variety of watercraft, including stand-up paddleboards.

58 North Fork Payette, McCall Town Run

Distance: 2 miles
Difficulty: Class II+
Craft: Canoe, kayak, raft
Approximate paddling time: 1–2 hours
Flows: 1,000–3,500 cfs (**Gauge:** North Fork Payette at McCall)
Season: May, June
Put-in: Payette Lake spillway near Rotary Park (44.911369, -116.118803)
Takeout: Deinhard Lane bridge (44.897904, -116.112827)
Shuttle: The put-in and takeout are both in and around McCall and can be accessed via several routes. To get to the takeout, find Deinhard Lane near the south entrance to McCall and go west 0.8 mile. There's a dirt parking area on the north side of the road on river-left near the bridge. The put-in is at Rotary Park near the waterfront 1 mile west of downtown McCall. You can get there from the takeout by driving 0.5 mile east on Deinhard Lane and turning left (north) on Mission Street. Go 0.5 mile and turn left on Mather Street, which winds through forested neighborhoods near the river. The put-in below the spillway is 1 mile ahead.

For a couple miles below Payette Lake, the North Fork is a swift but relatively easy whitewater run where McCall locals go to get wet after work. There are no defined rapids, but there are plenty of rocks and eddies. Although it's straightforward, it can be a challenging place for beginners because of the shallow streambed, cold water, and potential for deadfall coming into play in the event of a swim. The run has some nice eddies for kayakers to practice squirts and some decent catch-on-the-fly surf waves at certain water levels.

Distance: 13 miles
Difficulty: Class I
Craft: Canoe, kayak
Approximate paddling time: 1 day
Flows: 1,000–1,500 cfs (**Gauge:** North Fork Payette at McCall)
Season: May, June, July
Put-in: Sheep Bridge (44.891179, -116.109532)
Takeout: Hartsell Bridge (44.790053, -116.140539)

Shuttle: To get to the takeout from Cascade, drive north on ID 55 for 20.1 miles and turn left (west) on Smylie Lane. (The turn is 8.6 miles south of McCall.) Go 3.1 miles on Smylie Lane to the bridge. To get to the put-in, return to ID 55 and drive north 7.6 miles. Turn left onto Deinhard Lane and go 0.5 mile. Turn left on Mission Street and go 0.6 mile. Turn right again and travel a short distance on a dirt road to Sheep Bridge.

This is a scenic and gentle float on a meandering and wooded portion of the North Fork. It's one of the best canoe floats in the basin.

While there is no whitewater, there are a number of hazards created by logjams. Paddlers need to be alert and prepared to portage. It's a long float, and a whole day needs to be allocated. Because of its length and great scenery, it's also a great option for an overnight trip, but you need to be mindful of private property, particularly in the first 5 miles.

The first few miles below Sheep Bridge work through the southern outskirts of McCall, where you'll get occasional glimpses of riverside homes. After about 3 miles the run starts to feel much more remote, even though you'll never be more than a mile from a road. (West Mountain Road parallels the whole run to the west.) At mile 9 at a large logjam, the river splits into multiple channels and retains a braided character for 2 miles. You'll want to start in the left channel and work to the right via the braided network.

Water level depending, there are some great sandy beaches in the final 4 miles.

60 Kelly's Whitewater Park

Difficulty: Class II
Craft: Canoe, kayak, raft, surfboard, stand-up paddleboard, inner tube
Flows: 500–3,000 cfs (**Gauge:** Idaho Power, North Fork Payette at Cascade)
Season: May–Oct

Access: Kelly's is at the south end of Cascade off ID 55. You can't miss the timbered ranch-style entrance.
Additional information: kellyswhitewaterpark .com

With its grand opening in 2010, Kelly's was Idaho's first whitewater park and has become a popular recreation area for paddlers of various abilities. On a hot summer weekend the park is abuzz with activity.

Kelly's has five water features ranging from beginner to advanced, and the facility includes a 2,600-square-foot welcome center, which is perched over the river with huge glass windows and views of the river park.

The top wave at Kelly's can be challenging for intermediates, but it's a really good surf spot.

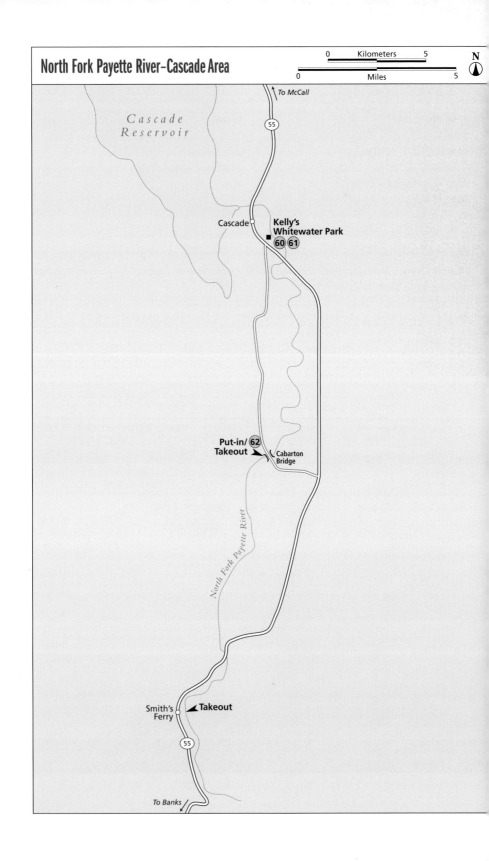

North Fork Payette River–Cascade Area

To McCall

55

Cascade Reservoir

Cascade

Kelly's Whitewater Park
60 61

Put-in/ 62 Takeout

Cabarton Bridge

North Fork Payette River

Smith's Ferry

Takeout

55

To Banks

Kelly's Whitewater Park is excellent for paddlers of all abilities.

The top wave is the park's most challenging, and can be kayaked and surfed. At most levels, the river-right side is more hole than wave, and the river-left side has a nice green curl. It's intimidating for intermediate paddlers, but it's a really good surf spot that's hosted several national championship kayaking events.

There's a man-made island below that has waves on either side. The waves closest to the visitor center are the park's easiest. The wave on the river-left side of the island is the park's best intermediate feature.

An old timber town, Cascade's biggest employer, the Boise Cascade Mill, closed in 2001 and ushered in an era of 20 percent unemployment. Shortly after the park's opening, Cascade mayor Dick Carter reported that the park had already started to prop up the local economy. Two tube and raft rental companies have taken root, as have a bed-and-breakfast and bistro.

61 North Fork Payette, Cascade to Cabarton

Distance: 10.5 miles
Difficulty: Class I
Craft: Canoe, kayak, stand-up paddleboard
Approximate paddling time: 3–5 hours
Flows: 500–2,000 cfs (**Gauge:** Idaho Power, North Fork Payette at Cascade)
Season: May–Oct
Put-in: Kelly's Whitewater Park (44.511225, -116.030972)

Takeout: Cabarton Bridge (44.413664, -116.032358)
Shuttle: From Banks drive 28.6 miles north on ID 55. Turn left onto Cabarton Road and go 1.7 miles to a developed boat ramp below the bridge. To get to the put-in at Kelly's Whitewater Park, return to ID 55 and continue north 7.5 miles. The timbered ranch-style entrance to the park is on the right. You could also put in at the lower ID 55 bridge to shave a mile off the float.

This is a beautiful, winding flatwater paddle with great views of the surrounding mountains and no rapids. Flows are reliably supplied through the summer by Cascade Reservoir. Because of the popularity of the region's whitewater paddles, this one is frequently overlooked, and you're almost certain to have it to yourself.

62 North Fork Payette, Cabarton

Distance: 9.6 miles
Difficulty: Class III
Craft: Canoe, kayak, raft
Approximate paddling time: 3–5 hours
Flows: 500–3,000 cfs (**Gauge:** USGS, NF Payette River near Banks)
Season: May–Oct
Put-in: Cabarton Bridge (44.413664, -116.032358)

Takeout: Smith's Ferry (44.302478, -116.087150)
Shuttle: To get to the takeout from Banks, take ID 55 north 19.1 miles to Cougar Mountain Lodge in Smith's Ferry. Note that the facilities behind Cougar Mountain Lodge and those across the road are fee areas. To get to the put-in, return to ID 55 and drive 9.5 miles north. Turn left onto Cabarton Road and go 1.7 miles to a developed boat ramp below the bridge.

The Cabarton is one of Idaho's Class III classics. The river parallels a railroad but leaves the highway for most of the run, making it feel more remote than it is. The water, released from the top of Cascade Reservoir, is also relatively warm in the summer. The run is extremely popular and guaranteed to be busy on hot summer weekends.

For the first 2 miles the river is fairly mellow, with some Class II riffles and a lot of flat water. At mile 2.3 the riverbed constricts and things get more exciting, leading

The Cabarton's Class II and III rapids are fairly straightforward, and its scenery is excellent.
PHOTO BY WENDY JONES

Kayakers navigate the currents at the entrance of Trestle Rapid. PHOTO BY WENDY JONES

into the first of two Class III rapids, Trestle. You'll know you're there when you see the railroad suspended over your head, but at that point you'll already be halfway through this relatively long rapid.

After Trestle, things calm down until mile 7, where ID 55 rejoins the river. For the next 1.5 miles it's a fairly active river, with some big waves and a few holes to avoid. Things culminate at Howard's Plunge, a steep and exciting Class III. From there it's another mile of flat water to the takeout at Smith's Ferry.

63 North Fork Payette, The North Fork

See map on page 97.
Distance: 15.9 miles
Difficulty: Class V
Craft: Kayak, cataraft
Approximate paddling time: 3–6 hours
Flows: 1,000–3,000 cfs (USGS, NF Payette River near Banks)
Season: Apr–Oct (dependent on dam releases)

Put-in: Highway pullout near Smith's Ferry (44.265742, -116.069752)
Takeout: Banks (44.084375, -116.116365)
Shuttle: From Banks, the takeout, drive 16.2 miles north on ID 55 to a pullout on the right near milepost 95. Murray Creek is across the river, and the launch site is down a steep embankment.

This is the granddaddy of Idaho's expert whitewater and where you'll see some of the best kayakers in the world honing their skills. There are rivers with harder rapids, and there are rivers with bigger water, but there are few anywhere that match the North Fork's combination of steep gradient, large volume, consistent dam-released water, and number of big Class V rapids in a 16-mile stretch.

The North Fork of the Payette is a legendary experts-only run suited primarily to whitewater kayaks.

Between Smith's Ferry and Banks there are eighteen named Class V rapids, and more than a dozen additional challenging drops that, on any other river, would have names of their own. The rapids are too numerous and complex to describe in detail here, but the river has been divided over the years into three sections: Upper Five, Middle Five, and Lower Five.

The Upper Five, from Smith's Ferry to Big Eddy, has steep, constricted rapids. It includes four named drops: Steepness, Nutcracker, Disneyland, and S-Turn. Nutcracker, located at milepost 93, is a long rapid that ends with a huge rock in the center and is generally considered the second most challenging on the river.

The Middle Five, from Big Eddy to Hound's Tooth, is the real meat of the run. Class V rapids come in rapid succession, and several are very challenging. They are Slide, Bad Jose, Know Where to Run, Chaos, Bouncer Down the Middle, Pectoralis Major, Jacob's Ladder, Golf Course, Screaming Left Turn, and Jaws. Jacob's Ladder, between mileposts 86 and 87, is the toughest of the river's eighteen rapids, and many accomplished boaters choose to portage. It feeds without hesitation into Golf Course to create a very long 0.5-mile rapid with two names.

The Lower Five, from Hound's Tooth to Banks, is the easiest and most frequently paddled section. It includes four named rapids: Hound's Tooth, Otter's Slide, Juicer, and Crunch. The put-in for this section is near milepost 84 in a big dirt pullout. The most common test segment for aspiring North Forkers is to put in below Hound's Tooth and paddle to the ID 55 bridge, above Otter's Slide. This 2-mile section, informally called the Warm Up, is very continuous Class IV+ paddling and offers boaters a taste of what the Lower Five's named rapids are like.

The North Fork has numerous big waves, holes, and constricted sections of chaotic water created by blasting the ID 55 roadbed on one side and the railroad on the other. Fed by irrigation releases from the top of Cascade Reservoir, the water is warm and consistent in the summer, usually flowing at around 2,000 cfs and gradually tapering off in late summer and fall. At 1,800 to 3,000 cfs it is solid Class V, and it's Class V+ above that. The North Fork has numerous hazards to speak of, but one of the most commonly experienced is its sharp, shallow rocks. For this reason, the first rule of thumb here is not to flip, and to roll quickly if you do. Between 1,000 and 1,800 cfs, the rapids are more manageable, but the rocks are also closer to the surface.

A growing contingent of Boise boaters are also running the North Fork in the winter, when it's flowing at 500 cfs and lower. At these flows the river is still plenty challenging and extremely rocky. Your boat is certain to take some abuse.

If you're new to this river, it's best to pair up with an experienced North Forker to show you the way.

Payette River

Below the confluence of the South and North Forks, the Payette River changes character and consists of more family-friendly whitewater, good play boating, and grassy hillsides. Most paddlers stick to The Main, the uppermost of the segments outlined below, but there's good paddling farther downstream as well.

If you're in the area during high water of about 8,000 cfs or more on the Horseshoe Bend USGS gauge, it's worth checking out a place kayakers call "The Bladder," an inflatable diversion dam that creates an excellent huge surf wave. To find it go to the south side of Horseshoe Bend on ID 55 and turn east onto a dirt road called Pioneer Road, following the river upstream for a little less than a mile. It's an industrial-looking area, but if the wave is in, you're probably not going to notice.

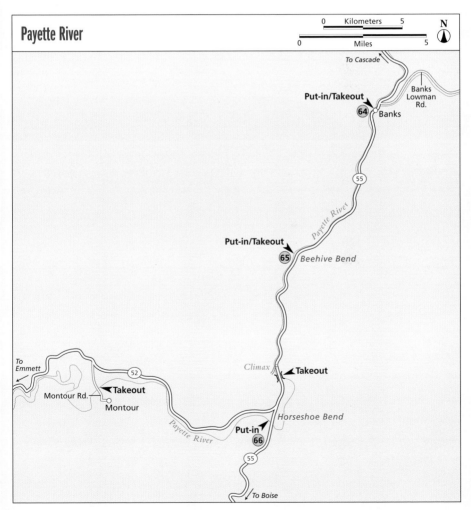

64 Payette River, The Main

Distance: 7.2 miles
Difficulty: Class III
Craft: Kayak, raft, whitewater canoe
Approximate paddling time: 3–5 hours
Flows: 500–10,000 cfs (**Gauge:** USGS, Payette River at Horseshoe Bend)
Season: Year-round if no ice; best Apr–Oct
Put-in: Banks (44.084375, -116.116365)

Takeout: Beehive Bend (44.006160, -116.179828)
Shuttle: The takeout at Beehive Bend is 8 miles south of Banks and 7 miles north of Horseshoe Bend on ID 55. Be careful pulling off and onto the highway here. The highway is busy, and Beehive Bend is located near a blind corner. To get to the put-in, drive 8 miles north on ID 55 to Banks, a fee area.

The Main Payette is one of the best and most popular Class III rivers in Idaho. On a hot summer weekend, the put-in at Banks is a sea of colorful rafts, kayaks, and shuttle vehicles. The river's pool-drop Class II and III rapids are fairly straightforward but

Go Left is the hardest of the Main Payette's excellent rapids.

pack plenty of punch for beginner and intermediate rafters and kayakers. Boaters paddling The Main need to at least have basic whitewater skills.

The river is runnable almost all year unless it's frozen, but it's most popular from June through August.

Shortly after the put-in are two Class II rapids. If you're having trouble at this point, you should consider getting out and hiking back to the put-in. The rapids only get more difficult.

The run's first and most challenging big drop, Go Left or You're Fired, is a Class III+ and comes at mile 2.7. It follows a long, slow pool and is easy to scout via the river-left bank. The line is obvious. Paddle down the tongue on river-left and avoid the holes.

At mile 3 is Bennett's Rock, a Class II+. At medium and low flows there's a huge hole in the center to center-left. The hole washes out at higher flows, but the rapid is generally run down the big wave train on the right. Mike's Hole, a Class III, is next at mile 3.9 and involves a right-to-left move to avoid the holes. Mixmaster and AMF, at miles 5.4 and 5.7, round out the run's more challenging drops. Both are a mix of big waves and a few holes, but the lines are straightforward. From there it's a gentle 2-mile float to the takeout on river-left.

65 Payette River, Lower Main

Distance: 5.5 miles
Difficulty: Class II
Craft: Canoe, kayak, raft
Approximate paddling time: 1–3 hours
Flows: 500–10,000 cfs (**Gauge:** USGS, Payette River at Horseshoe Bend)
Season: Year-round if no ice; best Apr–Oct
Put-in: Beehive Bend (44.006132, -116.179861)

Takeout: ID 55 bridge (43.938026, -116.193138)
Shuttle: The takeout is 1.8 miles north of Horseshoe Bend on ID 55. After crossing the bridge spanning the Payette, there's a large parking area and boat ramp on the left. To get to the put-in, return to ID 55 and go 5.5 miles north. Beehive Bend, a developed river access, is on the left.

The Class II float below Beehive Bend sees a lot less traffic than the Main Payette upstream, but it's a great section for beginner kayakers or rafters looking for a leisurely float. It also can be manageable for open canoes at low flows.

The river consists primarily of riffles, with the exception of a big Class II+, Climax, at mile 5, just before the takeout. Climax has some big waves, but the drop can be run pretty much down the middle.

Climax is also a good surf spot for kayakers and can be accessed for some park-and-play from a difficult-to-spot dirt parking area that's about 30 feet above the river. Watch for a small split between the guardrails. Climax is in at levels between about 3,500 and 7,000 cfs.

This section is also popular with personal watercraft and jet boats that access the river via the takeout boat ramp, so be mindful of the potential for motorized traffic.

66 Payette River, Montour Canoe Float

Distance: 9.2 miles
Difficulty: Class II
Craft: Canoe, kayak, raft
Approximate paddling time: 3–5 hours
Flows: 500–2,000 cfs
Season: Apr–Oct
Put-in: Horseshoe Bend (43.904398, -116.203383)
Takeout: Montour Road bridge (43.931524, -116.335132)
Shuttle: To get to the takeout, turn onto ID 52 at the north end of Horseshoe Bend and travel west. Go 9.1 miles and turn left onto Montour Road. The bridge is 1 mile ahead. There's a dirt road, parking, and primitive river access on the south side of the river, west of Montour Road. To get to the put-in, return to Horseshoe Bend and go south on ID 55 toward Boise. After crossing the bridge spanning the Payette River, turn right onto Old Emmett Road. There's a highway pullout beside the river. You could also continue farther downstream, where you'll find another pullout near the Boise Street bridge, just across the railroad tracks.

Because of a large diversion upstream from Horseshoe Bend, the first 3 miles of this run through a sagebrush–covered canyon can have less water than the bottom 6 miles. A hydro facility returns the missing flow at mile 3.5.

The run includes some easy Class II riffles, but is generally safe for open canoes and families, particularly later in the season. The riverbed is broad and sandy. There are a few islands covered with cottonwood trees, as well as sandbars and beaches. You also may encounter motorized traffic traveling upstream from Black Canyon Reservoir, which is about a mile below the takeout.

Snake River, Hells Canyon

Upstream of its confluence with the Salmon River, the Snake cuts through the deepest gorge in North America: Hells Canyon. He Devil Mountain, at 9,393 feet, is the tallest of the Seven Devils Mountains. At Granite Creek, 6 miles away, the rapids in the canyon bottom are 7,913 feet lower. The Grand Canyon, though by most standards more stunning, has 4,000- and 6,000-foot-tall walls on its south and north rims, respectively.

The 652,488-acre Hells Canyon National Recreation Area was established by Congress on December 31, 1975, and includes the 214,944-acre Hells Canyon Wilderness Area. The 66.3-mile section of the river below Hells Canyon Dam is also protected as a Wild and Scenic River.

Wild Sheep Rapid is one of two big rapids in Hells Canyon.

67 Snake River, Hells Canyon

Distance: 32 miles
Difficulty: Class III–IV
Craft: Kayak, raft, canoe
Approximate paddling time: 2–4 days
Flows: 7,000–70,000 cfs
Season: Year-round
Put-in: Hells Canyon Dam (45.253722, -116.696419)
Takeout: Pittsburg Landing (45.632475, -116.476016)
Shuttle: For kayakers a popular option on this run is to book a jet boat to shuttle up or down the river. There are also companies that will pick up your car and drop it at the takeout.

Otherwise, it's a 188-mile drive each way. To get to the takeout, go to Riggins and continue north on US 95 for 26.4 miles and turn left, crossing the old bridge. Immediately turn left, traveling upstream, and continue on FR 493 for 17 miles to Pittsburg Landing. The put-in at Hells Canyon Dam is northwest of Cambridge, Idaho. From the takeout, return to Riggins and continue south to New Meadows. Turn right in New Meadows to stay on US 95 and continue to Cambridge. In Cambridge, turn right (west) onto ID 71 and continue 39.8 miles to Hells Canyon Road. It's another 22 miles to Hells Canyon Dam.

This two- to four-day wilderness river trip is the most accessible in Idaho's system of permitted wilderness rivers. Rapids in Hells Canyon are big but fairly straightforward.

Due to hydroelectric production at Hells Canyon Dam, water levels in Hells Canyon can fluctuate drastically. Make sure to tie up your boats or drag them far above the waterline.

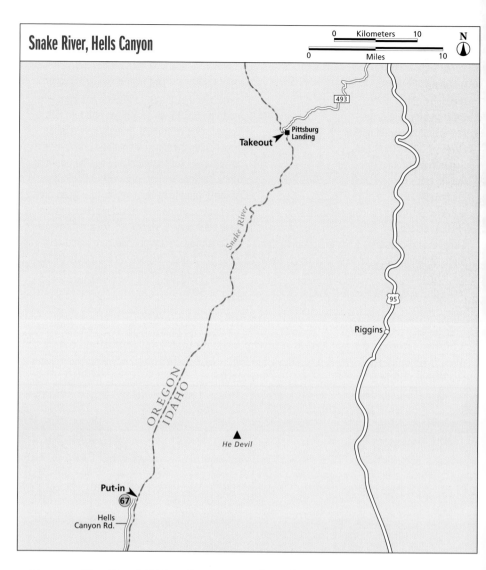

Most are Class II and III, but there are two big Class IVs: Wild Sheep and Granite. Wild Sheep is 6 miles below the put-in, and Granite 2 miles below that. Both are easy to scout or portage, and both deserve some respect. If you've been paddling smaller rivers recently, the size of the water in Hells Canyon may be surprising, particularly as the water approaches and exceeds 20,000 cfs.

Hells Canyon Dam is a hydroelectric facility that releases water based on the power grid's demand, and water levels in Hells Canyon are subject to extreme fluctuations. Boaters should always tether boats securely and leave equipment well above the water line. At levels over 30,000 cfs, rapids become considerably more pushy, and the run is not as suitable for intermediates. Below 10,000 cfs there are a number of play waves for kayakers, including an outstanding surf wave at Bernard Creek.

The Snake River in Hells Canyon is a federally protected Wild and Scenic River.
PHOTO BY KEVIN LEWIS

Paddlers can also float the 36 miles below Pittsburg Landing to Heller Bar (see Lower Salmon Canyons takeout). This lower part of the canyon contains Class II rapids and considerable flat water where upstream winds can be difficult to work against.

Permits are required to float Hells Canyon from Memorial Day weekend through September 10 and can be obtained by entering a forest service lottery each December and January. Self-issued permits are required during the remainder of the year. Look up Four Rivers Lottery for more information.

Salmon River Basin

The Salmon River and its tributaries are world renowned for their whitewater and wilderness. At 425 miles, the main stem of the Salmon is the longest free-flowing river in America that's within one state and drains nearly the entire heart of central Idaho.

The Salmon is a storied place overflowing with history and ecological significance. It drains all or portions of the Sawtooth, Frank Church–River of No Return, and Gospel Hump wilderness areas and contains two of the nation's most prized Wild and Scenic Rivers, the Middle Fork and Main stems of the Salmon, both winding through deep and extremely remote canyons. There's not a single road between the Salmon River's headwaters to the south and the Lochsa River to the north, a linear distance of 150 miles.

Dubbed the River of No Return by early settlers, the Salmon River was an impediment to the Lewis and Clark Expedition when it arrived near the present-day city of Salmon in August 1805. Having traveled ahead of the rest of the expedition and arriving at what is now Lemhi Pass on the spine of the Bitterroot Mountains, Meriwether Lewis wrote that he saw "immense ranges of high mountains still to the west of us with their tops partially covered with snow." He was looking into what is now the wild and rugged Salmon River country of Idaho.

After working downstream past the present-day city of Salmon, the Salmon River canyon closed in, and the river's rapids intensified. The whitewater, coupled with the canyon's sheer rock walls, convinced the expedition to find a safer route to the Pacific,

The Salmon River is born in the rugged mountains of central Idaho. The upper canyon is pictured here from the White Cloud Mountains looking downstream toward Challis.

and the explorers traveled back over the mountains and headed farther north into the Bitterroot Valley of Montana before crossing the mountains once more into the headwaters of the Lochsa River.

The remote nature of the Salmon River and its canyons also attracted a peculiar breed of people who lived solitary and eccentric lives. Idaho's river canyon dwellers date back to Territorial days and are a unique group that, until the 1980s, included canyon contemporaries with names like Beaver Dick, Cougar Dave, Wheelbarrow Annie, Buckskin Bill, and Free Press Frances. Fiercely independent loners, they lived eccentric lives on their own terms. Many of their homesteads can still be visited by river travelers today.

The Salmon River, as its name suggests, was also once home to millions of salmon that returned some 900 miles from the Pacific to spawn, die, and renew the circle of life. Their populations decimated by dams on the Columbia and Snake Rivers downstream, they now number in the tens of thousands, and all of Idaho's remaining wild salmon are protected under the Endangered Species Act.

Upper Salmon River Basin

The Salmon River's headwaters lie in the Sawtooth and White Cloud Mountains, some of the most picturesque of Idaho's numerous stony spines. The serrated ridges of the Sawtooths, in particular, easily rank as Idaho's most celebrated mountain range.

In 1972, in response to a proposed strip mine in the heart of the White Cloud Mountains, Congress established the 756,000-acre Sawtooth National Recreation

The Sawtooth Mountains stand sentinel over the town of Stanley in the midst of the 756,000-acre Sawtooth National Recreation Area.

Area to protect and showcase the region's stunning natural beauty and recreational assets. With resulting strict management of livestock grazing, development, and resource extraction, the Salmon River benefits and runs clear, clean, and cold in its upper reaches.

Paddling in the upper basin includes jaw-dropping vistas on tranquil glacial lakes, swift currents on the upper Salmon's meanders, and some outstanding Class III and IV whitewater in the canyon below Stanley. Camping at USDA Forest Service campgrounds is some of the best anywhere. Portions of the Salmon River near Challis and the city of Salmon also provide excellent canoeing and recreational paddling.

Redfish Lake is among the most popular destinations for paddlers in the upper Salmon River basin. Photo by Jeff Cole

68 Sawtooth Valley Lakes

Distance: 1–6 miles
Difficulty: Flat water
Craft: Canoe, kayak, stand-up paddleboard
Approximate paddling time: 1–8 hours
Season: May–Oct
Little Redfish Lake launch site: Mountain View Campground (44.161781, -114.905538)
Redfish Lake launch site: Redfish Lake Lodge (44.142798, -114.922983)
Stanley Lake launch site: Stanley Lake Inlet Campground (44.244688, -115.064834)
Access: From Stanley, the Redfish Lake area is 4.3 miles south on ID 75. Turn right onto Redfish Lake Road. Little Redfish Lake and Mountain View Campground are 0.5 mile ahead on the right. To get to Redfish Lake and Redfish Lake Lodge go 1.7 miles from the highway on Redfish Lake Road and turn right on FR 213, following signs for the lodge. Parking, docks, and facilities are 0.5 mile ahead.

To get to Stanley Lake, drive 5 miles west of Stanley on ID 21. Turn left on FR 455, following signs for Stanley Lake, and go 3.6 miles. Turn left on FR 697 at the west end of the lake, passing Lake View Campground, and go 0.25 mile to Stanley Lake Inlet Campground and ample parking, as well as a dock, to access the lake.

The glacial lakes of the upper Sawtooth Valley are some of the most scenic and magnificent in the Pacific Northwest. Created by the terminal moraines from glaciers that

It's difficult to imagine a more scenic place to paddle than Little Redfish Lake.

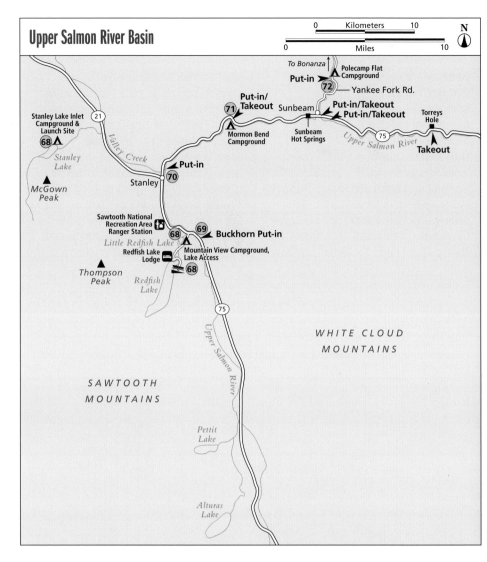

0   Kilometers   10

0   Miles   10

N

To Bonanza

Polecamp Flat Campground

Put-in

72   Yankee Fork Rd.

Put-in/Takeout

71   Sunbeam

Put-in/Takeout
Put-in/Takeout

Torreys Hole

Stanley Lake Inlet Campground & Launch Site

21

68

Mormon Bend Campground

Sunbeam Hot Springs

75   *Upper Salmon River*

Takeout

Valley Creek

Stanley Lake

Put-in

70

Stanley

McGown Peak

Sawtooth National Recreation Area Ranger Station

68   69   Buckhorn Put-in

Little Redfish Lake

Redfish Lake Lodge

Mountain View Campground, Lake Access

68

Thompson Peak

Redfish Lake

75

Upper Salmon River

WHITE CLOUD MOUNTAINS

SAWTOOTH MOUNTAINS

Pettit Lake

Alturas Lake

descended from the 10,000-foot spires of the Sawtooth Mountains, the lakes have clear, cold water and incredible views of the peaks' serrated granite ridges.

There are numerous glacial lakes in the Sawtooth range, but the five most accessible are Alturas, Pettit, Redfish, Little Redfish, and Stanley Lakes. All of these mountain tarns are worth paddling, but Redfish Lake is most popular and usually swarms with motorboats, kayaks, stand-up paddleboards, and other craft during the peak of the summer season. In 2003 personal watercraft were banned from Alturas and Pettit Lakes, so they're a good bet if you consider small buzzing watercraft a nuisance.

Little Redfish Lake is small but offers some of the best views of the Sawtooth Mountains. It usually isn't very busy. For scenery, Stanley Lake is also one of the best.

Paddle these stunning mountain lakes early in the morning to catch the alpenglow as it washes over the Sawtooths with soft pink-orange light.

An array of rentals are available at Redfish Lake Lodge, where you're sure to see people sunbathing, swimming, barbecuing, and paddling. Rentals are also available in nearby Stanley.

Mount Heyburn towers over Redfish Lake, named for the shimmering glow created by tens of thousands of sockeye salmon that historically returned from the Pacific every year to spawn.

69 Upper Salmon, Buckhorn to Stanley

Distance: 5.5 miles
Difficulty: Class II+
Craft: Canoe, kayak, raft
Approximate paddling time: 2 hours
Flows: 500–2,000 cfs (**Gauge:** None)
Season: June, July
Put-in: Buckhorn Bridge (44.163809, -114.887220)

Takeout: Rest area south of Stanley (44.209734, -114.931265)
Shuttle: The takeout, a large highway pullout with restrooms, is 0.5 mile south of Stanley on ID 75. The put-in is 4.5 miles farther south on ID 75 in a pullout on the northwest side of Buckhorn Bridge, which spans the Salmon River.

From the Sawtooth Fish Hatchery downstream to Stanley, the Salmon River has relative seclusion from the nearby highway. It also has fairly continuous Class II rapids and riffles. The riverbed is wide, and the run does not have the benefit of a few key tributaries that join the river farther downstream. In other words, it is generally rocky, particularly early or late in the season. This is a good, but not frequently paddled, option for technically proficient canoeists, kayakers, and rafters looking for a shallow but mellow cruise.

70 Upper Salmon, Stanley to Mormon Bend

Distance: 6 miles
Difficulty: Class I–II
Craft: Canoe, kayak, raft
Approximate paddling time: 2 hours
Flows: 500–3,000 cfs (**Gauge:** USGS, Salmon River below Yankee Fork)
Season: May–Oct
Put-in: Valley Creek confluence (44.225069, -114.928853)
Takeout: Mormon Bend Campground (44.262536, -114.843816)

Shuttle: The takeout at Mormon Bend Campground is 6.7 miles north/northeast of Stanley on ID 75. There's a developed boat ramp and ample parking. To reach the put-in, return on ID 75 back toward Stanley and go 6.5 miles to the bridge spanning Valley Creek near the Stanley Museum. There's ample parking in highway pullouts near the bridge. You could also put in at the rest area south of town (see Buckhorn to Stanley takeout) to add a mile to the float.

In the 6 miles below Stanley, the Salmon River leaves behind the sweeping mountain views of the Sawtooth Valley and enters a canyon with a mix of timbered and sagebrush-covered slopes. The river is swift, but shouldn't pose any significant

The scenic float from Stanley to Mormon Bend is the mellowest of the upper Salmon's paddling options.

problems for paddlers in open canoes or any other type of craft. This is the best option on the upper Salmon for beginners and can be busy during the peak of the summer season.

The float starts by going past businesses and riverside homes in Lower Stanley and works around a few corners into the Salmon River canyon. There are a number of hot springs along the Salmon River, but one of the best is at mile 2.7 on river-left. It's small and almost sure to be crowded, but worth a stop if it isn't.

There's a boat ramp and ample parking at the Mormon Bend takeout.

During mid-summer flows, the upper Salmon River below Stanley is suitable for a range of watercraft, not just rafts or kayaks.

71 Day Stretch

Distance: 15 miles
Difficulty: Class III–IV
Craft: Kayak, raft
Approximate paddling time: 3–5 hours
Flows: 500–10,000 cfs (**Gauge:** USGS, Salmon River below Yankee Fork)
Season: Apr, May, June, July, Aug
Put-in: Mormon Bend Campground (44.262555, -114.843780)

Takeout: Torrey's Hole (44.255669, -114.593486)
Shuttle: To reach the takeout from Stanley, drive 21 miles downriver on ID 75 to Torrey's Hole, where there's ample parking, restrooms, and a boat ramp. To reach the put-in, drive back upriver 14.8 miles to Mormon Bend Campground, where there's a developed boat ramp and parking.

The Day Stretch is the quintessential whitewater run in the upper Salmon River basin. With a mix of four distinct Class III and IV rapids, and a few Class II riffles and strong eddy lines, the run can be divided into an upper Class IV section and a lower Class III section. Most of the run is roadside, so the upper and lower floats can easily be combined or paddled separately.

From the put-in at Mormon Bend, the river works lazily for about 3 miles before arriving at a Class II rapid beneath the bridge. From there it's another mile to the toughest rapid of the run, Shotgun, a Class IV with steep gradient and lots of granite boulders. About 2 miles below Shotgun is Sunbeam, another Class IV created in 1936 when Sunbeam Dam was blasted using dynamite to restore salmon in the upper Salmon River basin. For kayaks, there's a sneak on river-right, but rafts usually run the meat of the drop. Level depending, lots of rafts flip.

The Day Stretch on the Salmon has several put-in and takeout options. This is the confluence of the Yankee Fork and the Salmon River, just below Sunbeam Dam.

Sunbeam Dam was blasted in 1936 to restore upper Salmon River salmon runs. The dam now creates a Class IV rapid that deserves a scout.

Below the dam there are two excellent put-ins and takeouts maintained by the forest service. The first is at the confluence with the Yankee Fork, the second another mile downstream. Class III paddlers should start at one of these two access points.

The next rapid, Piece of Cake, a Class III, comes quickly and consists of a big tongue that feeds into several small holes and waves. The final Class III, Warm Springs Narrows, is three-quarters of the way through the run. After floating across a long pool, the river enters a gorge. At 0.75 mile, Warm Springs Narrows is long, but the waves and holes are scattered. After this, it's a lazy 4-mile float to the takeout at Torrey's Hole on river-left. (There's also a kayaker's takeout that climbs a steep embankment on river-left immediately after Warm Springs Narrows.)

The Day Stretch can be run at hugely varying levels, and its difficulty varies accordingly. At low water, it's very rocky, but navigable. At high water, most of the holes wash out, but the water is fast, powerful, and very cold.

As a point of interest, a researcher named John Parsons, who was working on a Salmon River field guide in 2012, helped identify the precise geographic center of the state of Idaho. He pinpointed a spot a few miles north of Torrey's Hole, the takeout for this run. Welcome to the center of Idaho.

72 Yankee Fork

Distance: 3.3 miles
Difficulty: Class IV
Craft: Kayak
Approximate paddling time: 1 hour
Flows: 500–3,000 cfs (**Gauge:** USGS, Yankee Fork Salmon River near Clayton)
Season: May, June
Put-in: Polecamp Flat Campground (44.303360, -114.720263)
Takeout: Confluence with Salmon River at Sunbeam (44.269779, -114.734460)

Shuttle: To reach the takeout from Stanley, drive 13 miles downriver on ID 75 to Sunbeam. Just below the Yankee Fork bridge, the road has a pulloff and primitive boat ramp. To reach the put-in, turn onto Yankee Fork Road from ID 75 in Sunbeam and travel 3.1 miles to Polecamp Flat Campground. Turn right into a dirt parking area at the campground entrance. Put in directly across Yankee Fork Road from the campground.

The Yankee Fork is unique among central Idaho's big-water rivers: a small, short, easily accessible creek with great scenery and relatively easy rapids. In 3 miles this swift, cold, and continuous stream tumbles more than 250 feet over numerous granite boulders and ledges. At high flows, the Yankee Fork's narrow streambed carries more than 2,000 cfs and becomes a romp of continuous waves and holes. At medium flows, around 1,000 cfs, there are dozens of catch-on-fly surf waves and eddies to hop between.

The Yankee Fork can be paddled at low water, but it's best during spring runoff, when it's a continuous romp of waves and holes.

The steep, continuous rapids below Five Mile Creek—upstream from the standard Yankee Fork paddle—merit careful scouting.

The Yankee Fork is a runoff river whose feeder streams originate high in the Salmon River Mountains. Its season is short and begins in mid-May and runs through most of June in a good year. Because of the narrow streambed and recent forest fires, the run generally attracts new wood each spring. Scout from the road on your way to the put-in.

For the first mile the rapids rank as continuous Class III. The hardest series of the run comes not long after passing the bridge, the run's approximate halfway point. It's a long Class IV with continuous whitewater for 0.5 mile. After passing a swift blind bend at Blind Creek Campground, the river leaves the road for its culminating drops. The takeout is on river-left at the confluence with the Salmon River.

For expert kayakers, there's another short and infrequently paddled run a few miles upstream from the town of Custer. From the put-in at Fivemile Creek, the Yankee Fork tumbles steeply through a tight, constricted canyon with a few low-angle slides, a wood-choked waterfall, and a long rapid created by a giant landslide. It's a short, remote, and dangerous stretch of Class V and should be scouted top to bottom before being attempted.

73 Upper Salmon, Challis Paddle

Distance: 14.2 miles
Difficulty: Class I
Craft: Canoe, kayak, raft, drift boat
Approximate paddling time: 4–6 hours
Flows: 800–2,000 cfs (**Gauge:** USGS, Salmon River at Salmon)
Season: July–Oct
Put-in: Challis Bridge Boat Ramp (44.470275, -114.199915)
Takeout: Watts Bridge Boat Ramp (44.632003, -114.145549)

Shuttle: To get to the takeout from Challis, drive 10.4 miles north on US 93. There's a developed boat ramp and river access river-right on the downstream side of the bridge. To get to the put-in, return to US 93 heading south and go through Challis for a total of 13 miles from the takeout at Watts Bridge. Just after crossing the Salmon River, turn left to access a developed boat ramp and parking area.

This unassuming stretch situated between the Challis area's agricultural fields and the base of the Lost River Range is more scenic than you might expect when passing through the area on US 93. The river flows through a thick cottonwood forest and nudges up against beautiful pastel-hued cliffs. It also offers great views of the mountains to the west above Challis.

The water is swift but mellow, and there are a number of downed trees to keep you on your toes. The channel is braided in several areas, but all are generally clear of obstructions.

The Salmon River in this reach can be floated in the spring when the water's high, but that would raise the stakes on a trip that should be relaxing, not stressful. Try this one in the fall when the cottonwoods are gold or in the summer when the cool river and abundant trees offer a great way to beat the heat. The character of the Salmon River above and below this stretch is fairly consistent. Enterprising paddlers can explore with relative safety, particularly in July, August, and September, when flows are more manageable.

The Salmon River near Challis is more scenic than you might think driving past on the highway. PHOTO BY JAY KRAJIC

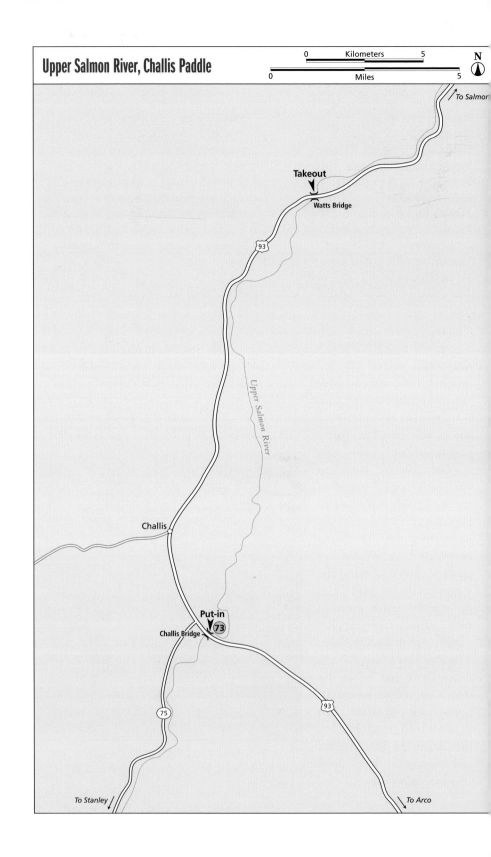

0   Kilometers   5

0   Miles   5

N

To Salmon

Takeout

Watts Bridge

93

Upper Salmon River

Challis

Put-in

73

Challis Bridge

75

93

To Stanley

To Arco

74 Upper Salmon, Shoup Bridge to Island Park

Distance: 6.2 miles
Difficulty: Class I
Craft: Canoe, kayak, raft, drift boat, stand-up paddleboard
Approximate paddling time: 2–3 hours
Flows: 800–4,000 cfs (**Gauge:** USGS, Salmon River at Salmon)
Season: July–Oct
Put-in: Shoup Bridge (45.098070, -113.893765)

Put-in: Island Park (45.177175, -113.898871)
Shuttle: The takeout is in downtown Salmon just off US 93. The turn into Island Park is the west, upstream, side of the main bridge at the center of town. To get to the put-in, go east through town and then turn right to stay on US 93 heading south. Go 5.3 miles and turn right into a developed boat ramp facility on the upstream side of the bridge.

The city of Salmon is a place right out of a western storybook. With broad pastures stretched out beneath the stunning backdrop of the Bitterroot Mountains and the Salmon River running through the middle of town, there's not much not to like about Salmon.

In the 60 miles from Challis to Salmon, the Salmon River's character doesn't change much. It's roadside almost the entire length and has stretches of Class I and II water. It's a very big and pushy river in the spring, but in the summer and fall the river rolls along with some gentle wave trains. The main hazards to avoid are man-made irrigation diversions, and there are dozens of paddling options and access points. The only two areas where the river gets away from the highway for any extended distance, however, are in Challis and Salmon.

There are quite a few paddling options in the Salmon area, starting with a 6.2-mile paddle from Shoup Bridge to Island Park downtown. This is one of the most popular stretches of the Salmon River in the Salmon area, and although it skirts the edge of the city the development doesn't encroach on the river much. There's a notable irrigation diversion just below the put-in on river-right. Stay left to avoid it. From there to the takeout, it's fairly smooth and scenic sailing. When you arrive at Island Park, take the left channel. The right is too shallow to float at all but the highest flows.

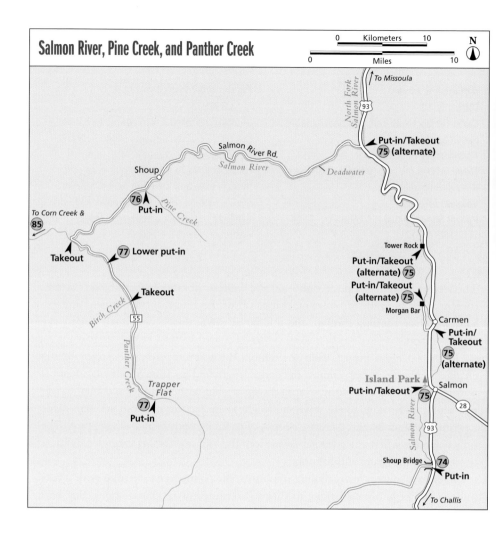

Salmon River, Pine Creek, and Panther Creek

75 Upper Salmon, Island Park to North Fork

Distance: 21 miles
Difficulty: Class I
Craft: Canoe, kayak, raft, drift boat, stand-up paddleboard
Approximate paddling time: 2 hours
Flows: 800–4,000 cfs (**Gauge:** USGS, Salmon River at Salmon)
Season: July–Oct
Put-in: Island Park (45.177175, -113.898871)
River access: Carmen (45.231280, -113.894040)
River access: Morgan Bar (45.253822, -113.907319)
River access: Tower Rock (45.311360, -113.906761)

Takeout: North Fork (45.405089, -113.995297)
Shuttle: The takeout at North Fork is 21.2 miles north of Salmon on US 93. Tower Rock is 9.8 miles north of Salmon. Carmen Bridge is 4 miles north. To get to Morgan Bar, go 3.8 miles north of Salmon and turn left (west) onto Fairgrounds Road. You'll pass the fairgrounds on your left and go 0.5 mile. The road will bear to the right and become Stormy Peak Road. Take this winding dirt road, staying within eyeshot of the river, for 1.6 miles. Morgan Bar will be on your right. To get to the put-in, return to Salmon via US 93. The turn into Island Park is on the west, upstream, side of the bridge.

In the 21 miles between Salmon and North Fork, there are a number of floatable sections on the Salmon River, all of them Class I and ideally suited to open canoes and recreational craft once spring runoff has ebbed. There are a total of ten river access points and boat ramps on this stretch, so a wide variety of floats can be put together.

Perhaps the single most popular family-friendly paddle in the Salmon area is the 4.4-mile float from Island Park in downtown Salmon to Carmen Bridge. During the peak of the summer floating season, this stretch can become crowded with people bobbing down the river in all manner of craft. It's very safe, but paddlers should watch out for a couple of irrigation diversions. There's another river access point, Morgan Bar, 1.9 miles below Carmen on river-left that offers more parking and restrooms.

Paddlers interested in extending their trips can explore the entire stretch of river between Salmon and North Fork, a distance of 22 miles. Below the Tower Rock Boat Ramp the river becomes braided in places, and paddlers need to stay on their toes to avoid drifting into small channels that could accumulate logjams.

Following is a quick mileage reference for some of the popular Salmon-area paddles.

- Shoup Bridge to Island Park: 6.2 miles
- Island Park to Carmen: 4.4 miles
- Morgan Bar to Tower Rock: 4.4 miles
- Tower Rock to North Fork: 11.2 miles

Salmon River Road leads downstream to the Middle Fork takeout and the Main Salmon put-in. North Fork is also a good takeout for paddlers traveling from more mellow paddles upstream.

You can also paddle downstream another 3 miles below North Fork to Deadwater, where the Salmon River's currents are almost completely stilled during normal summer flows. The Deadwater Picnic Area is 3.6 miles down Salmon River Road from North Fork.

76 Upper Salmon, Pine Creek

Distance: 6.7 miles
Difficulty: Class III
Craft: Kayak, canoe, raft
Approximate paddling time: 2–3 hours
Flows: 800–6,000 cfs (**Gauge:** USGS, Salmon River at Salmon)
Season: May–Aug
Put-in: Pine Creek (45.364214, -114.299870)

Takeout: Panther Creek (45.315179, -114.404860)
Shuttle: From Salmon take US 93 north 21.2 miles to North Fork and turn left onto Salmon River Road. Go 26.5 miles to Panther Creek. To get to the put-in, return 6.7 miles to Pine Creek. There's a large pullout near the bridge on river-right.

A lot of whitewater boaters pass this stretch by on their way to the Main Salmon put-in or after taking off the Middle Fork of the Salmon. That's too bad. It's a good Class III day trip in a beautiful canyon, and it's got a few great play spots for kayakers.

There are a dozen or so good Class II and III rapids, but the biggest are Pine Creek just below the bridge at the put-in and Dutch Oven Rapid at mile 4.1. The entire run is roadside and easy to scout while setting up shuttle.

77 Panther Creek

Distance: 12 miles
Difficulty: Class III-V
Craft: Kayak
Approximate paddling time: 2-4 hours
Flows: 500-1,000 cfs (**Gauge:** None)
Season: May, June
Upper put-in: Trapper Flat (45.162584, -114.289736)
Upper takeout: Birch Creek (45.254198, -114.320867)

Lower put-in: Above Hot Springs Creek (45.295689, -114.352346)
Lower takeout: Panther Creek (45.315179, -114.404860)
Shuttle: From Salmon take US 93 north 21.2 miles to North Fork and turn left onto Salmon River Road. Go 26.5 miles to Panther Creek. From there continue up Panther Creek Road 3 miles for the lower run. Go 10 miles to put on below most of the Class V. Go 12 miles to put in for some tough Class V whitewater.

Panther Creek has two very different personalities, a really intense upper and a Class III+ lower. In either case, this is a small mountain stream with a short runoff window.

The upper section, from Trapper Flat to Birch Creek, is very continuous and technical Class IV and V paddling. There's at least one portage around a danger-ous boulder-sieve rapid. The rap-ids are continuous, long and shallow, and paddlers should be very wary of broaching and pinning. To avoid the Class V, put in below the big rapids, all of which are concentrated in the top couple of miles of the run.

Following a few miles of flat water after Birch Creek, the river picks up again at Hot Springs Creek for 3.2 miles of fairly continuous and enjoy-able Class III/IV paddling until you reach the confluence with the Salmon River.

Though it could be paddled as a single trip, Panther Creek is seldom run from top to bottom. The upper and lower are so different that boat-ers tend to gravitate toward one or the other.

Lower Panther Creek is continuous whitewater.
PHOTO BY WENDY JONES

Middle Fork of the Salmon River Basin

The Middle Fork and its tributaries are the beating heart of wild Idaho. Nearly the entire basin is within the boundaries of the 2.4-million-acre Frank Church–River of No Return Wilderness Area, which until 1994 was the largest designated wilderness in the lower forty-eight states (now exceeded only by Death Valley in California). The Middle Fork was also one of the original eight rivers protected as a Wild and Scenic River with passage of the Wild and Scenic Rivers Act in 1968. This is a wild place with unimaginable beauty and some of the finest rivers in the country, including the legendary Middle Fork itself.

With the exception of a few floats near its headwaters, paddling in the Middle Fork basin is a commitment. The standard trip down the Middle Fork's 96 miles takes a week, and trips on its tributaries require boaters to either charter an airplane shuttle at a backcountry airstrip or paddle out on the Middle Fork, and that requires a highly sought after permit.

The Middle Fork of the Salmon River's 100 miles of wilderness paddling is legendary. Cliffside Rapid is only one of dozens of rapids waiting to test paddlers. Photo by Kevin Lewis

153

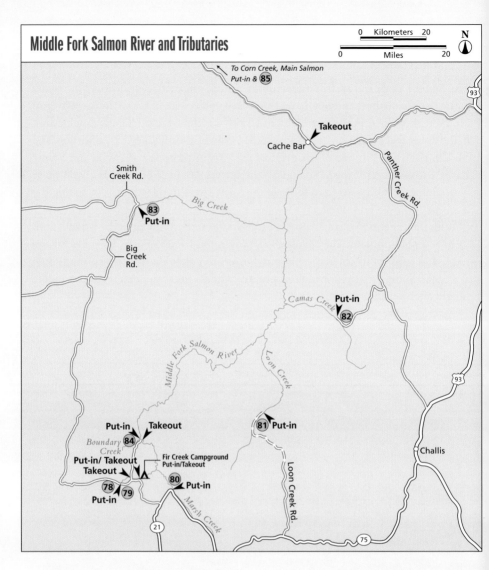

0   Kilometers   20

0   Miles   20

N

To Corn Creek, Main Salmon
Put-in & 85

93

Takeout

Cache Bar

Panther Creek Rd

Smith
Creek Rd.

Big Creek

83
Put-in

Big
Creek
Rd.

Camas Creek   **Put-in**
82

Loon Creek

Middle Fork Salmon River

93

Put-in   **Takeout**   81 **Put-in**

Boundary 84
Creek
Put-in/ Takeout   Fir Creek Campground
Takeout   Put-in/Takeout

Challis

78 79   80 **Put-in**
Put-in

Loon Creek Rd.

21

Marsh Creek

75

The streams that form the Middle Fork's upper headwaters, Bear Valley and Marsh Creeks, are small and meander through postcard-perfect meadows riddled with wildflowers. They tumble quickly into steep-walled canyons and join to form the Middle Fork, which steadily grows into a large river over its deeply incised course.

The wilderness and natural beauty of the place is the most appealing part for many visitors, but the canyon also has a rich cultural history. There are numerous old cabins, homesteads, and Native American pictographs to visit. There are also outstanding hot springs.

As this is wilderness, it is also an ever-changing landscape. There have been dozens of forest fires in the Middle Fork basin in the past decade alone. Once-forested mountainsides have experienced massive landslides, resulting in more than fifteen new or altered rapids, and every new season brings another opportunity for change.

Importantly, the Middle Fork is one of the only river basins in the entire Pacific Northwest where wild salmon are truly wild. Fisheries managers have refrained from stocking the Middle Fork with hatchery-bred salmon as they have for almost every other river. For this reason it is widely considered one of the best barometers for the health of wild salmon, an endangered species, in the Columbia River Basin.

With clean and clear water, challenging rapids, and spectacular scenery over the course of its 100 free-flowing miles, the Middle Fork easily earns a lofty status among America's rivers.

78 Bear Valley Creek, Upper Meanders

Distance: 3.5 miles
Difficulty: Class I
Craft: Canoe, kayak, stand-up paddleboard
Approximate paddling time: 2–4 hours
Flows: 100–500 cfs (**Gauge:** None)
Season: June–Sept
Put-in: Downstream of bridge near Bear Valley Campground (44.412037, -115.372519)
Takeout: FR 568 (44.427577, -115.330652)
Optional takeout: Fir Creek Campground (44.428227, -115.285114)
Shuttle: Upper Bear Valley Creek is accessed via Bear Valley Road (FR 579), a dirt road, from ID 21 and is often closed by snow until late May or early June. The well-signed turnoff

(look for signs to Boundary Creek) is 23 miles west of Stanley and between mileposts 109 and 110. Continue 9.4 miles and turn right on FR 568, following signs for Boundary Creek. Continue 0.8 mile to the bridge. There's a large parking and river access area downstream of the bridge on river-right. To get to the put-in, return to Bear Valley Road and continue west 2.8 miles to the bridge near Bear Valley Campground. There's a short access road on the west side of the bridge with parking and access to the creek. The turnoff to Fir Creek Campground, the alternate takeout, is 7.9 miles from ID 21 on the right. The campground is 0.75 mile ahead on FR 579A.

This is an extremely beautiful and easy float. If you're paddling here in late June or early July, you may see chinook salmon completing the final miles on their homeward

Upper Bear Valley Creek, probably the easiest float in the upper Middle Fork of the Salmon basin, makes for a beautiful day trip.

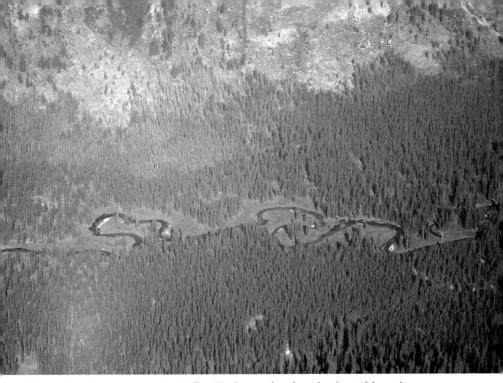

Before it drops into a canyon, Bear Valley Creek meanders through a beautiful meadow.

journeys. You may also see bald eagles, deer, elk, or moose. In fact, don't be surprised if you see all of these in a couple hours on the river.

Of the river paddles in the upper Middle Fork and upper Salmon, this is probably the easiest, and it is as beautiful as the others if not more so. It can be paddled using inflatables, hard-shells, canoes, or stand-up paddleboards.

Bear Valley Creek is a classic meandering stream that has cut considerable oxbows and oxbow lakes into the surrounding meadows. It's a small stream, so there is a danger of river-wide logs and sweepers, but the channel is generally clear of obstructions.

The recommended float from Bear Valley Campground to the bridge on FR 568 is relatively short, but you'll want to pack a lunch and take your time to soak up this pristine and beautiful part of Idaho. To add 3.6 miles to your trip, continue downstream to Fir Creek Campground. Be aware, though, that the final mile gets mildly more difficult, approaching Class II, as the creek begins to enter the canyon. And once past the campground you are committed to the Class III canyon below because that's where the road ends. Water level depending, you may also be able to put in along Elk Creek farther to the west.

79 Bear Valley Creek, Canyon

Distance: 13.2 miles
Difficulty: Class II–III
Craft: Kayak, canoe, raft
Approximate paddling time: 5–7 hours
Flows: 500–2,000 cfs (**Gauge:** None)
Season: June, July
Put-in: Fir Creek Campground (44.428227, -115.285114)
Takeout: Above Dagger Falls (44.528066, -115.283995)
Shuttle: The takeout for this run is 0.5 mile upstream of the standard put-in for the Middle Fork at Boundary Creek and is well signed. From ID 21 turn onto Bear Valley Road (FR 579) between mileposts 109 and 110. The turn is 23 miles west of Stanley. Continue on Bear Valley Road 9.4 miles and turn right on FR 568, following signs for Boundary Creek. Continue 9.6 miles and turn right, following signs for Dagger Falls, which is 0.7 mile farther. To reach the put-in, return to Bear Valley Road and turn left back toward ID 21. Go 1.5 miles and turn left on FR 579A. Fir Creek Campground is 0.75 mile ahead.

After meandering through scenic mountain meadows at more than 6,000 feet, Bear Valley Creek twists into a steep-walled, timbered canyon and begins its descent toward Marsh Creek, where the two waterways join to become the Middle Fork.

The creek is swift and the riverbed fairly undefined for the first 4 miles until it merges with Marsh Creek. In fact, most of the rapids, including some good Class IIIs, are on the upper Middle Fork after the Marsh Creek confluence.

The recommended takeout is above Dagger Falls. You'll know you're there when you arrive at a pack bridge suspended over the river. Dagger Falls can be run, but it's got some sticky holes and lots of jagged rocks below 5 feet (about 5,000 cfs) on the Middle Fork Lodge gauge. Above 5 feet, it's big, but paddlers can usually safely navigate the chute on the left.

Don't miss the hot springs just before the Marsh Creek confluence on river-right.

80 Marsh Creek

Distance: 15.8 miles
Difficulty: Class III-IV
Craft: Kayak, canoe, raft
Approximate paddling time: 1 day
Flows: 1,800–20,000 cfs (**Gauge:** Middle Fork Lodge)
Season: May, June, July
Put-in: Cape Horn Road (44.396008, -115.169505)
Takeout: Above Dagger Falls (44.528066, -115.283995)
Shuttle: The takeout is a 0.5 mile upstream of the standard put-in for the Middle Fork at Boundary Creek and is well signed. From ID 21 turn onto Bear Valley Road (FR 579) between mileposts 109 and 110. The turn is 23 miles west of Stanley. Continue on Bear Valley Road 9.4 miles and turn right on FR 568, following signs for Boundary Creek. Continue 9.6 miles and turn right, following signs for Dagger Falls, which is 0.7 mile farther. To reach the put-in, return to ID 21 and travel 3.2 miles east toward Stanley. If the road's open, turn left on Cape Horn Road and then take a quick left on FR 083 and travel it 0.5 mile to its end. If the road's snowed in, put in on Cape Horn Creek just off ID 21 or at the bridge on Cape Horn Road.

When the road to Boundary Creek is snowed in, this is the standard put-in for trips on the Middle Fork, but Marsh Creek can also be done as an unpermitted day trip.

If there's a lot of snow, you'll have to put on Cape Horn Creek right off ID 21, and it's an extremely small stream. In fact, you may find it difficult to believe you can float a boat on it at all, but Cape Horn Creek quickly joins Marsh Creek, and a number of additional creeks add considerable volume before Marsh Creek enters the canyon 1.5 miles downstream.

Marsh Creek is swift, with a fairly undefined streambed. It has a number of blind corners prone to collecting wood, and paddlers need to stay on their toes and be prepared to portage. New wood is deposited annually from avalanches, and early-season paddlers must be prepared to deal with it. This has been the cause of some unfortunate early-season fatalities.

The confluence with Bear Valley Creek comes at mile 6.4, and most of the run's Class II and III rapids are after that.

The recommended takeout is above Dagger Falls. You'll know you're there when you arrive at a pack bridge suspended over the river. Dagger Falls can be run, but it's got some sticky holes and lots of jagged rocks below 5 feet (about 5,000 cfs) on the Middle Fork Lodge gauge. Above 5 feet, it's a big rapid, but the chute on the left generally goes. The portage for rafts is very challenging.

81 Loon Creek

Distance: 20.4 miles (plus 50 miles on the Middle Fork)
Difficulty: Class V
Craft: Kayak
Approximate paddling time: 1–2 days
Flows: 500–1,000 cfs (**Gauge:** None; approximately 3–5 feet on the Middle Fork Lodge gauge)
Season: June–July
Put-in: Loon Creek Ranger Station (44.602121, -114.806854)
Takeout: Middle Fork confluence (44.807955, -114.812177)

Shuttle: To reach the takeout at Cache Bar from the city of Salmon, take US 93 for 21 miles and turn left onto Salmon River Road at North Fork. Continue 40.7 miles to Cache Bar. To get to the put-in from Stanley, drive 13 miles downriver along ID 75 and turn left at Sunbeam on Yankee Fork Road. Go 8.6 miles and turn left on Loon Creek Road. Follow Loon Creek Road 25 miles, crossing Loon Creek Summit. Pass Loon Creek Ranger Station and travel to the end of the road.

Loon Creek is a beautiful, remote stretch of river with a good mix of challenging rapids and mellow miles where you can enjoy the abundant beauty of the Frank Church–River of No Return Wilderness.

Much of the drainage has burned during recent wildfires, which have impacted the area's visual aesthetics. There have also been enormous avalanches that have deposited hundreds of trees in the river. Approach blind corners and horizons with caution.

For about the first 10 miles, Loon Creek is swift and continuous and has a few good Class III and IV rapids with the ever-present danger of logjams.

The middle section, where you'll pass Falconberry and Biggs ranches on the left, is relaxed and provides an opportunity to collect yourself for the hardest rapids of the run. About 3 miles below Biggs, at mile 13, the canyon closes in and the whitewater picks up, starting with a long Class IV rock garden followed by a Class V a couple miles later. Both should be scouted.

The river's final and hardest series begins after the river passes Bennett Creek Pack Bridge at mile 18. This is a mile-long rapid through a tight gorge and contains some powerful holes and tight slots.

Loon Creek Hot Springs and the Middle Fork are another couple miles downstream, and once at the Middle Fork you'll need to have planned ahead. You either have to have a permit to paddle the remaining 50 miles on the Middle Fork or have chartered an air taxi to pick you up at Lower Loon Airstrip, reported to be one of the more challenging backcountry airstrips in Idaho.

82 Camas Creek

Distance: 11.2 miles
Difficulty: Class V
Craft: Kayak
Approximate paddling time: 1–4 days
Flows: 500–1,000 cfs (**Gauge:** None; approximately 3–5 feet on the Middle Fork Lodge gauge)
Season: June
Put-in: Below Duck Creek (44.855935, -114.535418)
Takeout: Cache Bar (45.318626, -114.636654)

Shuttle: To reach the takeout at Cache Bar from the city of Salmon, take US 93 for 21 miles and turn left onto Salmon River Road at North Fork. Continue 40.7 miles to Cache Bar. To reach the put-in, drive 14 miles upstream to Panther Creek. Follow Panther Creek Road 36 miles to Rooker Basin and turn right (west) on Silver Creek Road (FR 108). Follow Silver Creek Road 14 miles to Camas Creek Road (still FR 108). Continue 2.7 miles to the road's end 0.5 mile below Duck Creek. If the gate at Meyers Cove is locked, start there. This adds a couple miles of flat water.

Camas Creek is a swift, continuous, challenging stream. Of the Middle Fork's tributaries it offers the best expert-level paddling and includes a dozen Class IV rapids as well as several steep and constricted Class Vs. Plan on a full day of paddling and scouting, plus another couple of days to paddle the remaining 40 miles on the Middle Fork after the confluence.

Camas Creek starts calm, but things pick up early in the run once the canyon walls close in with Camas Falls, a recommended portage. The river is stunningly beautiful, but you'll have a tough time enjoying the scenery because the river is so continuous. Things slack off a few miles above the confluence with the Middle Fork.

As with the other creeks in the area, you must have a permit to float out on the Middle Fork.

83 Big Creek

Distance: 35 miles (plus 20 miles on the Middle Fork)
Difficulty: Class IV
Craft: Kayak
Approximate paddling time: 2–4 days
Flows: 500–2,000 cfs (**Gauge:** None; approximately 3–5 feet on the Middle Fork Lodge gauge)
Season: June, July
Put-in: Big Creek Airstrip (45.138305, -115.313189)
Takeout: Cache Bar (45.318626, -114.636654)
Shuttle: To reach the takeout at Cache Bar from the city of Salmon, take US 93 for 21 miles and turn left onto Salmon River Road at North Fork. Continue 40.7 miles to Cache Bar. From here it is advisable to return to Salmon to take a chartered flight to the put-in at Big Creek Airstrip. If driving, you'll need to go 60 miles back to Salmon, another 60 miles south to Challis, and turn right onto ID 75. Continue 58 miles to Stanley and turn right onto ID 21. Go 58 miles to Lowman and turn right onto Banks Lowman Road. Go 34 miles to ID 55 and turn right and continue 37 miles to Cascade. Turn right on Warm Lake Road and go 37 miles to Johnson Creek Road. Follow Johnson Creek Road north for 25 miles to Yellow Pine. From Yellow Pine take Profile Creek Road 23 miles to Big Creek Road and the Big Creek Airstrip via Profile Summit.

Of the Middle Fork's tributaries, Big Creek has the best Class IV rapids, but it also has the most arduous shuttle, 380 miles if you drive it, and that's only possible if the roads aren't snowed in. The only sensible way to do this trip is to leave a car at Cache Bar, the Middle Fork takeout, and charter a Cessna from the city of Salmon to drop you at Big Creek Airstrip.

The first 10 miles are very small and swift, and downed trees are a constant hazard. Plan to do a lot of portaging. The creek picks up numerous tributaries in this reach and grows fast. Monumental Creek joins at mile 11.6 and adds a significant amount of water. Though you need to stay on your toes, the amount of wood in the river from here down to the Middle Fork decreases significantly.

Coxey Hole at mile 17.6 signals your arrival at a tough rapid, which follows about 0.5 mile later. From there to Taylor Ranch at mile 28.5 the river mellows, and you'll be able to relax and enjoy the beautiful canyon. Three miles after the ranch, granite walls close in as you enter Big Creek Gorge, an incredible 5 miles of continuous Class IV that ends at the Middle Fork.

A permit is required to paddle the final 20 miles out on the Middle Fork and can be obtained through the Four Rivers Lottery.

84 The Middle Fork

Distance: 100 miles
Difficulty: Class IV–IV+
Craft: Kayak, raft, canoe
Approximate paddling time: 1 week
Flows: 1,000–20,000 cfs (**Gauge:** Middle Fork Lodge)
Season: Apr–Oct
Put-in: Boundary Creek Boat Ramp (44.531726, -115.294169)
Takeout: Cache Bar Boat Ramp on Main Salmon (45.318626, -114.636654)

Shuttle: To reach the takeout at Cache Bar from the city of Salmon, take US 93 for 21 miles and turn left onto Salmon River Road at North Fork. Continue 40.7 miles to Cache Bar. To get to the put-in, return 60 miles to Salmon, then another 60 miles south to Challis and turn right onto ID 75. Continue 58 miles to Stanley and turn right onto ID 21. The well-signed turnoff to Boundary Creek is 23 miles ahead on the right, where you'll take Bear Valley Road 9.4 miles and turn right on FR 568, following signs for Boundary Creek, another 11 miles.

The Middle Fork is one of the most prized multiday wilderness trips in America for good reason. It is secluded, beautiful, and flows through the heart of wild Idaho. It also has outstanding Class IV rapids that can be run at a variety of levels.

Paddling the Middle Fork of the Salmon River is highly popular for good reason.

A spring launch on the Middle Fork often means a snowy start on Marsh Creek because the road to the launch site at Boundary Creek is still snowed in.

Floating the Middle Fork is a great opportunity to observe a wild river's growth as it descends from its headwaters. There are no dams, and the river flows under natural cycles, peaking in late May or early June and getting rocky by mid-July. While the Middle Fork at medium flows is an accessible Class IV river, it becomes considerably more difficult and continuous at peak runoff, when it is considered Class IV+. At low flows of around 1,000 cfs at Middle Fork Lodge, most rafters, and some kayakers, choose to fly into Indian Creek and start their trips there to avoid the river's rocky upper rapids. Most paddlers take a week to paddle the Middle Fork, but at peak flows kayakers have been known to do the whole thing in one very intense day.

From the put-in at Boundary Creek the Middle Fork is steep and fairly continuous for about 25 miles. This is where inexperienced rafters often get themselves into trouble, particularly at high water. Velvet Falls, Elkhorn, Powerhouse, and Pistol Creek are good rapids in this section. The gradient relaxes from 40 feet per mile to 23 feet per mile after Indian Creek.

Rapids pick up again after Tappen Ranch. Standouts in this section are Tappen Falls and Haystack. The best whitewater of the trip comes after the Big Creek confluence, in Impassable Canyon, so named because there's no trail along the river, not because of the whitewater. A few of the standout rapids in Impassable Canyon include Porcupine, Redside, Cliffside, and Rubber.

The standard Middle Fork put-in at Boundary Creek is often snowed in until mid-June, and when this is the case boaters must start on Marsh Creek at ID 21. Marsh Creek is a small stream that includes blind corners prone to collecting wood, and rafters in particular need to be ready for this hazard. (See Marsh Creek description on page 159 for more information.)

Paddling on the Middle Fork is strictly managed by the USDA Forest Service. If you want to float the 96 miles from Boundary Creek to the Main Salmon during prime season, May 28 to September 3, you have to luck into a permit through the Four Rivers Lottery. Permits are also required year-round. There are seven issued per day during off-season on a first-come, first served basis.

There are several excellent mile-by-mile guides to the Middle Fork that go into far more detail about the canyon's rapids, camping, culture, geology, and history than these pages allow. *The Middle Fork of the Salmon River: A Comprehensive Guide* is one of the best.

Main Salmon

The Salmon River bisects Idaho where practically no roads do. From Salmon to Riggins, it flows mostly west for more than 125 miles, and for the majority of that journey is within the Frank Church–River of No Return Wilderness Area.

At normal summer flows, the Salmon River has big but relatively friendly Class III and IV rapids and miles of enjoyable floating in a gorgeous steep-walled gorge.

Big Mallard is just one of more than a dozen really good rapids on the Main Salmon.
Photo by Wesley Keller

85 Main Salmon

Distance: 85 miles

Difficulty: Class III–IV (IV above 20,000 cfs, IV(V) above 50,000 cfs)

Craft: Raft, kayak, canoe, drift boat

Approximate paddling time: 1 week

Flows: 4,000–80,000 cfs (**Gauge:** Salmon River at White Bird)

Season: Apr–Oct

Put-in: Corn Creek Boat Ramp (45.369976, -114.687774)

Takeout: Vinegar Creek Boat Ramp (45.459576, -115.892964)

Shuttle: At 411 miles, this is the longest shuttle in Idaho, and paddlers should consider using one of the state's excellent professional shuttle services. They'll pick your car up at Corn Creek and drive it to the takeout at Vinegar Creek. To reach the takeout, drive to Riggins and take Salmon River Road upriver 25.5 miles to Vinegar Creek, a well-developed boat ramp. To get to the put-in, return to Riggins and go south through McCall to Banks. Turn east and go to Stanley, then north/northeast to Challis and north again to Salmon. From Salmon go north on US 93 21.2 miles and turn left onto Salmon River Road. Go 45.8 miles to the end of the road and the Corn Creek Boat Ramp. The shuttle is 383 miles through Missoula, Montana.

The Main Salmon is a western classic. Flowing for 85 miles through the heart of the Frank Church–River of No Return Wilderness Area, the Main has a dozen big-water Class III and IV rapids set in an unspoiled canyon overflowing with pioneering history.

Coined the River of No Return because it was a one-way trip for early settlers traveling the canyon downstream, the Main Salmon is a family-friendly wilderness whitewater trip at most levels and has beautiful sand beaches, a remote canyon, and fantastic pool-drop rapids. It flows through the second deepest gorge in North America; only Hells Canyon on the Snake River is deeper. It is also a federally designated Wild and Scenic River.

Though it can be done by kayak-

Buckskin Bill was one of Idaho's eclectic river personalities. His home on the Salmon River can be visited during a Main Salmon trip. PHOTO BY WESLEY KELLER

ers as an intense day trip during peak flows, most paddlers take six or seven days to float through this remote part of Idaho and savor the wilderness. There are no

The Salmon River is revered for its white sand beaches. PHOTO BY WESLEY KELLER

dams on the Salmon River, and the flow fluctuates according to the seasons, cresting at 80,000 cfs or more in late May or early June and dipping to a few thousand cfs in late summer and fall. At high water, with a few notable exceptions, most of the rapids wash out. At medium and low flows, rapids are more defined. Most consist of big wave trains punctuated with big holes. The run is generally considered Class III below 20,000 cfs and Class IV above that. At high water, above 50,000 cfs, a Class V rapid forms at Whiplash, a drop that's fairly tame at lower levels. Other good rapids include Bailey, Split Rock, Big Mallard, and Elkhorn.

If you want to float the 85 miles from Corn Creek to Vinegar Creek during prime season, June 20 to September 7, you have to luck into a permit from the Four Rivers Lottery, administered by the USDA Forest Service. No more than eight parties are allowed per day during this time. Permits are also required year-round, though there is no limit to the number issued outside of the summer lottery season.

There are a number of excellent books and mile-by-mile guides available for the Main Salmon, and they are highly recommended to take full advantage of the area's rich history, superlative hiking, and wonderful camping.

South Fork of the Salmon River Basin

The South Fork of the Salmon River and its tributaries are remote, beautiful, and chock-full of challenging, world-class whitewater. The basin includes a solitary town, Yellow Pine, which at the time of the 2010 census had a population of 32. Yellow Pine and its charming dirt main street is a 50-mile, 3-hour drive from the city of Cascade, so paddlers heading into the area should stock up on provisions and plan to do some camping.

Settled by fur trappers and miners, the South Fork basin was heavily logged during the middle of the twentieth century, and more than 800 miles of logging roads were built across the drainage. Resulting erosion produced widespread sediment pollution in the rivers and severely degraded the basin's high-quality fish habitat.

Though a shadow of its former vitality, the South Fork today is a river that is regaining its strength. Though only small parts of the basin are designated wilderness, it is remote and wild, and several of the rivers leave roads behind for considerable distances.

The South Fork flows north from its headwaters in the Salmon River Mountains and joins the Main Salmon River at Mackay Bar.

The South Fork of the Salmon has some of the best whitewater in Idaho. The lower canyon, pictured, is also very remote.

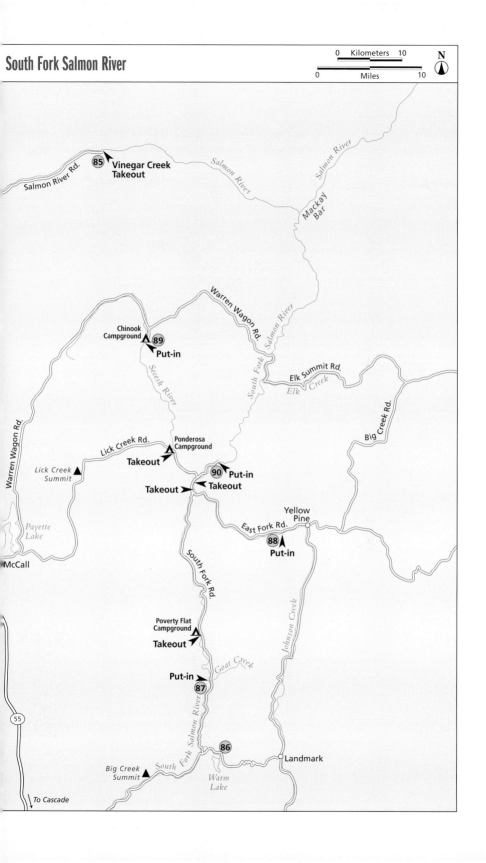

South Fork Salmon River

85 Vinegar Creek
Takeout

Salmon River Rd.

Salmon River

Salmon River

*Mackay
Bar*

Warren Wagon Rd.

Chinook
Campground **89**
Put-in

Salmon River

South Fork

Steesh River

Elk Summit Rd.

Elk Creek

Big Creek Rd.

Lick Creek Rd.   Ponderosa
Campground
Takeout

*Lick Creek
Summit*

Warren Wagon Rd.

90 Put-in
Takeout

Takeout

*Payette
Lake*

McCall

Yellow
Pine

East Fork Rd.

88 Put-in

South Fork Rd.

Johnson Creek

Poverty Flat
Campground
Takeout

Goat Creek

Put-in
87

55

South Fork Salmon River

86

Landmark

*Big Creek
Summit*

South Fork Salmon River

*Warm
Lake*

To Cascade

86 Warm Lake

Distance: 1-4 miles
Difficulty: Flat water
Craft: Canoe, kayak, stand-up paddleboard
Approximate paddling time: 1-5 hours
Season: May-Oct

Launch site: Shoreline Campground
(44.652482, -115.665490)
Access: From Cascade take Warm Lake Road 26.2 miles east. Shoreline Campground, a boat ramp, and docks are on the north side of the lake.

Nestled high in the Salmon River Mountains 26 miles east of Cascade, Warm Lake is a picturesque and secluded body of water where you've got great odds of seeing moose, deer, elk, or black bears. The lake also has abundant rainbow, brook, lake, and bull trout, as well as mountain whitefish and kokanee.

There are several lodges, developed campgrounds, and private cottages with docks along the lake's shores, but early-morning paddlers may have the place to themselves. At 0.5 mile wide and 1.5 miles long, the 640-acre lake is situated at 5,290 feet and offers great views of the surrounding mountains.

87 South Fork, Goat Creek Run

Distance: 6.7 miles
Difficulty: Class IV-V
Craft: Kayak, canoe
Approximate paddling time: 3-4 hours
Flows: 500-4,000 cfs (**Gauge:** USGS, South Fork Salmon at Krassel)
Season: Apr-June
Put-in: Goat Creek (44.758985, -115.684430)

Takeout: Poverty Flat Campground (44.823179, -115.704118)
Shuttle: To reach the takeout from Cascade, take Warm Lake Road 23 miles to South Fork Road and turn north. Poverty Flat Campground is 13.5 miles ahead. To reach the put-in, return upriver 5.6 miles to Goat Creek. There's a 10-foot-high culvert beneath the road that helps signal your arrival.

At high water this run on the upper South Fork packs some heat. At medium flows, it's still plenty challenging but becomes more manageable for most advanced boaters. It has a tight streambed with continuous rapids flowing through a remote canyon. There is no easy escape valve, so pack a spare paddle and plenty of food and water.

The action starts after about 2 miles when several big avalanche paths come into view above the river, with a long Class IV rapid. After passing the avalanche chutes, wood is a constant and ever-changing hazard on this run and portaging may be necessary.

Not long after passing the avalanche paths, the river enters its crux section, a continuous rapid that ends at Double Drop, a Class V pair of ledges. The Swimming Hole, a powerful ledge hole, is about 1.5 miles below Double Drop.

Aside from the named rapids, the South Fork has a number of long, continuous rapids that make for a

Double Drop at low water is steep but manageable. It becomes a very tough rapid as the water level rises.

fun, challenging day trip. It is Class IV at about 500 to 1,000 cfs and Class V above that. Boaters new to the run should plan their first trips at low to medium flows or tag along with someone who's familiar with the run.

88 East Fork of the South Fork

Distance: 12 miles
Difficulty: Class IV-V
Craft: Kayak
Approximate paddling time: 3-6 hours
Flows: 500-3,000 cfs (**Gauge:** None)
Season: Apr-June
Put-in: 2.2 miles below Yellow Pine (44.955790, -115.536609)
Takeout: East Fork Road bridge (45.009827, -115.713246)
Shuttle: The takeout is 14.4 miles below Yellow Pine on East Fork Road. It is also near the end of South Fork Road, the only paved road in the area. From South Fork Salmon Road, turn right onto East Fork Road and go less than 0.5 mile to a pullout on the upstream side of the bridge. To get to the put-in, continue upstream 11 miles on East Fork Road. From milepost 47, continue 0.75 mile. There's a pullout on the south side of the road, with a short walk down to the river. Intermediate boaters should put on at Caton Creek, about 2.5 miles downstream.

The East Fork of the South Fork boasts tough, roadside whitewater that gradually gets easier the farther downstream paddlers go. It starts with a very difficult Class V rapid called Flight Simulator and continues for about 6 miles of continuous Class IV rapids. The next 6 miles are predominantly Class III.

The top rapids on the East Fork of the South Fork include very tough paddling for expert kayakers.

At low flows, Flight Simulator is a technical Class IV+ rapid, but paddlers shouldn't underestimate it. When the water is bank-full or higher, it is a long, continuous, and powerful Class V with very sticky hydraulics.

For less experienced boaters or experts wary of running Flight Simulator at high water, Caton Creek is a good alternative put-in. Paddlers running from Caton Creek down will still face some huge water and powerful holes, particularly in the first several miles.

For expert paddlers there are additional runs on the tributaries above Yellow Pine. The East Fork of the South Fork from Vibika Creek to Johnson Creek is continuous Class IV with downed trees and steep drops. It has a short window and can be paddled near peak runoff.

The upper miles of Johnson Creek, which joins the East Fork of the South Fork at Yellow Pine, contain numerous Class V and V+ rapids that are chock-full of logs. The 5-mile lower section of Johnson Creek, from Yellow Pine Airport down to the East Fork of the South Fork, is Class III. The put-in is about 0.5 mile upstream from the airport bridge, but don't put on above there unless you're prepared for very difficult whitewater. Deadhorse Rapids, a big Class V, is just upstream.

89 Secesh River

Distance: 14.5 miles
Difficulty: Class V/V+
Craft: Kayak
Approximate paddling time: 1 day
Flows: 1,000–2,000 cfs (**Gauge:** None)
Season: Apr–June
Put-in: Chinook Campground (45.212349, -115.809118)
Takeout: Ponderosa Campground (45.062079, -115.760563)
Shuttle: To get to the takeout from McCall, go east on Lick Creek Road, over Lick Creek Summit, 28.4 miles. If Lick Creek Summit is closed due to snow, go south on ID 55 to Cascade and turn left (east) on Warm Lake Road. Take Warm Lake Road 23 miles to South Fork Road and turn north, going 34 miles. Turn west on Lick Creek Road and go 4.5 miles to Ponderosa Campground. To reach the put-in from McCall, go north on ID 55 1.2 miles and turn right (east) on Warren Wagon Road. Go 37 miles to Chinook Campground.

Of the South Salmon basin's abundant difficult whitewater, the Secesh is the most challenging. It is a demanding and tiring day trip that also requires a lengthy shuttle. Be wary of this run at high water. It would be a shame to take a kayak along for an otherwise beautiful hike.

The first several miles after the put-in include some swift Class III, but the river steepens and gets ever more difficult as it goes, working its way into continuous Class IV and V rapids in the heart of the canyon. There's a trail along the river-left bank the entire length of the run that serves as a welcomed safety valve and portage route.

The first rapid starts a couple miles below the put-in, and the paddling gets tougher at Loon Creek, mile 3.5, where there's a pack bridge suspended above the river. From Loon Creek down, the river gets progressively harder still.

At mile 10, the water pools, and a falls are visible pouring down Tobacco Can Creek high on the canyon wall on the left. This signals the beginning of The Miracle Mile, the top of which must be portaged. The portage is on the left. After carrying around the top of the rapid, there's a brief window of Class IV before the river works around a bend and drops into the heart of the rapid, a long, tough cascade full of rocks, holes, and wood. From there it's another 3 miles of continuous whitewater to the confluence with Lick Creek and Ponderosa Campground, the takeout.

The final 5 miles of the Secesh from Ponderosa Campground to the confluence with the South Fork of the Salmon make a good Class IV day trip. This bottom section is roadside and can easily be scouted while setting up shuttle.

90 South Fork of the Salmon, Canyon

Distance: 32 miles (plus 21 miles on Main Salmon if paddling out)
Difficulty: Class IV–V
Craft: Kayak, raft
Approximate paddling time: 2–3 days
Flows: 1,000–10,000 cfs (**Gauge:** USGS, South Fork Salmon at Krassel)*
Season: Apr–July
Put-in: End of East Fork Road (45.048169, -115.663565)
Takeout: Vinegar Creek Boat Ramp (45.459576, -115.892964)
Shuttle: To reach the takeout from McCall, go north on ID 55 to Riggins and turn right on Big Salmon Road. Go 25 miles upstream to the end of the road at Vinegar Creek. To reach the put-in from McCall, take Lick Creek Road 33 miles, over Lick Creek Summit, to the confluence with the South Fork. Turn left and drive to the end of the road. If Lick Creek Summit is closed due to snow, drive south from McCall to Cascade and turn east on Warm Lake Road and travel 23 miles to South Fork Road. Go north on South Fork Road 33 miles. Turn left on East Fork Road and drive to the end of the road. Kayakers can also charter a plane to pick them up at Mackay Bar and fly them back to the Yellow Pine Airport, but some additional shuttling logistics are involved along the East Fork of the South Fork.
*Note that the flow at Krassel is only a rough indication of what's happening on the lower South Fork, which also picks up the flow from the East Fork of the South Fork and Secesh Rivers.

This fantastic two- to three-day trip doesn't get the fanfare of Idaho's Middle Fork or Main Salmon Rivers, but it's just as beautiful and has tougher (which for some means better) whitewater. At peak runoff, the rapids are enormous, and at medium flows there are still two Class V rapids with which to contend. Both would be difficult to portage with a raft. For this reason raft trips on the South Fork are less common. Rafters who commit to this remote multiday river often aim for low water in early July, when there's still some—but not much—runoff left. This river is largely the domain of self-support kayakers, especially when the water is high.

At low flows, the South Fork is an enjoyable Class III–IV trip with

At low to medium water, the South Fork is a technical paddle. At high water, all those rocks become big holes. PHOTO BY WENDY JONES

Elk Creek Rapid at low to medium water is still a challenging drop. Photo by Wendy Jones

numerous boulders and very tight slots. From medium to high flows, the river has some of the biggest water in Idaho and is a committing Class V expedition. You're sure to fall into some holes. Watch out for Devil Creek Rapid at mile 5.5 and Fall Creek Rapid at mile 28.5, just a few miles before the Main Salmon confluence. Both can be scouted from the left. Fall Creek Rapid has three distinct sections. In the final part the river drops over a succession of ledges and slams into the river-left wall.

Though this run is very remote and secluded, there's a bridge spanning the river at Elk Summit Road 13 miles into the trip. This can serve as a spot to leave a car full of camping provisions. It is, however, a long drive via Warren Summit or Elk Creek Summit, both of which will probably be snowed in early in the season.

Boaters floating the South Fork of the Salmon and exiting onto the Main Salmon must obtain a tributary permit. Contact the Krassel Ranger District at (208) 634-0616 for permit information. Paddlers may also be able to charter a backcountry flight back to Yellow Pine Airport from Mackay Bar to avoid the 21-mile float out on the Main Salmon.

Note that readings on the Krassel gauge do not include flows from the Secesh or East Fork of the South Fork of the Salmon Rivers. At 1.5 to 3.5 feet, the run is mostly Class III and IV. From 3.5 to 6 feet it is Class IV+ with two Class Vs. It is Class V above 6 feet.

Little Salmon Basin

The Little Salmon drains the western edge of the Salmon River Mountains, some of the snowiest mountains in central Idaho, and runoff usually starts a little earlier than other parts of the state.

Flowing from south to north, the Little Salmon begins as a meandering stream in a beautiful meadow along US 95 downstream of New Meadows and drops abruptly over a series of challenging Class V+ waterfalls before settling into the continuous Class IV character that defines most of its descent toward Riggins and the Salmon River.

During salmon and steelhead fishing seasons, the lower miles of the Little Salmon downstream of Rapid River become extremely crowded with anglers. Boaters need to be mindful that they're sharing the river and give anglers wide berth.

91 Little Salmon, New Meadows

Distance: 8.5 miles
Difficulty: Class I
Craft: Canoe, recreational kayak
Approximate paddling time: 3–4 hours
Flows: 500–1,000 cfs (**Gauge:** Little Salmon River at Riggins)
Season: May–Oct
Put-in: Zim's Road bridge (45.038794, -116.288679)

Takeout: US 95 pullout above waterfalls (45.124211, -116.295679)
Shuttle: The takeout is 11.2 miles north of New Meadows on US 95. There's a pullout on the right, just above a series of waterfalls. To get to the put-in, return via US 95 6.6 miles and turn right (west) on Zim's Road, following signs for Zim's Hot Springs. The put-in bridge is 0.6 mile ahead.

The Little Salmon meanders gently downstream of New Meadows. There are a few riffles to navigate and fences to duck or portage, but the run on this meandering stream is a mellow and scenic cruise for open canoeists or recreational kayakers and includes great views of the surrounding mountains. The water is very slow, but spring paddlers should be wary of the fences, which may lack clearance when the water is high.

The upper meanders of the Little Salmon River are a worthwhile cruise for recreational paddlers.

92　Little Salmon, Upper Steeps

Distance: 3 miles
Difficulty: Class V+
Craft: Kayak
Approximate paddling time: 2 hours
Flows: 1,000–2,500 cfs (**Gauge:** Little Salmon River at Riggins)
Season: Apr–June
Put-in: US 95 pullout (45.124211, -116.295679)

Takeout: US 95 pullout (45.154149, -116.297703)
Shuttle: From Riggins go 20.8 miles upriver on US 95 to a roadside pullout beside the Little Salmon. This is the takeout. To reach the put-in, continue 3 miles upstream to another highway pullout above the top waterfall.

This series of waterfalls on the upper Little Salmon is experts-only fare. The falls are full of shallow, jagged rocks, so landing zones aren't clean, and the rapids are very tight, complex, and continuous.

The biggest falls are contained in the first 1.5 miles below the put-in, but river access along busy US 95 is challenging. There's a good highway pullout beside the river 3 miles down. You can also paddle down to Hazard Creek for a 6-mile trip.

93 Hazard Creek

Distance: 1 mile
Difficulty: Class IV
Craft: Kayak
Approximate paddling time: 20 minutes
Flows: 500–1,500 cfs (**Gauge:** None)
Season: Apr–June
Put-in: Hard Creek confluence (45.182973, -116.283869)
Takeout: Little Salmon confluence (45.183493, -116.300983)

Shuttle: The turnoff to Hazard Creek is 19 miles south of Riggins on US 95. It is 15.8 miles north of New Meadows. Take Hazard Creek Road 0.25 mile to the bridge. The put-in is another mile up the road. You can put on at the bridge, but if you cross and drive into the dispersed camping area on the right, you can also put on at the Hard Creek confluence.

Hazard Creek is a great short creek run that can serve as a fun, fast start to a trip on the Little Salmon. It's a tight, swift, and cold mountain stream, and fairly continuous.

The gorge is difficult to scout, and river-wide logs are a real hazard. For this reason paddlers must be confident they can catch small eddies in very fast, continuous water before attempting this run.

Hazard Creek is a tight, swift, continuous mountain stream.

94 Little Salmon River

Distance: 19 miles
Difficulty: Class IV
Craft: Kayak, canoe, raft
Approximate paddling time: 4–6 hours
Flows: 500–5,000 cfs (**Gauge:** Little Salmon River at Riggins)
Season: Apr–June
Put-in: Hazard Creek (45.183493, -116.300983)
Alternative put-in/takeout: US 95 rest area (45.342745, -116.350885)
Takeout: Riggins (45.425587, -116.311657)

Shuttle: There are a number of good put-in and takeout options along this stretch, but there's also a lot of private property, so please be respectful. The main takeout is at the boat ramp on the Salmon River in Riggins. To reach the upper put-in drive south on US 95 for 19.5 miles and turn left (east) on a dirt road that leads to the confluence of Hazard Creek and the Little Salmon River. There's also a highway rest area at mile marker 189, 6.5 miles south of Riggins, that serves as a good put-in or takeout.

For the entirety of its 19 miles the Little Salmon has continuous Class III and IV rapids. It is the epitome of a Class IV river and at high water packs some heat. It consists of long, steep boulder gardens with a sprinkling of stout holes. Paddlers need to be comfortable running continuous Class IV whitewater before attempting this run.

A flood scoured the canyon and rearranged rapids in the late 1990s, making some more difficult and others easier. Notably, a rapid a mile below the put-in called Amphitheater Hole is no longer a recirculating nightmare. It's still a stout drop, but the riverbed was rearranged sufficiently to remove the powerful hydraulic.

The lower portion of the Little Salmon, below Rapid River, is very popular for salmon and steelhead anglers in the spring, and paddlers need to share the river respectfully.

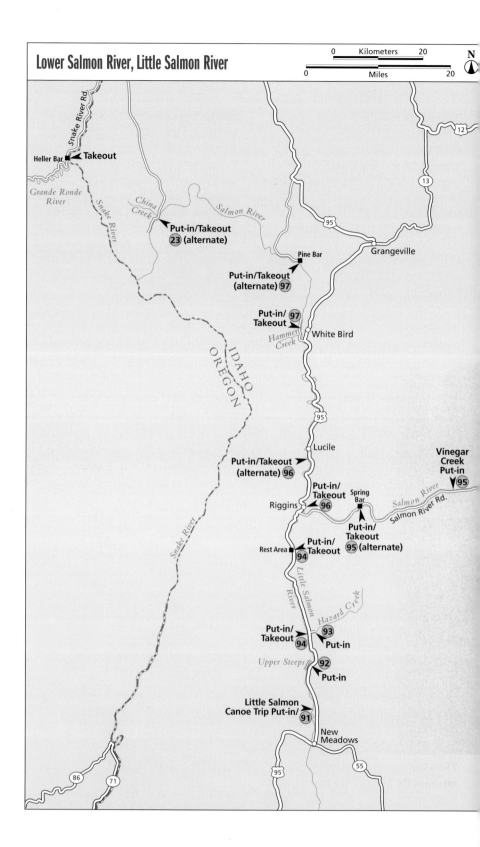

Lower Salmon River, Little Salmon River

Lower Salmon

The section of the Salmon River known as the Lower Salmon begins at Vinegar Creek, 25 miles above Riggins, and flows more than 100 miles to its confluence with the Snake River on the Idaho-Oregon border.

There are several good day trips on the Lower Salmon near Riggins and a wonderful Class II–III multiday trip below Whitebird. The canyon has outstanding surfing for kayakers at a variety of levels.

The Lower Salmon is a big river and can flow at more than 100,000 cfs during peak runoff following big snow years. The river and its canyon are remarkable, with white sand beaches, steep canyon walls, arid flora, and pool-drop rapids. It isn't technically wilderness, but portions of the Lower Salmon are very wild and remote.

Riggins is the hub for all the activity and has a number of river outfitters from which to choose, as well as good restaurants and accommodations. After runoff has ebbed, camping on the sand beaches along the Salmon River above Riggins is excellent. There is also good camping up Hazard Creek on the Little Salmon.

The white sand beaches of the Lower Salmon River offer some of the finest riverside camping anywhere. PHOTO BY KEVIN LEWIS

95 Lower Salmon, Vinegar Creek

Distance: 25 miles
Difficulty: Class III–IV
Craft: Canoe, kayak, raft, drift boat
Approximate paddling time: 5–7 hours
Flows: 4,000–80,000 cfs (**Gauge:** USGS, Salmon River at White Bird)
Season: Apr–Oct
Put-in: Vinegar Creek (45.459691, -115.892863)

Takeout: Riggins (45.425587, -116.311657)
Shuttle: The takeout is in Riggins at a well-developed BLM boat ramp in the center of town. To reach the put-in, drive south on US 95 1 mile and turn left (east) onto Big Salmon Road. The put-in is 25 miles upstream, at the end of the road. To put in at Spring Bar, go 10.3 miles up Big Salmon Road.

In the 25 miles from Vinegar Creek to Riggins, the Salmon River has several big rapids that are fairly spread out. They're straightforward, but at high water are huge. The rapids below Spring Bar are the location of the annual Big Water Blowout, a festival held the first Saturday in June each year.

Good rapids in this section are Vinegar Creek, 0.5 mile below the put-in; French Creek at mile 7; Ruby at mile 17.5; and Lake Creek at mile 18.8, just above Lake Creek Bridge, the first bridge travelers find driving upstream. Boaters looking to run the biggest water on this stretch can put in at Spring Bar 10 miles above Riggins and drop into Ruby a couple miles later.

This section also has some of the best kayak surfing in the region. Mill, Peace, Cat's Paw, Couch, and Gold Hole waves are all located on this stretch, and that's not even all of the named surf spots. Mill Wave is good at lower flows of about 4,000 cfs and is just upstream of Riggins, across from the old mill. Both Peace and Cat's Paw are below Lake Creek Bridge on Salmon River Road, about 6 miles upstream of Riggins, and are good at about 4,000 cfs. Couch Wave is 16.8 miles upstream of Riggins and is in at a wide variety of levels, about 7,500 to 26,000 cfs. Gold Hole is 23.9 miles up the Salmon River and is in between 5,500 and 13,000 cfs. Beware of Gold Hole below 7,000 cfs. It is a very sticky hole at lower levels.

During peak spring runoff, even the flat water on the Salmon River churns and boils.

96 Lower Salmon, Riggins to Whitebird

Distance: 32 miles
Difficulty: Class III–IV
Craft: Canoe, kayak, raft, drift boat
Approximate paddling time: 4–8 hours
Flows: 4,000–80,000 cfs (**Gauge:** Salmon River at Whitebird)
Season: Apr–Oct
Put-in: Riggins (45.425587, -116.311657)
Alternative put-in/takeout: Lucile (45.525321, -116.304914)
Takeout: Hammer Creek (45.764957, -116.324561)

Shuttle: To reach the takeout at Hammer Creek from Riggins, take US 95 26.8 miles north along the Salmon River. Turn left onto Old Highway 95, following signs for Hammer Creek, and after 0.75 mile turn left again onto Doumecq Road. Cross the bridge and follow Doumecq road 1.8 miles downriver to Hammer Creek. To reach the put-in/takeout at Lucile, follow US 95 north from Riggins 8.5 miles. There's a developed boat ramp just south of Lucile. The put-in is at the boat ramp in Riggins.

For 30 miles below Riggins the Salmon River runs parallel with US 95 through a steep-walled arid canyon. There are a number of developed river access points that make various trip combinations a cinch. The best whitewater is in the first 8.5 miles from Riggins to Lucile, but there's also a big Class IV rapid, Blackhawk, 17.5 miles below Riggins.

From Riggins to Lucile, the rapids are big but straightforward and are predominantly Class III, Class IV at higher water. Timezone is at mile 1.5, Chair Creek at mile 4.2, and Fiddle Creek at mile 5.3.

At high water the Salmon River flows at 80,000 cfs or more in this section, and currents are extremely powerful. Use caution above 25,000 cfs. The run is also very popular for float boaters fishing for salmon and steelhead in the fall, late winter, and spring.

For kayakers there's excellent surfing on this stretch. A great ledge-hole with eddy service forms just below Race Creek on river-left a mile into the trip. It's in between 25,000 and 55,000 cfs. The wave at the top of Chair Creek Rapid is enormous and can be surfed at about 25,000 to 30,000 cfs. The second and third waves at Chair Creek can be surfed a bit lower, at about 15,000 to 20,000 cfs.

97 Lower Salmon, Canyons

Distance: 51.5 miles (plus 19.5 miles on the Snake River)
Difficulty: Class II–III (IV(V) at high water)
Craft: Canoe, kayak, raft, drift boat
Approximate paddling time: 3–7 days
Flows: 4,000–80,000 cfs (**Gauge:** USGS, Salmon River at Whitebird)
Season: Apr–Oct
Put-in: Hammer Creek (45.764957, -116.324561)
Alternative put-in/takeout: Pine Bar
Alternative put-in/takeout: Eagle Creek Road (45.971802, -116.730966)
Takeout: Heller Bar (46.088666, -116.983400)
Shuttle: To get to Heller Bar from Riggins, drive north on US 95 114 miles to Lewiston. Cross the Snake River into Clarkston and go south on ID 129 to Asotin. From Asotin take Snake River Road 22 miles to Heller Bar. This is the most commonly used takeout for the Lower Salmon Canyons.

To get to Eagle Creek Road from Riggins, you'll need a good map. Take US 95 77 miles north to Winchester and turn left on the US 95 business route. Take Olander Road south out of Winchester and use your map to navigate a network of forest roads to Eagle Creek Road, which descends via rough terrain into the canyon. Four-wheel drive is recommended.

To get to Pine Bar from Riggins, take US 95 north 42 miles to Cottonwood. Find Graves Creek Road and take it 15 miles, bearing left at the river, to the developed boat ramp at Pine Bar. Four-wheel drive is recommended.

To reach the put-in at Hammer Creek from Riggins, take US 95 26.8 miles north along the Salmon River. Turn left onto Old Highway 95, following signs for Hammer Creek, and after 0.75 mile turn left again onto Doumecq Road. Cross the bridge over the Salmon River and follow Doumecq Road 1.8 miles downriver to Hammer Creek.

The Lower Salmon Canyons are probably Idaho's most underrated multiple-day river trip. It flows through three arid canyons and has beautiful sand beaches and steep canyon walls. The Class II and III rapids are best in late summer when the state's other runs have withered.

Like other runs on the Salmon, water levels vary from 4,000 to 80,000 cfs or more, and the river's character changes dramatically according to level. It is Class III up to about 10,000 cfs, Class IV between 10,000 and 25,000 cfs, and Class IV(V) above 25,000 cfs.

In the spring when the water's high, a very powerful Class V rapid develops at Slide, an otherwise innocuous Class III located near the confluence of the Salmon and Snake Rivers. This rapid is guaranteed to flip rafts and drift boats above 25,000 cfs. It can be recognized by the huge landslide that creates the rapid, as well as a power line that crosses the river just upstream. It would be a very difficult portage for rafts. At low and medium flows, the toughest rapid is Snow Hole, 30 miles below the put-in.

Although it is remote and road-free for most of its length, there are several put-in and takeout options, including the possibility for a 15-mile day trip on the upper

The Canyons on the Lower Salmon could be the most underrated multiday river trip in Idaho.
Photo by Kevin Lewis

section. They are at Pine Bar via Graves Creek Road 15 miles down, Eagle Creek Road 40 miles down, and, farthest downstream and the most common takeout, Heller Bar on the Snake River.

Clearwater River Basin

The Clearwater River Basin is the north end of the Big Wild, an area stretching more than 200 miles north to south through the pristine heart of wild Idaho. By annual discharge, it's the largest tributary of the Snake River and has correspondingly big whitewater during spring runoff.

The Clearwater and its tributaries drain the western side of the Bitterroot Mountains and the Selway-Bitterroot Wilderness Area. The Middle Fork of the Clearwater and its two main tributaries, the Lochsa and Selway Rivers, are also three of the original eight Wild and Scenic Rivers designated in 1968 with passage of the Wild and Scenic Rivers Act.

The Clearwater basin is brimming with history. It is here that Lewis and Clark met the Nez Perce Indians who nurtured the expedition back to health and escorted it to the Pacific. It is also here, in the town of Pierce, that gold was first struck in Idaho in 1860, triggering a deluge of European settlement throughout the state.

The Clearwater was more than a homeland for the Nez Perce; it was the birthplace of the Nez Perce people. The story goes that a monster was stomping through the land and eating all the animals. Coyote fooled the monster into swallowing him. Using a set of stone knives, Coyote cut apart the monster from the inside to release all the trapped animals. Upon emerging from the monster's remains, Coyote cut the monster into pieces and threw them upon the land. These pieces became people. But the nearby land was still uninhabited. Fox asked Coyote about this. As Coyote washed the blood of the monster off his hands, the drops became the Nez Perce people.

Not far upstream from Kamiah on the river-right side of the Clearwater River, there's a place called Heart of the Monster, the place where the Nez Perce came into existence.

Selway River Basin

The Selway River's headwaters are in the Frank Church–River of No Return Wilderness Area—the same wilderness that cradles the Main and Middle Forks of the Salmon River. In fact, the Selway's headwaters are less than 10 miles, and some 6,000 vertical feet, north of Corn Creek—the launch site for a weeklong wilderness trip on the Main Salmon River.

About 30 to 40 miles north of the Selway's headwaters, at a campground called Paradise, the Selway begins to form into a small river. Another 50 miles downriver during the peak of spring runoff, it becomes a very big river that thunders over Selway Falls at more than 20,000 cfs before working on toward its confluence with

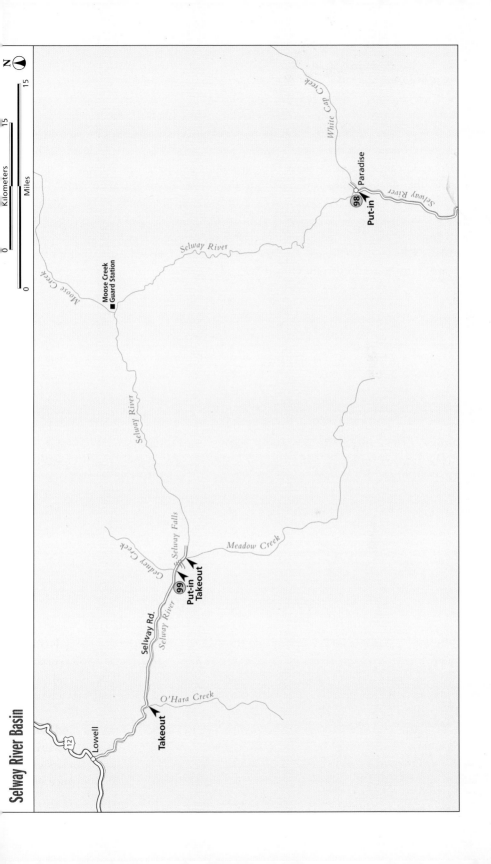

Selway River Basin

the Lochsa River, where the two waterways combine to form the Middle Fork of the Clearwater.

There are only two standard paddling runs in the Selway River basin: the revered wilderness trip from Paradise to Race Creek and the Class II–III day trip downstream of Selway Falls. But the basin has loads of additional opportunities for adventurous paddlers. Portions of the upper Selway above Paradise have been paddled. So have Moose Creek, a major tributary that joins from the north, and Meadow Creek, a creek that drains a huge basin and joins the Selway River just above Selway Falls. These are all major expeditions on rivers that are not frequently paddled. Meadow Creek in particular has long portions of Class V.

Protected as a Wild and Scenic River, and mostly encased in the 1.3-million-acre Selway-Bitterroot Wilderness Area, the Selway is one of the wildest and most remote parts of the lower forty-eight United States.

98 Selway River, The Selway

Distance: 47 miles
Difficulty: Class IV–IV+
Craft: Kayak, raft, canoe
Approximate paddling time: 3–5 days
Flows: 1,600–20,000 cfs (becoming Class IV+ above 20,000 cfs) (**Gauge:** USGS, Selway River at Lowell)
Season: May–July
Put-in: Paradise (45.860605, -114.744095)
Takeout: Above Selway Falls (46.045934, -115.295134)
Shuttle: This is another run for which it makes sense to hire a shuttle driver. Check shuttle quest.com for the latest listings. If you're determined to work it out on your own, prepare for a 250-mile ordeal that may not be passable if the Bitterroots Mountains are still smeared in snow. To get to the takeout, go to Lowell, Idaho, via US 12 and find Selway Road. The put-in is 19 miles upriver. To get to the put-in, return to US 12 and head east toward Missoula. When you arrive in Lolo, Montana, turn south on US 93 and go to Darby; 4.2 miles south of Darby turn right onto MT 473. Go 14.4 miles and turn right on Nez Perce Road. Take Nez Perce Road up and over Nez Perce Pass, traveling a little more than 40 more miles to the put-in.

The Selway is one of Idaho's coveted wilderness river trips, and of them it's the most difficult to get a permit. Only one trip permit is issued per day during the regulated season, May 15 to July 31, and a portion of those are reserved for commercial outfitters. You can float before May 15, but the road to the put-in is usually covered with snow into June. After July 31 the river is usually too rocky to float a raft.

The Selway is a nationally designated Wild and Scenic River that flows through the heart of the Selway-Bitterroot Wilderness Area. From its headwaters on the spine of the Bitterroot Mountains, it quickly grows into a big river during spring runoff and has very big and complex rapids when the water is high.

There are more than a dozen good rapids, but most of the challenging drops are in the 5 miles below Moose Creek confluence, which nearly doubles the river's flow. Double Drop, Ladle, and Little Niagara are the standouts, and Ladle in particular warrants a scout. Rapids are fairly continuous following Ladle, so it's a nasty spot to flip a raft or go for a swim.

The Selway has a relatively short window. In late May and early June, the water is often high, and canceled trips are common. By late July, you'll be hard pressed to float a raft through the maze of boulders. Late June is a fairly dependable window.

Boaters tend to refer to Selway flows by referencing the stick gauge near the put-in at Paradise. At 1 to 3 feet (850–1,500 cfs at Paradise and 1,500–8,000 cfs at the USGS gauge), it's Class III and IV. At 3 to 6 feet (1,500–4,500 cfs at Paradise and 8,000–20,000 cfs at the USGS gauge), it's solid Class IV. Above 6 feet (4,500 at Paradise and 20,000 cfs on the USGS gauge), it starts to take on Class V characteristics. Call (406) 821-3269 for the latest readings from Paradise.

The Selway is one of America's most revered wilderness rivers. Only one permit is issued per day during peak season. PHOTO BY KEVIN LEWIS

Wetter than Idaho's other permitted wilderness rivers, the Selway basin has western red cedar, hemlock, grand fir, and Douglas fir trees and is considered by many to be one of the premier wilderness river trips in the country.

99 Selway River, Lower

Distance: 10.7 miles
Difficulty: Class II–III
Craft: Canoe, kayak, raft
Approximate paddling time: 3–5 hours
Flows: 1,000–20,000 cfs (**Gauge:** USGS, Selway at Lowell)
Season: Apr–Oct
Put-in: Gedney Creek (46.056956, -115.314424)

Takeout: O'Hara Creek (46.086621, -115.517537)
Shuttle: From US 12 at the confluence of the Lochsa and Selway Rivers, go 6.8 miles upriver on Selway Road to O'Hara Creek, where there's a bridge across the Selway and good camping at O'Hara Creek Campground. This is the take-out. The put-in at Gedney Creek, below Selway Falls, is another 10.7 miles upriver.

Below Selway Falls, the Selway River relaxes and whisks swiftly toward its confluence with the Lochsa River. It's an excellent intermediate kayak or raft run when the water's high, but it's even better as a relaxing and beautiful late-season canoe trip on gin-clear water.

Roadside its entire length, the lower Selway can easily be scouted while setting up shuttle. To add 7 miles, take out at Lowell at the Lochsa-Selway confluence.

Lochsa River Basin

The Lochsa River is probably the Clearwater basin's best-known paddling destination. It parallels a heavily traveled highway—the only east-west thoroughfare across Idaho for hundreds of miles. This is a conduit that provides paddlers access to the Lochsa's legendary big water, but also to several outstanding steep creeks in the basin's headwaters.

True to its name, *Lochsa* is a Nez Perce word meaning "rough water," and the river has more than sixty rapids between Powell and Lowell, a distance of 70 miles. Powell and Lowell are also the only places along the Lochsa with any services, and only Lowell sells gas.

The Lochsa's pre-European history is one of abundant salmon and salmon fishing by Native American anglers. This is also one of the first places Lewis and Clark arrived in what is now Idaho. Their journals describe the confluence of the Crooked Fork and White Sand Creek (also known as Colt Killed Creek) as a place where they killed a horse to stave off starvation.

Today the Lochsa and its surrounding canyon is an accessible place that, if not wild, is relatively pristine and boasts some of the best big-water kayaking and rafting in Idaho.

The Lochsa River is a premier destination for big-water paddlers, who travel from around the globe every spring to test its surging currents.

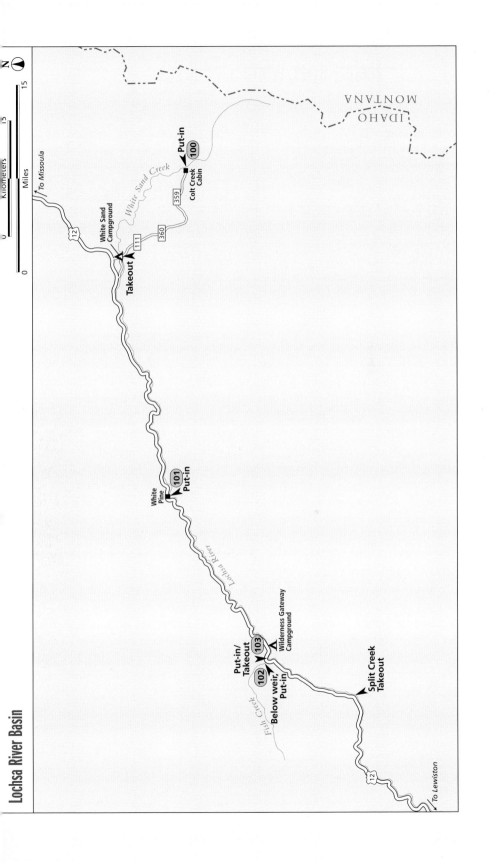

100 Lochsa River, White Sand Creek

Distance: 12.7 miles
Difficulty: Class III–IV
Craft: Kayak, decked canoe, small raft
Approximate paddling time: 4–6 hours
Flows: 500–2,000 cfs (**Gauge:** None)
Season: June
Put-in: Colt Creek Cabin (46.433518, -114.540594)
Takeout: White Sand Campground (46.507431, -114.687270)
Shuttle: To find the takeout, turn off US 12 at mile 163.5. Take FR 111 1.2 miles to the bridges that cross Crooked Fork and White Sand Creek, which join and form the Lochsa just downstream. You can take out at the bridge or at the campground just downstream on river-right. To get to the put-in, head toward Elk Summit on FR 111. Turn right onto FR 360 4.1 miles from the takeout bridge. Go 5.5 miles, up and over Savage Pass, and turn left onto FR 359. The put-in is 5.5 miles of switchbacks into the canyon away.

This lower section of White Sand Creek, not to be confused with the Class V+ run that can be accessed by hiking 4 miles upstream, flows through a beautiful, remote canyon and primarily features continuous technical Class III and IV whitewater. It's generally good to go when the Lochsa is flowing at medium flows of about 6,000 to 12,000 cfs. At high water, when White Sand has about 1,500 cfs or more, things get a lot more difficult, and the run ranks a solid Class IV+. Because of the remote setting, cold water, and possibility for river-wide trees and sweepers, it should only be attempted by advanced and expert boaters.

At medium flows most of the Class IV is concentrated in the first 3 to 4 miles where the run is tighter and more technical. After passing Storm Creek on river-right it's still very continuous, but things start to open up a bit. The river backs off to Class II for its last several miles before joining with the Crooked Fork to become the Lochsa River. Either take out at the FR 360 bridge or at White Sand Campground on river-right downstream.

There are two additional experts-only runs for which Colt Creek Cabin is the takeout. Both require hiking, and both are arduous all-day expeditions. Upper White Sand Creek can be accessed by crossing the pack bridge at Colt Creek Cabin and hiking upstream 4 miles. To paddle Big Sand Creek, leave a car at the Colt Creek Pack Bridge and return to FR 360. Go 4 miles south, to Swamp Creek, and hike downhill for 3 miles to the creek. Both of these are expert steep creeks with committing, hazardous rapids and multiple portages.

101 Lochsa River, Upper

Distance: 19.5 miles
Difficulty: Class IV
Craft: Canoe, kayak, raft
Approximate paddling time: 4–6 hours
Flows: 1,000–20,000 cfs
Season: Apr–July
Put-in: White Pine (46.452520, -115.079113)

Takeout: Fish Creek (46.334516, -115.344820)
Shuttle: The takeout at Fish Creek is near mile marker 120 on US 12. To get to the put-in at White Pine, go 19.3 miles east on US 12. The turnoff is at mile 138.5 and can be a little tricky to spot.

Of the two primary whitewater sections on the Lochsa River, the upper is considered more difficult. It definitely has different character than the Goat Range downstream. The whitewater is swift and more technical, and moves are required to avoid falling into some big holes. As the water rises, the rapids blend into one another with little room for recovery if you flip a raft or swim.

Lost Creek, Lone Pine, Castle Creek, and Ten Pin are among the run's numerous rapids. Boaters should watch for Onno's Hole about 4 miles into the run (between mile markers 131 and 132). The center tongue feeds into a large hole. Castle Creek about 4.5 miles below the put-in is probably the run's most difficult. It's long and contains numerous large holes.

The upper Lochsa is also a much longer trip than the Goat Range, but at high flows paddlers can easily do both with a lunch stop. Wilderness Gateway Campground has excellent camping and is a popular place for boaters to gather in the spring. There's also good camping up Fish Creek.

In addition to this run and the Goat Range just downstream, there are less frequently paddled Class III options upstream of White Pine and downstream of Split Creek. It's all roadside and easy to set up put-ins and takeouts.

102 Fish Creek

Distance: 0.75 mile
Difficulty: Class IV
Craft: Kayak
Approximate paddling time: 15 minutes
Flows: 400–2,000 cfs (**Gauge:** None)
Season: Apr–June
Put-in: Below weir (46.339359, -115.353792)
Takeout: Lochsa confluence (46.333367, -115.346243)

Shuttle: The takeout is where Fish Creek meets the Lochsa River near mile marker 120 on US 12. To reach the put-in, drive upstream along Fish Creek for 0.75 mile. There's a meadow on the left and a primitive trail that accesses the fish weir. Put in below the weir. If you arrive at the Fish Creek trailhead, backtrack a few hundred yards until you find the weir.

At 0.75 mile long, Fish Creek isn't much of a run by itself, but it's a popular start to the lower Lochsa for kayakers. There's a fish weir near the end of the road, and you'll need to put in below it.

Fish Creek is very continuous Class IV creeking and culminates with a pair of ledges at the pack bridge near the Lochsa confluence. This run is essentially one very long Class III–IV rapid.

103 Lochsa River, Goat Range

Distance: 8.9 miles
Difficulty: Class IV
Craft: Canoe, kayak, raft
Approximate paddling time: 3–5 hours
Flows: 1,000–20,000 cfs
Season: Apr–July
Put-in: Fish Creek (46.334516, -115.344820)
Takeout: Split Creek (46.230395, -115.416888)

Shuttle: The entire Lochsa is roadside along US 12, which connects Lewiston, Idaho, to Lolo, Montana. The takeout at Split Creek is at mile 112. To get to the put-in, return to the highway and head upriver to mile marker 120, where there's a large paved staging area and restrooms.

While the upper whitewater run on the Lochsa is considered more difficult, the lower, which boaters call the Goat Range, is probably more fun—and popular. The riverbed is constricted, and the rapids rear back with enormous waves and holes—but

Pipeline near mile marker 114 is well named. It's an incredible surf wave at certain water levels.

Lochsa Falls can be a formidable test for paddlers during high water. PHOTO BY KEVIN LEWIS

they're fairly straightforward. Rapids like Killer Fang Falls, House Wave, Grim Reaper, Lochsa Falls, and Split Creek will keep paddlers on their toes.

The Goat Range also has one of the best surf waves in Idaho. Pipeline, near mile marker 114, is just upstream of Old Man Creek and at medium and high flows is a huge glassy wave. Eddy service is lousy, but at certain levels the surfing is incredible. It's best between 4,000 cfs and 7,000 cfs but can be surfed at a variety of flows. At 8,000 cfs and above it's a fast wave well suited to longer boats, and as the water drops it becomes an increasingly sticky hole.

Roadside its entire length, the Goat Range stands out as one of Idaho's most fantastic and accessible whitewater day trips.

In addition to this run and the Upper Lochsa, there are less frequently paddled Class III paddling options upstream of White Pine and downstream of Split Creek. It's all roadside and easy to set up put-ins and takeouts.

Main Stem Clearwater

The Lochsa and Selway Rivers converge in Lowell to form the Middle Fork of the Clearwater, which continues downstream to Kooskia, where it picks up the South Fork and becomes, simply, the Clearwater River. It flows nearly 100 miles on its course to meet the Snake River in Lewiston, Idaho, and picks up a number of tributaries, including Lolo Creek and the Potlatch River, both popular whitewater kayaking runs.

The Clearwater River is also popular among salmon and steelhead anglers, who are commonly seen along much of the river's length in drift and jet boats. There are abundant boat ramps and public access points to accommodate the consistent and diverse use.

The Clearwater River affords numerous paddling opportunities over its entire 100 miles.

104 Middle Fork of the Clearwater

Distance: 23 miles
Difficulty: Class I–II
Craft: Canoe, kayak, raft
Approximate paddling time: 3–7 hours
Flows: 2,000–20,000 cfs (**Gauge:** Add Lochsa and Selway USGS gauges.)
Season: May–Oct
Put-in: Lowell (46.139278, -115.601953)
Put-in/takeout: Highway pullout 13.5 miles from put-in (46.148975, -115.833750)

Takeout: Kooskia (46.146924, -115.980352)
Shuttle: The takeout is at the junction of ID 12 and US 12 in Kooskia. There's a boat ramp on river-right just downstream of the bridge. To get to the put-in, drive 23 miles upstream to Lowell. There's a highway pullout just downstream of the confluence of the Selway and Lochsa Rivers.

This is a 23-mile section and can be broken into several smaller paddles. In general, the upper half has more tree cover and feels more remote and wild. The canyon surrounding the lower half is more open, and the valley more pastoral.

The Middle Fork is one of four Idaho Rivers designated Wild and Scenic with passage of the Wild and Scenic Rivers Act in 1968. It is big, broad, beautiful, and fairly well cared for. It also has a lot of calm water interspersed with Class II rapids. At high water this section can be very pushy. By mid- to late June, it's a delightful open canoe run or mellow raft or kayak float through a beautiful valley. Although fairly straightforward, it should only be attempted by accomplished boaters in the spring, when it flows at 60,000 cfs or more. There is no gauge relating directly to this run. For the most accurate reading, look at the Lochsa and Selway gauges and practice some basic math skills.

The Middle Fork of the Clearwater is one of America's original Wild and Scenic Rivers.

Middle Fork Clearwater River

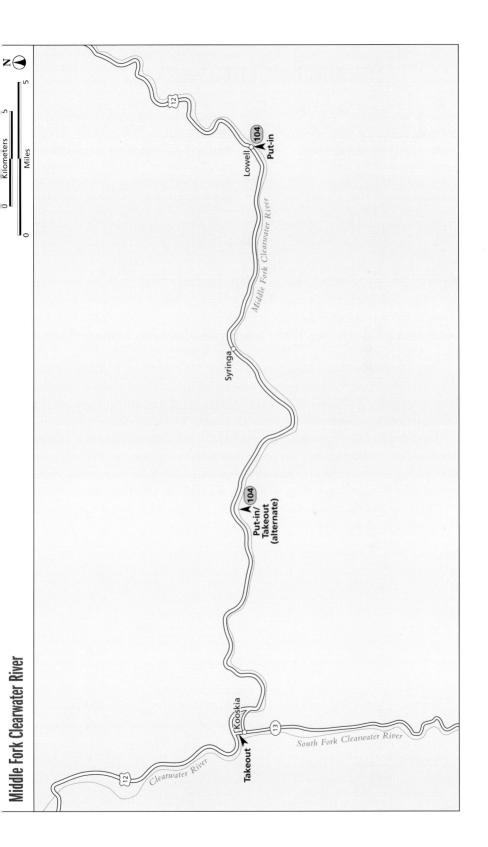

105 Clearwater River, Canoe Stretch

Distance: 6.5 miles
Difficulty: Class II
Craft: Canoe, kayak, raft, drift boat
Approximate paddling time: 2–4 hours
Flows: 5,000–15,000 cfs
Season: July–Oct
Put-in: Long Camp Boat Launch (46.276056, -116.097564)

Takeout: Five Mile Boat Launch (46.354757, -116.163332)
Shuttle: The takeout at Five Mile is 10.5 miles west of Orofino on US 12, 11.9 miles downstream from Kamiah. The put-in at Long Camp is 5.4 miles downstream from Kamiah and 17.3 miles upstream from Orofino.

From Kamiah to Lewiston, a distance of 60 miles, the Clearwater River flows along US 12 and is accessible from more than a dozen boat ramps. The lower Clearwater is a very big river in spring and carries between 50,000 and 100,000 cfs. While its rapids top out at Class II, this river is best for open canoes and other recreational craft July through October, when it generally runs about 5,000 to 15,000 cfs.

The Clearwater passes through the heart of the Nez Perce Indian Reservation and has beautiful sand beaches in a canyon that's equal parts stunning and understated. There are vertical cliff walls in places, but for the most part it's got rolling grassy ridges and ravines full of pine trees.

Most of the run's whitewater is concentrated in the 30 miles between Kamiah and Orofino. Below Orofino the valley broadens and the river relaxes a bit. The suggested float goes through one of the more constricted sections of the canyon and contains several Class II rapids. It can be scouted from the highway. (**Note:** Significant portions of the Clearwater River Valley burned in 2015 wildfires. This should not impact the safety of paddling, but may affect the scenery.)

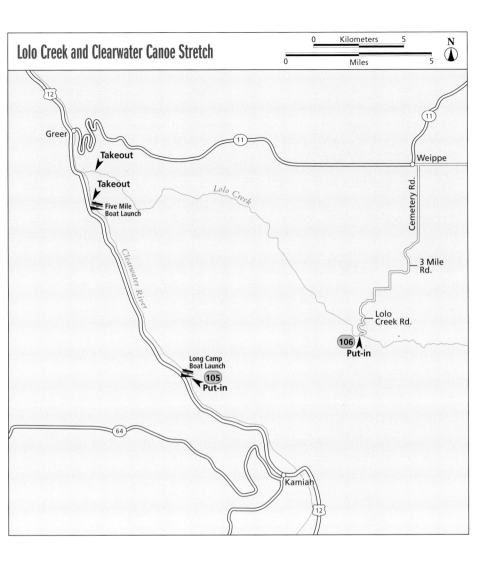

Lolo Creek and Clearwater Canoe Stretch

Greer

Takeout

Takeout

Five Mile
Boat Launch

Lolo Creek

Clearwater River

Long Camp
Boat Launch

105
Put-in

64

Kamiah

12

Weippe

Cemetery Rd.

3 Mile
Rd.

Lolo
Creek Rd.

106
Put-in

11

12

N

Kilometers

Miles

106 Lolo Creek

Distance: 13 miles
Difficulty: Class IV+
Craft: Kayak
Approximate paddling time: 6–8 hours
Flows: 300–1,000 cfs (**Gauge:** USGS, Lolo Creek near Greer)
Season: Apr–June
Put-in: Lolo Creek Road (46.293999, -115.974866)
Takeout: Lower Lolo Creek Road (46.372375, -116.167868)
Shuttle: From Orofino take US 12 east 7.6 miles and turn north across the bridge to Greer. From Greer take ID 11 (Greer Grade Road) 0.75 mile east and, before the first big switchback, turn right onto Lower Lolo Creek Road, a gravel road. Follow the road a little less than a mile to a bridge that crosses Lolo Creek. This is the takeout. Check the stick gauge while you're there. To get to the put-in, return to ID 11 and climb the grade via a number of switchbacks to the Weippe Prairie. Go a total of 14 miles and turn right (south) on 3 Mile Road. (The turn is 2.8 miles west of Weippe.) Take 3 Mile Road 5.4 miles and turn right on Lolo Creek Road, which is signed but easy to miss. Take Lolo Creek Road 3.9 miles into the canyon, where you'll arrive at a bridge, the put-in.

For 13 miles above its confluence with the Clearwater River, Lolo Creek flows through a remote, steep-walled, mossy canyon. There are no roads or trails, so it's a committing run with continuous Class III and IV whitewater. As the water rises, it gets very pushy and becomes Class V. There are also abundant downed trees that shift from year to year. You're almost guaranteed to have to portage some of them.

Rapids start early and remain continuous almost the entire length of the creek. Rapids also get progressively harder for the first half of the trip. If you find yourself in trouble early, it may be best to hike back up along the creek to your car. Hiking up the canyon walls to get out would be an epic misadventure.

The named action starts a couple miles into the run with YMCA, where there's a slot river-left at the bottom. The current wants to push boaters through the slot, which isn't problematic unless there's wood in it, and there frequently is. Make sure to scout the bottom of this drop.

After another mile you'll arrive at Zig Zag, easily identifiable by huge logs protruding from the river-left bank. Lame Duck isn't much farther downstream. Six miles into the canyon, you'll arrive at Little Schmidt and Big Schmidt, where there are almost always river-wide logs. The Schmidts make for a long, tough rapid. They can be portaged, but the portage is an ordeal.

After the Schmidts, it's a few miles of continuous Class III to a rapid created by a 1997 landslide. The resulting drop, 11 miles into the trip, is very steep and not very clean, though it's been run plenty. The portage is easy. From there to the takeout, Lolo Creek is swift but the difficulty backs off.

There's a new USGS gauge on Lolo Creek. According to research by North Idaho kayaker Todd Hoffman, watch for minimum runnable flows of about 200 cfs. Lolo

Lolo Creek's rapids get increasingly tough during the first half of the trip. This is what the creek looks like at 750 cfs.

Creek has Class IV characteristics up to about 1,000 cfs. It's Class V from about 1,200 to 1,600 cfs, and isn't recommended above that.

Paddlers need to be clear about Lolo Creek's hazards and the level of commitment needed, but it is a fantastic and beautiful run that stands out as one of Idaho's best. (**Note:** Significant portions of Lolo Creek canyon burned during wildfires in August 2015 and likely will cause additional wood hazards as well as the possibility of landslides that could create new rapids.)

107 Potlatch River

Distance: 16 miles
Difficulty: Class IV-V
Craft: Kayak
Approximate paddling time: All day
Flows: 1,000-3,000 cfs (**Gauge:** USGS, Potlatch River near Spalding)
Season: Feb-May
Put-in: Little Boulder Campground (46.772643, -116.457383)
Takeout: Cedar Creek (46.650054, -116.549021)
Shuttle: To get to the lower takeout at Cedar Creek, head northeast from the town of Kendrick on ID 3 to its junction with Cedar Ridge Road (also designated CR P1 and Southwick Road). Cedar Ridge Road follows the river. Go 6.6 miles to the mouth of Cedar Creek, where there's limited parking near the bridge spanning Cedar Creek. The put-in at Little Boulder Campground is 4 miles east of Deary, which is located at the junction of ID 3 and ID 8. Continue on ID 3, which turns right (east) at the junction. At Helmer, turn south onto Park Road (FR 1963). Continue 2.3 miles to the river. There is parking on the left just before the bridge.

This is the backyard proving ground for Moscow, Idaho, kayakers and is a great expert-level whitewater run through a secluded canyon. The Potlatch has an extremely early season that usually starts in February and runs through late April.

There's a large rapid in the upper section known as Coleman Falls. It's the second big drop below the put-in and is marked by a large tributary on river-right. In 2013 the traditional "easy" line through the bottom was blocked by a log, and this increases the difficulty considerably. Portaging involves running the first part of the rapid and catching a small eddy on the left, then portaging around a large boulder.

Below Coleman Falls there are several more Class IV rapids before an old bridge, one of a couple midway access points to the run. The second is about 3 miles farther downstream. (Don't attempt to drive into the lower midway access point if the road is muddy.)

Below the lower access there are three Class III rapids, the third being the most difficult.

The Potlatch is an early-season run that cranks up in late February or early March and usually finishes by the end of April. Spikes are possible outside the normal season with heavy rains.

From the stick gauge at the put-in, the minimum level is about 3 feet. At flows below 4 feet the bottom 10 miles becomes scrappy and cumbersome, so much so that many boaters prefer the difficult hike out of the canyon at one of the midway points. At flows above 4.5 feet the upper part of the run increases in difficulty to Class IV+ or V.

The USGS gauge near Spalding is more than 30 miles downstream and does not correlate well with the stick gauge at the put-in. As a rough estimate, look for about 1,000 cfs on the Spalding gauge as a minimum.

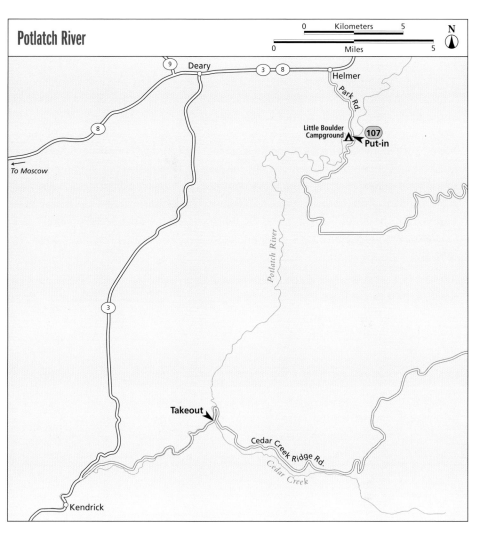

Boaters looking for mellower paddling on the Potlatch can try the lower canyon between Cedar Creek and Kendrick High School. The water is mostly Class II, and the banks are mostly private land. Please be respectful.

—Todd Hoffman

South Fork of the Clearwater Basin

The South Fork of the Clearwater River is primarily an experts-only whitewater run. Strong open canoeists may be able to do trips in the lower basin near Kooskia, but the South Fork is really the domain of kayaks, rafts, and whitewater canoes.

The South Fork begins near the town of Elk City, one of Idaho's most off-the-beaten-path municipalities, and flows for 62 miles to the Middle Fork of the Clearwater at Kooskia. The South Fork historically was one of Idaho's most prolific producers of chinook salmon, but an early 1900s dam near the town of Harpster, combined with sediments from historic mines and logging activity in the upper basin, severely impacted the health of the river—and the fishery. Its whitewater is outstanding.

Almost the entire South Fork is roadside, and all of its major rapids can be scouted from the highway.

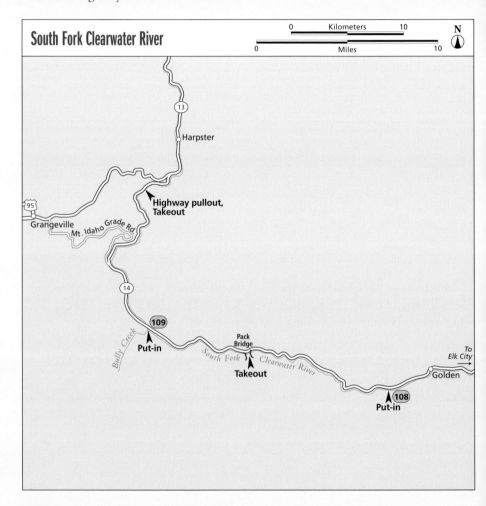

South Fork Clearwater River

108 South Fork of the Clearwater, Golden Canyon

Distance: 9.7 miles
Difficulty: Class V
Craft: Kayak
Approximate paddling time: 3–5 hours
Flows: 500–2,000 cfs (**Gauge:** South Fork Clearwater at Stites)
Season: Apr–July
Put-in: Below Coyote Falls (45.798209, -115.716866)
Takeout: Pack Bridge near Mile Marker 19 (45.825341, -115.885403)

Shuttle: The takeout is 34.5 miles south of Kooskia via ID 13 and ID 14. Stay left at the Y 15.3 miles south of Kooskia to turn onto ID 14 and stay along the river. From Grangeville the takeout is 21 miles east/southeast via Mt. Idaho Grade Road, which turns onto ID 14 at the bottom of the canyon. From the ID 14 bridge the put-in is 9.7 miles upriver on ID 14. Watch for the rock hanging over the highway and Coyote Falls just upstream.

At medium flows Golden Canyon is a challenging Class V day trip, and it gets much more challenging at high water of about 1,500 cfs or more. It takes on Class IV characteristics at low water, but paddlers still need to be on the lookout for several Class V rapids. Roadside, it can and should be scouted top to bottom before putting on. The run is steep, boulder-choked, and hazardous.

Most boaters choose to portage the first big rapid, Coyote Falls, which is just upstream of the large rock hanging over ID 14 and marks the beginning of the run. You can and probably should put in below this nasty rapid.

About midway through is the second significant rapid, Chuck Rollins. The final Class V, Fish Jump, is near the end and includes a near river-wide hole at the bottom. Don't let the three named rapids lull you into complacency. This run is chock-full of long, continuous, and powerful rapids and can run at 5,000 cfs or more, well above recommended flows.

109 South Fork of the Clearwater, Mickey Mouse

Distance: 10.7 miles
Difficulty: Class IV–IV+
Craft: Canoe, kayak, raft
Approximate paddling time: 3–5 hours
Flows: 500–3,000 cfs (**Gauge:** South Fork Clearwater at Stites)
Season: Apr–July
Put-in: Highway pullout near Bully Creek (45.840153, -115.996064)

Takeout: Highway pullout 6.2 miles below bridge (45.948497, -115.999618)
Shuttle: The run is about 15 miles south of Kooskia on ID 13 and 11 miles east of Grangeville on ID 13. The takeout is just upstream from the intersection of ID 13 and ID 14. To get to the put-in, take ID 14 south along the South Fork for 13 miles.

Though easier than Golden Canyon upstream, this lower whitewater run on the South Fork of the Clearwater has several big rapids that can pack some wallop.

The rapids above the ID 14 bridge are fairly short but intricate. Blackerby Rapid, just below the bridge 4.3 miles into the run, is a long and tough drop at any level, but

The South Fork of the Clearwater flows through a beautiful and deep timber-enshrouded canyon.

at high water is probably Class V. The river makes a soft left bend at the top, and the current feeds into a stout hole on the outside of the bend. That's the toughest part of the rapid, but the whitewater continues for the better part of a mile. This would be a dangerous place to swim. Another good series starts 9.8 miles below the put-in.

Because it is roadside, put-ins and takeouts are arbitrary, but rafters should run most of the way to ID 13, where there's easier takeout access. The takeout referenced below is about 2 miles upstream of the highway junction.

The Class IV Mickey Mouse section of the South Fork Clearwater, though nowhere near as difficult as its upstream counterpart, is still plenty challenging for most paddlers. PHOTO BY WENDY JONES

North Fork of the Clearwater Basin

The North Fork of the Clearwater is a hidden gem that not many paddlers know about. For whitewater boaters it's got an array of paddling opportunities ranging from big-water Class III and IV to Class IV and V creeking, as well as opportunities for a couple of wild and remote expeditions that few paddlers will ever undertake. It also has some extremely good surfing at certain water levels.

For all its incredible paddling, the North Fork doesn't get as much use as other Idaho areas because it's so far from the beaten path. Paddlers heading into the basin must top off their fuel tanks and stock up on provisions before they go.

For boaters heading to the North Fork from southern Idaho, access is via ID 11 through Weippe, Pierce, and Headquarters into the lower basin. For north Idaho and northwest Montana boaters, it makes sense to wait until Hoodoo Pass opens (often not until early July) and enter the top of the basin by crossing the Bitterroot Range from I-90 in Montana. This latter option will almost certainly ensure missing peak runoff, but the North Fork's creeks are usually runnable through mid-July, and the North Fork itself can be paddled much longer into the summer.

The North Fork drainage is dominated by hemlock, grand fir, and western red cedar forests, and the upper basin tributaries contain some of the largest stands of old growth left in the entire Clearwater River basin. Once the most productive steelhead fishery in Idaho, the North Fork's anadromous fish were cut off from the main stem of the Clearwater in 1973 with construction of Dworshak Dam, the third tallest dam in the United States, located near Orofino.

In addition to paddling, the North Fork has abundant opportunities for hiking, backpacking and camping, horseback riding, and world-class fly fishing on highly revered blue-ribbon trout streams.

The North Fork of the Clearwater is a beautiful off-the-beaten-path river.

110 North Fork of the Clearwater, Black Canyon

Distance: 11 miles
Difficulty: Class IV
Craft: Canoe, kayak
Approximate paddling time: 3–5 hours
Flows: 1,000–3,000 cfs (**Gauge:** None)
Season: May–early July
Put-in: Hidden Creek Campground
(46.831843, -115.178886)
Alternative put-in: Elizabeth Creek
(46.790336, -115.220349)

Takeout: FR 255 bridge (46.717635, -115.256815)
Shuttle: The takeout is near Kelly Forks Guard Station at the confluence of the North Fork and Kelly Creek. To reach the put-in, take Black Canyon Road upstream for 6.6 miles to Elizabeth Creek or 10.7 miles to Hidden Creek Campground. Kelly Forks is 86 miles via the North Fork Clearwater from Pierce. It is 51 miles via Hoodoo Pass from I-90 in Montana.

The North Fork through Black Canyon is clear, cold, and jaw-droppingly beautiful. It's also chock-full of wood. Scout carefully while setting up shuttle.

The entire run is roadside, so put-ins and takeouts are arbitrary, but the best whitewater is below Elizabeth Creek and remains fairly continuous for 6.5 miles to

From Elizabeth Creek down to Kelly Forks, the North Fork of the Clearwater is a tight, exciting whitewater trip.

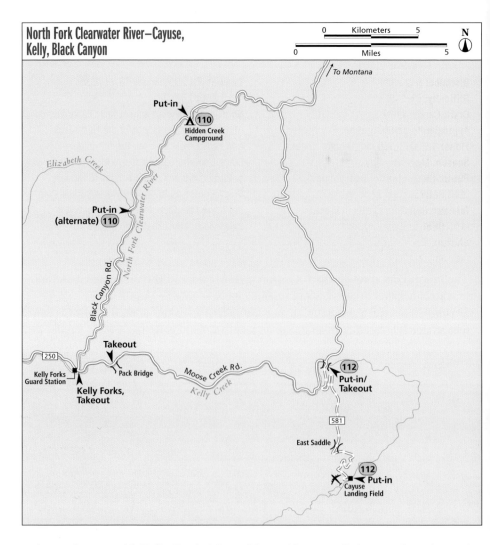

the confluence with Kelly Creek. Most of the rapids can easily be seen from the road except for two of the biggest, both of which are near the end of the run. One has a nasty hole toward the end of the drop.

Black Canyon starts in a broad and beautiful valley that gradually descends into a deep canyon where avalanche paths dump numerous logs into the river each year. They pile up in tight channels and outside corners, and while most of the river generally has navigable lines, because of the wood this is not a place where swimming is even remotely okay.

There is no gauge for Black Canyon, but watch for flows of about 4,000 cfs and above at the Canyon Ranger Station gauge on the North Fork of the Clearwater.

111 Cayuse Creek

Distance: 8.3 miles
Difficulty: Class III+
Craft: Canoe, kayak
Approximate paddling time: 3-6 hours
Flows: 400-1,500 cfs (**Gauge:** None)
Season: May-July
Put-in: Cayuse Landing Field (46.667757, -115.068020)
Takeout: FR 581 bridge (46.719939, -115.085615)
Shuttle: From Kelly Forks Ranger Station at the confluence of the North Fork Clearwater

and Kelly Creek, take Moose Creek Road (FR 255) 11 miles upstream along Kelly Creek. Moose Creek Road turns left, but stay on the main road, which becomes FR 581, and you'll arrive at a bridge spanning Kelly Creek. This is the takeout. To get to the put-in, continue on FR 581 for 7.8 miles, over East Saddle, to the Cayuse Landing Field where a bridge crosses Cayuse Creek. This road can often be closed well into June, or even early July, due to snow.

Cayuse Creek is a beautiful Class III paddle through a roadless gorge, but despite its relatively straightforward rapids it is not suitable for beginners or wobbly intermediates because of the remote setting, cold water, shallow rapids, and potential for logs and sweepers.

Shortly after leaving the Cayuse Landing Field, Cayuse Creek drops into a tight granite gorge containing several Class III rapids. The first is about 1.8 miles into the run, and the creek's rapids are continuous for the ensuing 2 to 3 miles. Things open up again about a mile before the Kelly Creek confluence at mile 4.5, and from there it's 4 miles of easy and splashy Class II to the takeout below the FR 581 bridge at Moose Creek confluence.

As with all small mountain streams, be wary of the potential for logs and sweepers, which shift from year to year. There is no gauge, but watch for flows of about 4,000 cfs or more at Canyon Ranger Station on the North Fork of the Clearwater.

Revered for its trout fishing, Cayuse Creek also has excellent Class III paddling in a tight granite gorge. Photo by Wendy Jones

The shuttle via FR 581 is steep and narrow and climbs more than 1,300 feet to a pass at East Saddle. It is often smothered in snow well into June, or even early July. A good trail parallels the river-left side of Cayuse Creek and another parallels the river-right side of Kelly Creek.

112 Kelly Creek

Distance: 8.9 miles
Difficulty: Class IV
Craft: Canoe, kayak
Approximate paddling time: 3–5 hours
Flows: 500–2,000 cfs (**Gauge:** None)
Season: May–July
Put-in: Above Clayton Creek on FR 255
(46.713004, -115.089579)

Takeout: Pack bridge above Kelly Forks Ranger Station (46.719498, -115.232883)
Shuttle: The takeout is upstream of Kelly Forks Ranger Station, which is located at the confluence of the North Fork and Kelly Creek. There's a pack bridge on Moose Creek Road (FR 255) 1.3 miles from the ranger station. To get to the put-in, continue upstream 8.8 miles to a dirt pullout above Clayton Creek Rapid.

This is a swift creek that starts with a bang. The toughest rapid, Clayton Creek, is right at the start and is a fairly pushy Class IV rapid. At high water the top of the drop becomes a river-wide hole. Several series of continuous Class III and IV rapids follow for the first half of the trip, and then the river relaxes for the duration of the run.

Kelly Creek's continuous Class III and IV rapids provide miles of entertainment.
Photo by Wendy Jones

Kelly Creek flows through a beautiful, tight canyon with dense conifers on one side and hillsides burned in the 1910 fire on the other. It is also one of the most revered fly-fishing streams in Idaho.

Moose Creek Road (FR 255) parallels Kelly Creek the entire length and makes scouting or portaging a cinch. There is no gauge on Kelly Creek, but watch for flows on the North Fork of the Clearwater at Canyon Ranger Station of about 4,000 cfs or more.

The whitewater paddle on Kelly Creek begins in a picturesque meadow and drops into a stunning valley, where evidence of the 1910 fire is still visible.
Photo by Wendy Jones

113 North Fork of the Clearwater, Tumbledown

Distance: 16.4 miles
Difficulty: Class III (V)
Craft: Canoe, kayak, raft
Approximate paddling time: 5–7 hours
Flows: 1,000–15,000 cfs (**Gauge:** North Fork Clearwater at Canyon Ranger Station)
Season: Apr–Aug
Put-in: Weitas Creek Pack Bridge (46.637294, -115.434859)
Takeout: Ermine Creek (46.759964, -115.505696)
Shuttle: There's good river access all along the North Fork of the Clearwater. There's a rough dirt road that leads to a riverside meadow and good raft access at Ermine Creek, which is 13.7 miles upstream from Aquarius Campground and 12.3 miles downstream from FR 250 and Oregrande Creek. This is the suggested takeout. To get to the suggested put-in, go 16.5 miles upstream to Weitas Creek. Additional access points can be found at Oregrande Creek and Washington Creek Campground. Note that Washington Creek is only 3.3 miles above Irish Railroad and a good access point if you want to run it.

This whitewater run on the North Fork of the Clearwater has classic Idaho big water and several outstanding surf waves. It also has a Class IV–V rapid, Irish Railroad, that should be scouted carefully.

The first series starts 3.5 miles below Weitas Creek and is 0.5 mile long, ending near the confluence with Oregrande Creek. Spray Creek comes at mile 9.3. After passing beneath the Washington Creek Campground bridge at mile 10.4, watch for Washington Creek Hole on river-left if the water's between 8,000 and 11,000 cfs. It's a great play spot with decent eddy access. Irish Railroad is near the end of the run at mile 14.1.

Note that because it is roadside, put-ins and takeouts are arbitrary, particularly for kayakers. Segments suggested here are designed to accommodate put-ins and takeouts for rafts. To avoid Irish Railroad, simply put in below it and continue down the Aquarius section (see description on page 222).

North Fork Clearwater River and Skull Creek

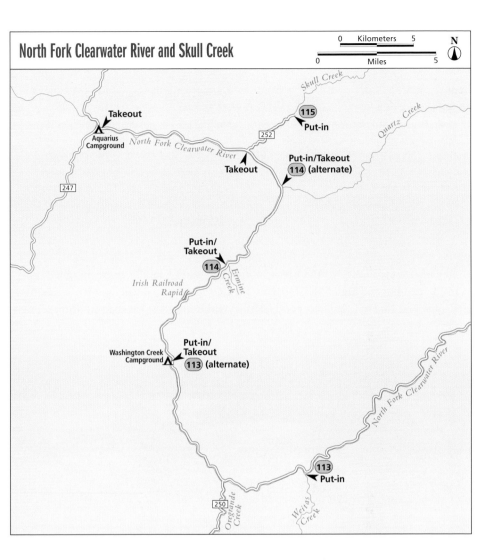

114 North Fork of the Clearwater, Aquarius

Distance: 13.6 miles
Difficulty: Class III
Craft: Canoe, kayak, raft
Approximate paddling time: 4–6 hours
Flows: 1,000–15,000 cfs (**Gauge:** North Fork Clearwater at Canyon Ranger Station)
Season: Apr–Aug
Put-in: Ermine Creek (46.759964, -115.505696)

Takeout: Aquarius Campground (46.840818, -115.618813)
Shuttle: The takeout at Aquarius Campground is just upstream from the bridge spanning the North Fork on FR 247. It is 25 miles downstream from Oregrande Creek. The suggested put-in at Ermine Creek is 13 miles upstream. Quartz Creek, another potential put-in, is 8.4 miles upstream.

The lower run on the North Fork is another big-water Class III gem with great surfing at medium and high flows. Quartz Creek, an alternative put-in, is 4.6 miles below Ermine Creek. There are four good Class III rapids spread across the run (three if you start at Quartz Creek). There's a long series just below the suggested put-in, and then

The North Fork has great surfing at certain levels, including here at Aquarius Campground.

Standard Class III whitewater froths on the North Fork Clearwater. PHOTO BY WENDY JONES

the river relaxes until you pass Skull Creek. You'll hit Lost Pete, Cougar, and Aquarius rapids in the final 5 miles.

This run is Class III at all but the highest water levels. The river's boulder garden rapids are defined at low and medium flows and become huge wave trains above 10,000 cfs. At high flows, the rapids are straightforward, but the river is very fast and powerful.

115 Skull Creek

Distance: 2.7 miles
Difficulty: Class IV
Craft: Kayak
Approximate paddling time: 1–2 hours
Flows: 500–1,000 cfs (**Gauge:** None)
Season: May, June
Put-in: Pullout upstream of bridge (46.848010, -115.446153)
Takeout: North Fork Clearwater confluence (46.827124, -115.485758)

Shuttle: The takeout is on North Fork Clearwater Road (FR 247) at the bridge crossing Skull Creek. It's 7 miles upstream of Aquarius Campground and 19.3 miles downstream of Bungalow Bridge at the Oregrande confluence. To reach the put-in, drive up FR 252 along Skull Creek for 2.5 miles and cross the bridge. There's a good dirt pullout beside the creek a few hundred yards farther.

Skull is a tiny, tight, super-fun creek with continuous drops and the possibility for wood hazards. FR 252 parallels the run from the North Fork up about 4 miles and makes shuttling and scouting fairly easy, although most of the bigger drops are in a small gorge that's tough to peer into. You'll need to get out of your car and scramble down the bank to get a good look.

The biggest rapids start about 0.5 mile below the put-in and remain continuous for about a mile. They can become Class IV+ at high water. The creek then mellows to Class III to the takeout at the confluence with the North Fork.

Skull Creek is a tight, exciting creek run that mellows in its final mile, pictured.
PHOTO BY WENDY JONES

116 Little North Fork of the Clearwater

Distance: 26 miles
Difficulty: Class V
Craft: Kayak
Approximate paddling time: 2–3 days
Flows: About 500–800 cfs (**Gauge:** None. Watch for levels of 2,700 to 4,200 cfs on the North Fork Clearwater at Canyon Ranger Station gauge.)
Season: Late June–early July
Put-in: 1268 Bridge on Adair Creek Road (47.073598, -115.808361)
Takeout: Cedar Creek (46.913026, -115.821008)
Shuttle: The Little North Fork has one of the longest, and without question the most complicated shuttle of any run in Idaho. It is close to 300 miles and involves a staggering number of poorly marked logging roads. Do not attempt this trip without USDA Forest Service maps of the Clearwater and St. Joe National Forests. If you use the *Idaho Gazetteer* there is a 100 percent probability you will end up lost, stuck, and out of fuel. Don't get in a hurry, and

keep vehicles together. Some roads shown on the map don't exist, and existing roads are not shown on the map. To make things worse, very few of the roads have signs.

To find the takeout, go to Clarkia on ID 3 and get out your forest service map to navigate the complex network of logging roads, generally driving east, into the Little North Fork drainage. Use the GPS coordinates above to do some homework before attempting this. You'll start on St. Joe National Forest Road 301, then FR 382. The zigs, zags, and number of forest roads continue to mount the farther you go. Travel slowly and keep your group together. To get to the put-in, return to Clarkia and head over Hobo Pass into the St. Joe basin. Go upriver to Avery on St. Joe River Road, cross the St. Joe to the south side, and return downriver 1.8 miles to Fishook Creek. Again, get out your forest service map, travel slowly, and keep your group together as you find your way to the 1268 Bridge.

The Little North Fork is a beautiful, remote, and challenging run for kayakers only. It flows generally south from the mountains of north Idaho through a roadless canyon and is a committing multiple-day expedition. Boaters need to carry survival gear and spare paddles.

Paddlers embarking on Little North Fork expeditions also need to be extremely cognizant of water levels. Too little and the upper will be too shallow. Too much and the lower gorge gets gnarly. Making matters more difficult, there's no gauge, but historic data from a defunct gauge shows that it generally runs at about 20 percent of flows at the North Fork of the Clearwater at Canyon Ranger Station. Anecdotal information from north Idaho boaters suggests that flows of approximately 2,700 to 4,200 on the North Fork translate into manageable whitewater on the Little North Fork. One trip at 5,300 on the North Fork gauge resulted in a long, dangerous swim and an arduous hike out of the Little North Fork canyon.

The upper reach of the Little North Fork has the character of a small headwaters stream with braided channels, brush banks, and deadfall. From the put-in to Rutledge Creek, 3.2 miles, you are sure to portage a dozen or so times. At Durham Creek, 4.3

miles after the put-in, the river becomes steeper and more channelized as it enters a narrow gorge.

At mile 9 you'll arrive at Spotted Louis Creek. From here down the river changes character with a defined channel, steeper gradient, and more volume from several large tributaries. The ensuing gorge consists of sharp corners that attract ample wood. Watch for one of the only good camping spots near Foehl Creek, mile 16.3.

About 22 miles below the put-in, you'll arrive at Crescendo Creek where the river steepens again and rapids become increasingly difficult with significant wood hazards. This 2-mile section ends in a large pool above Body Bag Rapid, Class VI. It's been run, but boaters are very selective about levels. A difficult portage is on the left.

Below Body Bag, the gradient picks up, and the gorge walls become steep and constricted for 2 miles to the takeout. There are several long sections where the river-left wall is completely vertical, and boaters should try to use river-right eddies to pause, scout, or portage. The next rapid is Eanie-Meanie, a Class V. Following Eanie Meanie is Minie-Moe, another Class V. Below Minie-Moe the river is nonstop Class III and IV whitewater, with several steep ledges that could attract wood.

If large amounts of wood in the water make you squeamish, this run is not for you. Carry survival gear in your PFD pocket.

—Todd Hoffman

117 Dworshak Reservoir, Dent Acres Campground

Distance: 1–20 miles
Difficulty: Flat water
Craft: Canoe, kayak, stand-up paddleboard
Approximate paddling time: 1–8 hours
Season: May–Oct
Launch site: Dent Acres Campground
(46.623345, -116.222038)

Access: From US 12 cross the Clearwater River to Orofino. Turn left onto ID 7 and after 0.2 mile turn right onto Dent Bridge Road. Stay on Dent Bridge Road, bearing left at the fork, for 15 miles until you reach Dent Bridge. The campground is another 2 miles past the bridge.
Additional information: Call Dent Acres Campground at (877) 444-6777.

For open water paddlers, Dworshak Reservoir is the only real option in the Clearwater River basin. Dworshak was created in 1973 when construction of 717-foot-tall Dworshak Dam was completed. This is the highest single-axis dam in North America and the third-highest dam in the United States. It impounds a reservoir 54 miles long with more than 180 miles of shoreline.

In addition to generating hydropower and ameliorating the threat of downstream flooding, Dworshak decimated the North Fork of the Clearwater's once-prolific runs of steelhead and salmon. As compensation, the Dworshak National Fish Hatchery—the largest fish hatchery in the world—was built below the dam at the confluence of the North Fork and main stems of the Clearwater.

When it's full, Dworshak is a beautiful reservoir confined to a timber-enshrouded valley. The level fluctuates a lot, however, and by mid-summer most years the reservoir has a bathtub ring of dirt lining its edges.

To sample Dworshak's fares, head to Dent Acres Campground, where there's a boat launch, docks, restrooms, running water, campground, park, and hiking trails. From there you can paddle west or north up fairly narrow and wooded channels that can offer protection from the main lake's open water.

North Idaho

When it comes to paddling, north Idaho is a state unto itself. Most of the region is unique geologically compared with the rest of Idaho, but it's also distinctive because rivers in the Panhandle aren't tributaries of the Snake River. Rather, they predominantly flow east into Washington State and directly into the Columbia River or, in the case of the Kootenai River, north into British Columbia. In many ways north Idaho is more similar to northwest Montana and southern British Columbia than southern or central Idaho.

The most significant architects of north Idaho's mountains and rivers were glaciers that stretched south as far as Lake Pend Oreille, which at 1,150 feet deep is the fifth-deepest lake in the United States. During the last ice age, about 15,000 years ago, the southern lobe of the Cordilleran Ice Sheet carved out the Purcell Trench, the primary north-south valley that dominates the landscape from Sandpoint north to Nelson, British Columbia. In addition to scraping out the impressive U-shaped valley, the glacier dammed the Clark Fork River behind a 2,500-foot ice dam and flooded valleys to the east beneath 2,000 feet of water, what geologists have coined Glacial Lake Missoula. When the ice dam broke, a catastrophic flood resulted. It's estimated the flow of this torrent was 9.46 cubic miles per hour, or 386 million cubic feet per second, and moved at between 30 and 50 miles per hour. The flood completely rearranged the topography of north Idaho, eastern Washington, and northeast Oregon.

North Idaho has an absolute wealth of paddling opportunities. With hundreds of lakes and miles of calm, meandering streams, flatwater paddlers could spend lifetimes exploring north Idaho's gentler paddling fare. While the region's biggest rivers are fairly flat, there are also excellent whitewater boating opportunities on the St. Joe, St. Maries, and Moyie Rivers, as well as on dozens of tributary streams and steep creeks.

St. Joe Basin

The 140-mile-long St. Joe River is steeped in Idaho's logging history. Around the turn of the twentieth century, the basin's abundant white pine forests attracted extensive logging, and by 1910 the area had seventy-two major sawmills. The St. Joe and its tributaries were transformed into a network of flumes and splash dams used to transport logs to the sawmills downstream.

Despite the heavy logging of the past, the St. Joe flows crystal clear through deep, shadowy forests and open meadows and has the best cutthroat trout fishery in north Idaho. In 1978 it was recognized for its outstanding scenery and wild character when 66 miles were added to the National Wild and Scenic Rivers System.

The St. Joe's 6,487-foot headwaters are at St. Joe Lake, a mountain tarn tucked into a cirque on the spine of the Bitterroot Mountains less than 0.5 mile from the Idaho-Montana border. It's the same country that gives birth to the North Fork of the Clearwater River, whose headwaters are less than a mile southwest from the St. Joe's.

With its mouth at 2,129 feet, the lower St. Joe is touted as the highest navigable river in the world and was used by steamships in the early twentieth century to transport goods and people up and down the river. Motorboats are still common on the lower St. Joe. It's also extremely well suited to flatwater canoeing, kayaking, and stand-up paddleboarding. Whitewater paddlers, meanwhile, concentrate most of their energy in and around the town of Avery, which is about 50 miles upstream of Lake Coeur d'Alene.

118 St. Joe, Heller Creek

Distance: 18 miles
Difficulty: Class IV
Craft: Kayak
Approximate paddling time: Full day
Flows: 800–1,500 cfs (**Gauge:** USGS, St. Joe at Red Ives Ranger Station)
Season: Late June, July
Put-in: Heller Creek (47.063531, -115.218994)
Takeout: Spruce Tree Campground (47.038969, -115.347048)
Shuttle: To reach the takeout, travel to Red Ives Ranger Station, which is 37 miles upstream

from the town of Avery on St. Joe River Road. Continue along the river for 1.7 miles until you reach the end of the road and Spruce Tree Campground. To get to the put-in, return to Red Ives Ranger Station and turn right up Red Ives Creek on FR 320. Follow the road for 11.8 miles, crossing a summit on the north side of Red Ives Peak, and descend to the bridge at Heller Creek. For information on road conditions contact the Avery Ranger Station at (208) 245-4517.

The Heller Creek section of the St. Joe is the river's uppermost whitewater run and leaves roads behind, traveling through remote, wild country. It is very scenic, filled with logs, and can be difficult to get to before runoff ebbs because the road is usually covered with snow until late June.

The run is primarily Class III with several Class III+ rapids, but most importantly it contains a large number of logjams that move from year to year. There is also a trail that parallels the river-right side of the St. Joe for most of the run that can sometimes be used for scouting or portaging. The put-in is on Heller Creek, which quickly feeds into the St. Joe.

Most of the whitewater is located in the middle third of the run, but boaters need to be on their toes throughout the trip to avoid unnecessary tangles with logs and a few rather large logjams. Make sure to take along basic survival gear and spare paddles, and enjoy some of the most remote country north Idaho has to offer.

—Todd Hoffman

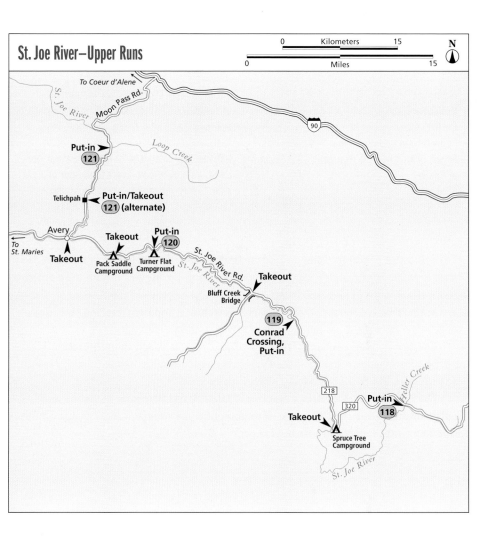

St. Joe River–Upper Runs

119 St. Joe, Tumbledown

Distance: 6.1 miles
Difficulty: Class IV
Craft: Canoe, kayak, raft
Approximate paddling time: 2–4 hours
Flows: 500–3,500 cfs (**Gauge:** USGS, St. Joe at Calder)
Season: Apr–July

Put-in: Conrad Crossing Campground (47.158741, -115.416411)
Takeout: Bluff Creek Bridge (47.186954, -115.488322)
Shuttle: The takeout is 22 miles east of Avery on St. Joe River Road. To get to the put-in, go 6.1 miles upriver to Conrad Crossing Campground.

From Conrad Crossing Campground to Bluff Creek, the St. Joe is a fantastic Class III–IV whitewater run. It's roadside its entire length but flows through deep forests and feels primitive. This is the most popular whitewater run on the St. Joe.

At low flows of about 800 to 1,500 cfs, it's technical and tight. During peak runoff of 2,000 cfs and up, it has huge standing waves and powerful holes.

The first 3 miles contain a few Class II and III riffles, and then the action kicks off with Tumbledown Falls, a Class IV. It starts with a boulder garden that leads into a sharp corner followed by a ledge with a sticky hole.

The ensuing miles contain a number of Class II and III rapids, including another rather distinct Class III+. Be wary of the potential for sweepers and logjams on this run. The wood shifts from year to year.

120 St. Joe, Skookum Canyon

Distance: 4.5 miles
Difficulty: Class III–IV
Craft: Canoe, kayak, raft
Approximate paddling time: 1–3 hours
Flows: 500–3,500 cfs (**Gauge:** USGS, St. Joe at Calder)
Season: Apr–July

Put-in: Turner Flat Campground (47.236482, -115.654303)
Takeout: Packsaddle Campground (47.231657, -115.729348)
Shuttle: The takeout at Packsaddle Campground is 4.5 miles east of Avery on St. Joe River Road. To get to the put-in, go 4.5 miles upriver to Turner Flat Campground.

This short float is another sampler of the St. Joe's abundant Class III rock gardens. It starts with a couple miles of flat water and then drops into about 2 miles of back-to-back Class II–III rapids, including one about midway through that approaches Class IV.

The St. Joe River canyon is often misty and beautiful.
PHOTO BY JAY KRAJIC

121 North Fork of the St. Joe

Distance: 10 miles
Difficulty: Class III+
Craft: Kayak
Approximate paddling time: 2-4 hours
Flows: 500-2,000 cfs (**Gauge:** None)
Season: Apr-June
Put-in: Loop Creek Bridge (47.353622, -115.736450)
Takeout: Avery (47.251380, -115.798161)
Shuttle: Exit I-90 at the Wallace, Idaho, visitor center exit and travel south, up Placer Creek, to FR 456. Go over Moon Pass and down the North Fork. The Lower takeout is at Avery. The midway takeout is at Telichpah Campground, 5 miles downriver from Loop Creek. Note that Moon Pass generally doesn't open until the last week of May or first week of June, depending on snow. For early-season runs, or those traveling from the south, the best access is via St. Maries.

The North Fork is a great river for intermediate paddlers with Class III skills. It is a mix of long sections of Class II swift water with a few Class III rapids. It has outstanding scenery, fun rapids, and nice play opportunities.

Referred to locally as the Little Joe, the North Fork can be run 10 miles from Loop Creek to the confluence with the main St. Joe at the town of Avery. The run is informally divided into two 5-mile-long sections. The top ends at Telichpah. The bottom begins there.

The first major rapid on the upper section is Big Dick, a Class III. It can be identified by a high bridge over a side canyon on river-left where Big Dick Creek cascades in.

About 2 miles above Telichpah Campground is the standout rapid of the run, No Sweat. It is a very long Class III+ with the crux move on a 90-degree right-hand bend. Just above Telichpah is another Class III, Telichpah Rapid, which ends at a nice takeout/put-in beach.

Immediately below Telichpah are a couple of small Class II and III rapids, then a swiftwater cruise to Avery.

There is no online gauge for the North Fork, but as a rule of thumb look for at least 4,000 cfs on the St. Joe at Calder gauge. There is a hand-painted gauge on the piling of the highway bridge at the North Fork's confluence with the St. Joe. Minimum level on that gauge is about 1 foot. The run gets juicy at 3 feet.

—Todd Hoffman

122 Slate Creek

Distance: 4.5 miles
Difficulty: Class V
Craft: Kayak
Approximate paddling time: 2–4 hours
Flows: 100–400 cfs (**Gauge:** None)
Season: Apr–June
Put-in: Slate Creek Road near Fritz Creek (47.303686, -115.928457)
Takeout: St. Joe River (47.257069, -115.937362)
Shuttle: If you're traveling from the east, exit I-90 at the Wallace visitor center exit. Work south following Placer Creek up a small canyon to FR 456. Take 456 over Moon Pass and down the North Fork of the St. Joe to the town of Avery. The takeout is 7 miles west of Avery. If traveling from the south or west, the takeout is 39.4 miles east of St. Maries. To get to the put-in, take St. Joe River Road east 1 mile and turn left (north) on Slate Creek Road (FR 225) at the Avery Ranger Station. Continue 6 miles, turning left at the fork on the canyon rim. Just after the road meets creek level, there's a small turnout to the left that leads to a primitive campground with the ruins of an old miner's cabin. A high-clearance or four-wheel drive is recommended.

Slate Creek is a steep, technical run best left to those with previous steep creeking experience. It flows through a deep, narrow canyon that is nearly impossible to exit on foot. At high flows, Slate Creek is big, pushy, and intimidating with large, unavoidable holes. At lower flows, it takes on pool-drop character with tight, technical rapids of exposed bedrock ledges and slides.

The run starts with a Class III+ slide, which is visible from the road not far below the put-in. The middle of the run remains very busy with ledges and slides. Several of the larger ledges can be very difficult to spot and only offer last-minute eddies. Stay alert, and don't run anything blind.

Where the West Fork of Slate Creek enters in a cascade on the right and a power line spans the canyon overhead is a two-part drop called Horseshoe Falls. It's Class V at higher flows. A short distance below is Triple Drop, a Class V that consists of a series of ledges that come in rapid succession. Another Class IV drop remains before another mile or so of continuous swift water.

Precise levels are difficult to determine on Slate Creek, but watch for flows of 4,000 cfs or more on the St. Joe at Calder gauge. If the water under the bridge at the takeout is about thigh deep or deeper, Slate Creek will be good to go.

—Todd Hoffman

Slate and Marble Creeks

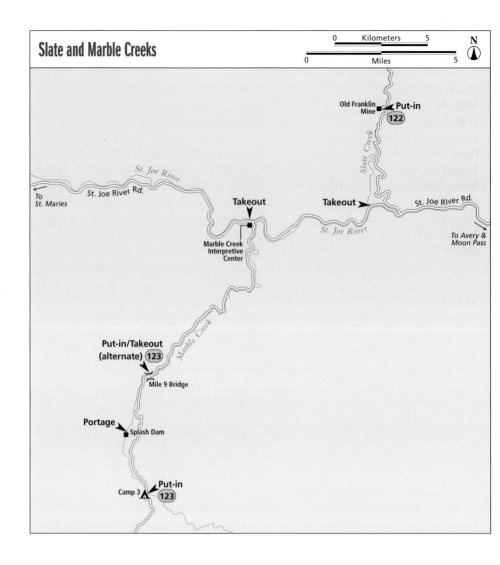

0 — Kilometers — 5
0 — Miles — 5

N

Old Franklin Mine ■ ◄ **Put-in**
(122)

Slate Creek

St. Joe River

To St. Maries

St. Joe River Rd.

Takeout ▼

Takeout ►

St. Joe River Rd.

St. Joe River

To Avery & Moon Pass

Marble Creek Interpretive Center

Put-in/Takeout (alternate) (123) ◄

Marble Creek

◄ Mile 9 Bridge

Portage ◄ ■ Splash Dam

Camp 3 ▲ **Put-in** (123)

123 Marble Creek

Distance: 13.5 miles
Difficulty: Class IV
Craft: Kayak
Approximate paddling time: 2–4 hours
Flows: 500–3,000 cfs (**Gauge:** None)
Season: Apr, May, June
Put-in: Camp 3 (47.124398, -116.097290)
Alternate put-in/takeout: Mile 9 bridge (47.178002, -116.095125)
Takeout: Confluence with St. Joe River (47.250064, -116.022064)

Shuttle: From St. Maries drive St. Joe River Road east 34 miles to the confluence of Marble Creek and the St. Joe River. To get to the put-in, take Marble Creek Road (FR 321) south 8.6 miles and bear to the left to stay on Marble Creek Road, crossing a bridge shortly after. The bridge is the put-in for the lower section. To get to the upper put-in, continue on Marble Creek Road 3.1 miles and bear right to get on Hobo Pass Road (still FR 321) and continue 1.9 miles to a second bridge.

Marble Creek, a tributary of the St. Joe, offers good intermediate-level paddling in a beautiful setting. The entire 13.5 miles can be run from Camp 3 to the confluence with the St. Joe River, but the most commonly run section is from the bridge at mile marker 9 down.

The top 4.6 miles above the bridge is mostly Class II to III swift water, with a portage around an old splash dam 2.3 miles below the put-in. The top flows through a secluded gorge where the road leaves the river and feels quite wild. The more commonly paddled 9 miles below the bridge are roadside and have the best whitewater.

Marble Creek is continuous Class III with a few Class IV rapids. The basin's abundant logs move around from season to season, so paddlers should stay alert. There is no online gauge for Marble Creek, but when the St. Joe is running 5,000 cfs or more, it's generally good to go.

If you're itching to learn about the area's rich logging history, the Marble Creek Interpretive Center at the takeout is a worthwhile stop.

124 St. Joe Canoe Floats

Distance: 2–15 miles
Difficulty: Class I
Craft: Kayak, canoe, stand-up paddleboard
Approximate paddling time: 2–8 hours
Flows: 500–3,500 cfs (**Gauge:** USGS, St. Joe at Calder)
Season: Apr–Oct
Access: Heyburn State Park (47.374103, -116.762261)

Shuttle: From St. Maries take ID 5 west 12.8 miles and turn right (north) onto Chatcolet Road. Go 2.4 miles to the park. From US 95, go east on ID 5 for 6.3 miles. Turn left (north) onto Chatcolet Road and go 2.4 miles to the park. There are additional access points, including Rocky Point Marina and Park, along ID 5 closer to St. Maries.

From Avery downstream to Lake Coeur d'Alene, a distance of roughly 60 miles, the St. Joe has numerous flatwater paddling options. From Avery to St. Joe City, a distance of 37 miles, the river is shallower and has long pools interspersed with Class II riffles.

The lower St. Joe is calm, but at high water it could still dangerous for unprepared paddlers.
PHOTO BY JAY KRAJIC

Currents can be powerful during spring runoff, but by July the water is mellow and chilly. From St. Joe City to Lake Coeur d'Alene, a distance of 25 miles, the river is deep, placid, and reflective.

The lowest reaches of the St. Joe also contain a peculiar phenomenon created when Post Falls Dam was constructed at the outlet of Lake Coeur d'Alene and raised the lake level, which backed water up around the St. Joe River Channel without inundating its raised banks. This in effect created new lakes that surround the St. Joe River.

Instead of a distinctive mouth or delta, the St. Joe flows in between several lakes with its banks intact. You really have to see and experience it, and that's the paddle detailed here. There are numerous access points between St. Maries and Heyburn State Park, but to get a feel for the area, simply plan an out-and-back trip from the state park.

From the park, paddle a mile east across Chatcolet Lake to the terminus of the St. Joe River and find your way into the channel. Continue paddling upstream as long or as far as you'd like, and keep your eyes peeled for motorized boat traffic. (For those opting to do a one-way shuttled paddle, the trip from St. Maries to Heyburn State Park is 14.5 miles, which is pretty long for a river with such sluggish current.)

125 St. Maries Whitewater Run

Distance: 14 miles
Difficulty: Class II–III
Craft: Canoe, kayak, raft
Approximate paddling time: 4-6 hours
Flows: 500-4,000 cfs (**Gauge:** USGS, St. Maries River near Santa)
Season: Apr, May, June
Put-in: ID 3 bridge at mile marker 72 (47.175653, -116.494538)
Takeout: 8 miles up St. Maries River Road (47.245320, -116.620389)

Shuttle: To get to the takeout from St. Maries, go south from the IGA on 1st Street, which will become St. Maries River Road. Go 8 miles (using the red painted mile markers) and look for a side road crossing the railroad tracks to the river's edge. To get to the put-in, return to St. Maries and take ID 3 for 12.4 miles to mile marker 72, which is on the bridge. There's a pullout on the upstream side of the bridge, but you'll have to cross some private property to access the river. Please be respectful.

The St. Maries River, which joins the St. Joe at the town of St. Maries, is a good spring float for intermediate whitewater paddlers. The whitewater is fairly straightforward, and the canyon is secluded and beautiful. Most of the run consists of Class II riffles and rapids, but it's remote and can be cold. For these reasons it should be attempted by strong intermediate paddlers.

The run starts with about 5 miles of swift, flat water in a broad valley. Midway through, the canyon begins to tighten and the gradient picks up at the first railroad bridge as the river works into an area called The Loops. The canyon meanders considerably in this area in a series of oxbows, and rapids are fairly long and continuous. They're formed by ledges and swift outside corners. Things get easier again after the second railroad bridge. The takeout is on the left following the third railroad bridge.

St. Maries and Lower St. Joe Rivers

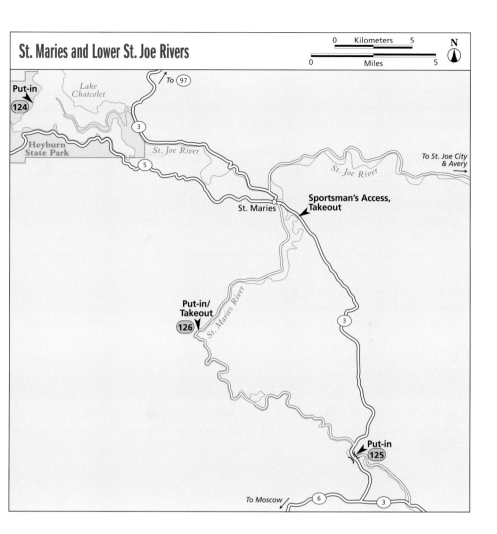

126 St. Maries Canoe Float

Distance: 8.4 miles
Difficulty: Class I
Craft: Canoe, kayak, stand-up paddleboard
Approximate paddling time: 2–4 hours
Flows: 500–2,000 cfs
Season: Apr–Oct
Put-in: 8 miles up St. Maries River Road
(47.245320, -116.620389)
Takeout: Sportsman's Access off ID 3
(47.307113, -116.542014)

Shuttle: The developed takeout with a dock and boat ramp is 1 mile south of St. Maries on ID 3. To get to the put-in, return to St. Maries and turn left at the IGA on 1st Street, which will become St. Maries River Road. Go 8 miles (using the red painted mile markers) and look for a side road crossing the railroad tracks to the river's edge.

The lower St. Maries is a placid, tranquil paddle. Its final miles are also deeper than the river's upstream counterpart, making for a longer paddling season. This section offers a lazy drift through pastoral bottomlands with scattered forests and wetlands.

The lower St. Maries is a placid river well suited to a variety of paddling styles.

Coeur d'Alene Basin

The Coeur d'Alene River has several very different personalities. The North Fork is a clear, cold and swift mountain stream that teems with fish and flows through a beautiful timber-enshrouded valley before settling into a deep and sluggish flow the rest of its journey to Lake Coeur d'Alene.

The South Fork is a swift stream that rushes through the heart of Idaho's Silver Valley, which was one of the world's leading producers of silver, lead, and zinc. The mining unfortunately resulted in toxic pollution that's worked its way downstream.

After the confluence of the North and South Forks, the main stem of the Coeur d'Alene River is calm, deep, and flows through extensive marshland and among a network of beautiful chain lakes. As with the South Fork, the main stem is undergoing extensive long-term cleanup from the mining pollution that traveled downstream with the river's currents.

The history of the cleanup goes something like this. In 1983 the US Environmental Protection Agency listed a 21-mile area in the South Fork of the Coeur d'Alene River basin as a Superfund site. The agency extended Superfund boundaries in 1998 to include areas throughout the 1,500-square-mile Coeur d'Alene basin, and cleanup is projected to take three decades at a cost of $359 million. Contamination related to mining in the upper South Fork basin has been found over 150 miles of the river system from Mullan, Idaho, through to the Spokane River reach of Lake Roosevelt, Washington, according to the EPA.

According to a 2014 report by the US Geological Survey, cleanup efforts are paying off, and concentrations of lead, cadmium, and zinc have dropped by 65 percent in the South Fork near the town of Pinehurst. Movement of heavy metals in the river, nevertheless, continues. About 400 tons of lead, 700 tons of zinc, and 5 tons of cadmium flow into Lake Coeur d'Alene each year, according to data collected from 2009 to 2013.

Coeur d'Alene River and Chain Lakes

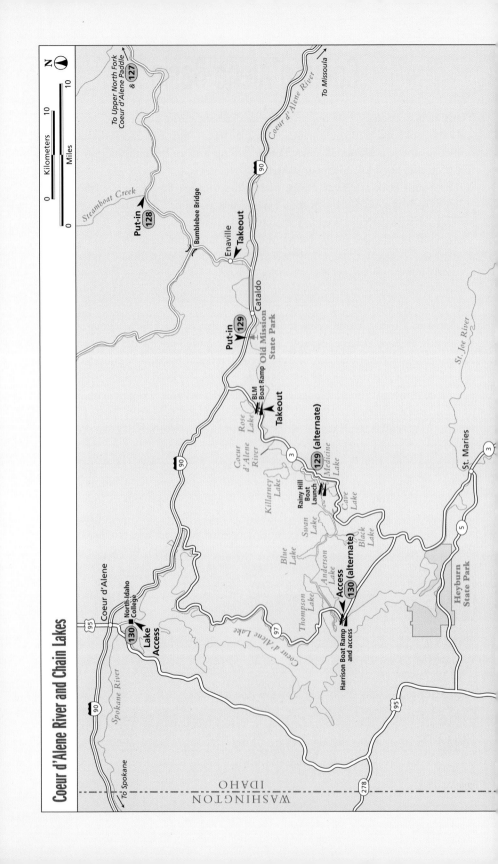

127 North Fork Coeur d'Alene, Upper

Distance: 25 miles
Difficulty: Class II
Craft: Canoe, kayak, raft, drift boat
Approximate paddling time: 3–8 hours
Flows: 500–2,000 cfs (**Gauge:** USGS, North Fork Coeur d'Alene River near Prichard)
Season: May–July
Put-in: Big Hank Campground (47.822411, -116.097037)

Alternative put-in: Sissions Creek Campground (47.743016, -116.007426)
Takeout: Downstream of Prichard (47.647957, -115.973191)
Shuttle: The takeout is 0.25 mile downstream from Prichard at the bridge crossing the North Fork. The takeout is on river-left on the downstream side of the bridge. To get to the Sissions Creek put-in, go 10 miles upstream. To get to the Big Hank put-in, go 19.6 miles upstream.

The North Fork of the Coeur d'Alene is a gem. Its upper reaches have beautiful, clear, swift water and flow through a remote timber-enshrouded valley that stretches more than 50 miles. There are several fantastic options for open canoes above Prichard. These sections include swift, cold water, blind corners, Class II rapids, and the potential for river-wide trees and sweepers. There are advanced open canoe runs and intermediate whitewater kayak runs.

From Prichard upstream for 25 miles the river is roadside, and access is easy. There are about a dozen different sportsman access points along the upper North Fork. Big Hank Campground, 18.5 miles from Prichard, is good. Sissions Creek, 9.4 miles above Prichard, is also good.

The Class II upper and Class I lower North Fork Coeur d'Alene provide diverse paddling opportunities.

128 North Fork Coeur d'Alene, Steamboat Creek to Enaville

Distance: 10 miles
Difficulty: Class I
Craft: Canoe, kayak, stand-up paddleboard
Approximate paddling time: 3-6 hours
Flows: 100-2,000 cfs (**Gauge:** USGS, North Fork Coeur d'Alene River at Enaville)
Season: June-Aug
Put-in: Steamboat Creek (47.660866, -116.152719)
Alternative put-in: Bumblebee Bridge (47.611225, -116.239669)

Takeout: Old River Road bridge (47.569486, -116.253407)
Shuttle: The put-in at Steamboat Creek is 11 miles up the North Fork of the Coeur d'Alene River from I-90. The Bumblebee Bridge put-in is 5.5 miles upstream from the interstate. The takeout is at the bridge spanning the North Fork on Old River Road, on the north outskirts of Enaville. There's a gravel parking area across the road from the river.

The lower reaches of the North Fork below Steamboat Creek (11.5 miles downstream of Prichard) are slow, deep, and suitable for beginners, open canoes, recreational kayaks, and stand-up paddleboards. This reach is extremely popular with family floaters, and you're sure to encounter people paddling all manner of craft. There are strict regulations prohibiting glass bottles on the river, as well as parking outside of designated areas.

The put-in at Steamboat Creek includes two large parking areas and a pond. Work around the pond to the right to reach a riverside access. For an even easier and shorter trip, start at Bumblebee Bridge, which results in a 4-mile paddle to the Old River Road bridge.

Note that the North Fork can flow at 20,000 cfs or more during spring runoff and is not a suitable family float at high water. Wait until late June for friendly flows. Nearly 100 percent of the land along the lower North Fork is privately owned. Please be respectful.

129 Coeur d'Alene, Chain Lakes

Distance: 1–37 miles
Difficulty: Class I
Craft: Canoe, kayak, stand-up paddleboard
Approximate paddling time: 1 hour to 2 days
Flows: 1,000–5,000 cfs (**Gauge:** USGS, Coeur d'Alene River near Cataldo)
Season: May–Oct
Put-in: Old Mission State Park (47.552690, -116.367086)
Takeout: BLM boat ramp (47.538335, -116.471344)

Additional access: Rainy Hill boat launch (47.473414, -116.588137)
Shuttle: To get to the upper BLM takeout on ID 3, exit I-90 at exit 34 and go south 3 miles to where the river and ID 3 merge. To get to the put-in at Old Mission State Park, return to I-90 and go east 5 miles to exit 39. The boat ramp is about 0.5 mile downriver (west) of the main park. To get to Rainy Hill, exit I-90 at exit 34 and go south 22.3 miles. Turn right (west) onto Rainy Hill Road. Rainy Hill Campground and the boat launch are 0.75 mile ahead.

The lower Coeur d'Alene River is slow, deep, and contemplative. It flows for 37 miles from the confluence of the North and South Forks to Lake Coeur d'Alene and past

Like other rivers in the area, the lower Coeur d'Alene is very calm and well suited to flatwater paddling.

Viewed upstream from the BLM boat ramp off ID 3, the Coeur d'Alene is beautiful and inviting.

ten chain lakes, all but two of which can be accessed via channels from the main river. It's truly a paddling paradise. There are more than a dozen access points along the lower Coeur d'Alene River that can be used in various combinations to produce a wide variety of trips.

Along with the lower St. Joe River, the lower Coeur d'Alene was once used by steamships transporting goods and people into and out of the heavily forested valleys of north Idaho. They made it almost the entire distance of the main stem of the Coeur d'Alene River, traveling to the Old Mission, which is just off I-90 about 25 miles east of Coeur d'Alene.

To sample the main Coeur d'Alene River, put on at the boat ramp at Old Mission State Park and paddle 6.25 miles to a BLM boat ramp off ID 3, just 3 miles south of I-90. To sample the chain lakes, try putting on at Rainy Hill Boat Launch, which will give you access to Medicine Lake, Cave Lake, and the main Coeur d'Alene River. Access channels to Swan and Black Lakes are also only about 4 miles downriver.

130 Lake Coeur d'Alene

Distance: 1–20 miles
Difficulty: Flat water
Craft: Canoe, kayak, stand-up paddleboard
Approximate paddling time: 1–8 hours
Season: Apr–Oct
Access: North Idaho College (47.674989, -116.796928)
Access: Harrison (47.453416, -116.787487)
Access: Heyburn State Park (47.373895, -116.762680)

Directions: North Idaho College is only 3 miles off of I-90. Exit the interstate and follow signs to the college. Harrison, located on the east shore of the lake, is a 34-mile drive from Coeur d'Alene. From Coeur d'Alene take I-90 west for 14 miles and exit onto ID 97. Take ID 97 south for 28 miles to Harrison. ID 97 also passes a half-dozen good access points between the interstate and Harrison.

With the beautiful city of Coeur d'Alene at its north end, Lake Coeur d'Alene is more than 25 miles long and almost 200 feet deep. It ranges in width from 1 to 3 miles and offers more than 100 miles of forested shoreline. Access options abound with seventeen boat launches and more than a dozen additional public access points.

You can access the south end of the lake from Heyburn State Park (see St. Joe Canoe Floats for more information). While this is technically on Chatcolet Lake, it's really the same body of water. The north end of the lake can easily be accessed from a number of boat launches and access points, but for a nice sandy beach aim for the North Idaho College campus, which is at the Spokane River lake outlet on the west edge of downtown Coeur d'Alene. Another good launch point is at the Coeur d'Alene River outlet in Harrison, from which you can paddle the main lake or work your way up the slow-moving Coeur d'Alene River.

This is a very large lake, and paddlers should be wary of heading for the open water, where it is easy to get more than a mile from shore. Afternoon winds can whip the lake into whitecaps, so be prepared and generally keep to the shoreline or protected coves and inlets.

A paddler keeps close to shore in Mica Bay, on the west side of Lake Coeur d'Alene.
PHOTO BY REMY NEWCOMB

Pend Oreille Basin

At 1,150 feet deep and formed by glaciers moving south from Canada, Lake Pend Oreille is among the deepest lakes on the continent. It's cradled by stunning mountain ranges to the east, north, and west and is home to a charming lakeside resort town, Sandpoint.

The lake's largest tributary, the Clark Fork, flows west out of Montana and finds its outlet at the Pend Oreille River, which flows west into Washington and then north into Canada, where it meets the Columbia River just on the north side of the US-Canada border.

The river system that feeds Lake Pend Oreille is large, but the geography within Idaho's northern panhandle is fairly confined. There are, however, an abundance of diverse paddling opportunities in the area. From gentle canoeing on the Clark Fork and Priest River to hair-raising steep creek kayaking on the upper Pack River, the Lake Pend Oreille area has a lot to offer.

Upper Priest Lake is the quintessential north Idaho kayak tour. PHOTO BY REMY NEWCOMB

Sandpoint Area Paddles

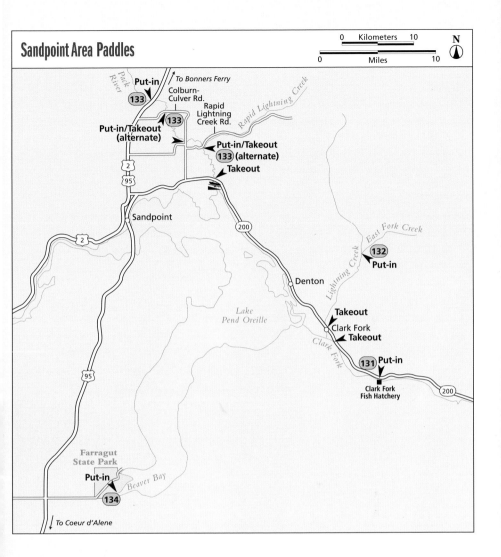

0 Kilometers 10

0 Miles 10

N

To Bonners Ferry

Pack River

Put-in
133

Colburn-Culver Rd.

Rapid Lightning Creek Rd.

Rapid Lightning Creek

Put-in/Takeout (alternate)
133

Put-in/Takeout
133 (alternate)

Takeout

2
95

Sandpoint

2

200

East Fork Creek

Lightning Creek

132
Put-in

Denton

Lake Pend Oreille

Takeout

Clark Fork

Takeout

Clark Fork

131 Put-in

95

Clark Fork Fish Hatchery

200

Farragut State Park

Put-in

Beaver Bay

134

To Coeur d'Alene

131   Clark Fork Cabinet Gorge Canoe Run

Distance: 6 miles
Difficulty: Class I (II at high water)
Craft: Canoe, kayak, stand-up paddleboard
Approximate paddling time: 2–4 hours
Flows: 10,000–50,000 cfs (**Gauge:** USGS, Clark Fork River below Cabinet Gorge Dam)
Season: Apr–Oct
Put-in: Clark Fork Fish Hatchery (48.086707, -116.080257)
Takeout: Johnson Creek Road (48.134682, -116.173670)
Takeout: Denton (48.202527, -116.251821)

Shuttle: The takeout is upstream from the town of Clark Fork, which is 25 miles east of Sandpoint on ID 200. From Clark Fork go south on Stephen Street for 0.7 mile and bear left onto Johnson Creek Road. The bridge is 0.25 mile ahead. There's a pullout on the river-left side of the river, upstream of the bridge. To get to the put-in, continue east on River Road (same road, different name) and go 6.5 miles. Turn left onto Cabinet Gorge Road. The turnoff to the hatchery is 1 mile ahead on the left.

From Cabinet Gorge Dam downstream to the town of Clark Fork, it's a mellow and beautiful 7-mile paddle through Cabinet Gorge, which marks the intersection of the Monarch Mountains to the south and the Cabinet Mountains to the north. This is also the location of the glacial ice dam that formed Glacial Lake Missoula, a 2,000-foot-deep glacial lake that inundated valleys hundreds of miles to the east and south.

To sample this popular paddling and fishing river, put in at the state fish hatchery on the south bank near the dam and float downstream to the bridge at Johnson Creek Road. If you're looking for a longer float, continue downstream past the town of Clark Fork and head through the delta at Lake Pend Oreille. Work your way right to get to a primitive boat ramp off ID 200 in Denton. This second option makes for a 13-mile trip.

This is a very big river subject to extreme flow fluctuations because of controlled flows from 208-foot Cabinet Gorge Dam. Flows during a recent July varied from 9,000 cfs at night to 20,000 cfs during the afternoon, when energy demand spikes. Average June flows are in the neighborhood of 70,000 cfs.

132 Lightning Creek

Distance: 8 miles
Difficulty: Class III+
Craft: Kayak, raft, canoe
Approximate paddling time: 2–4 hours
Flows: 900–4,000 cfs (**Gauge:** USGS, Lightning Creek at Clark Fork)
Season: Apr–June
Put-in: East Fork Creek (48.240694, -116.111060)

Takeout: ID 200 in Clark Fork (48.150737, -116.183252)
Shuttle: The takeout is on the southeast side of the ID 200 bridge in Clark Fork. To get to the put-in, head east on ID 200 and turn left (north) onto Main Street, following signs for Lightning Creek. Take Main Street 0.5 mile and turn left onto Lightning Creek Road (FR 419) and go 7.5 miles to East Fork Creek.

Lightning Creek is a swift and continuous Class III stream that flows south out of the Cabinet Mountains and joins the Clark Fork in the town of Clark Fork.

The paddle starts on East Fork Creek and joins Lightning Creek after a few hundred yards. The top half of the run is over a defined riverbed in a forested valley, but halfway down opens into a broad, braided river channel that has been scoured considerably by high water events. There are numerous trees in Lightning Creek that shift from year to year, so scout carefully.

Lightning Creek consists primarily of continuous Class III whitewater with only a few defined rapids. At low water it's technical and rocky with lots of eddies. At high water it's a big, roiling, and fast wave train from top to bottom.

—Todd Hoffman

Flows on Lightning Creek vary considerably, and high-water events have rearranged the riverbed. It's pictured here below navigable levels.

133 Pack River

Distance: 17.3 miles
Difficulty: Class I
Craft: Kayak, canoe, stand-up paddleboard
Approximate paddling time: 2-8 hours
Flows: 500-1,000 cfs (**Gauge:** USGS, Pack River near Colburn)
Season: June, July
Put-in: US 95 (48.421314, -116.499308)
Takeout: ID 200 (48.323784, -116.384995)
Shuttle: The takeout on ID 200 is 9.8 miles east of Sandpoint. The put-in is 9.3 miles north of Sandpoint on US 93. There's a dirt access area on river-left downstream of the bridge at the US 93 put-in. To access the intermediate takeouts/put-ins, locate Colburn Culver Road 2.2 miles south of the put-in on US 93. Head east 3 miles to reach the first takeout and 7.4 miles to reach the second. To reach the third, go east on Rapid Lightning Creek Road for 1.5 miles and locate the Pack River General Store. There's a highway pullout near the bridge across the river from the store. To get to the upper Pack whitewater runs, go 11.8 miles north from Sandpoint on US 93. Turn left onto Upper Pack River Road and continue upriver for 16 miles to Zuni Creek.

The Pack River tumbles from the Selkirk Mountains northwest of Sandpoint into Lake Pend Oreille. The lower Pack is a long-established canoe float, but its upper reaches also contain some fantastic Class V kayaking that includes a couple of bedrock slides—something that's rare in Idaho. To check out the Pack's Class V creeking, head up Pack River Road to Zuni Creek. The mile above Zuni Creek is Class V+. The 3 to 4 miles below Zuni Creek is Class IV to V and includes the slides.

The canoe paddle is a mellow, family-friendly paddle. Below US 95 the Pack meanders considerably and adds up to 17.3 miles of river in 8 linear miles. There are three intermediate put-in and takeout options along this sinewy stretch of river, two on Colburn Culver Road and one on Rapid Lightning Creek Road.

134 Lake Pend Oreille, Farragut State Park

Distance: 1–20 miles
Difficulty: Flat water
Craft: Canoe, kayak, stand-up paddleboard
Approximate paddling time: 1–8 hours
Season: Apr–Oct
Access: Beaver Bay in Farragut State Park
(47.955270, -116.567881)
Directions: From Sandpoint go south on US
95 for 25 miles and turn left (east) on Bayview

Road. The turn is 18 miles north of I-90 near
Coeur d'Alene. Take ID 54 east for 4 miles to
the park entrance. Once in the park, take S
Road 0.7 mile and turn right onto Beaver Bay
Road. Continue 1.6 miles to a parking area
and a protected waterfront.
Additional information: To reserve campsites
or cabins, or to get more information, call the
park at (208) 683-2425.

The 4,000-acre Farragut State Park is situated at the south end of Lake Pend Oreille, Idaho's largest lake—and at more than 11,000 feet deep, its deepest. The park has spectacular sandy beaches, pine forests, beautiful meadows, and ample camping.

Named for Admiral David Farragut ("Damn the torpedoes! Full steam ahead!"), the park occupies an area that was once a huge inland naval base and the second-largest naval training facility in the world. You can catch up on the area's naval history at the park's Brig Museum, but most importantly you can launch your craft of choice from Farragut and enjoy one of the more sheltered locations on this very large lake.

There are more than a dozen access points on Lake Pend Oreille. Paddlers must be cautious of the lake's open water, where an afternoon wind can whip up ocean-size swells. This is particularly true of the lake's eastern side, where the shoreline offers little protection from the open water and prevailing winds.

Farragut State Park offers relative seclusion from the open water of Lake Pend Oreille while also serving up impressive scenery.
Photo by Remy Newcomb

135 Priest Lake, the Thorofare

Distance: 5–15 miles
Difficulty: Class I
Craft: Canoe, kayak, stand-up paddleboard
Approximate paddling time: 1 to 2 days
Season: Late June–Oct
Access: Beaver Creek Portage Trail
(48.739345, -116.862830)
Access: Beaver Creek Boat Ramp (48.736054,
-116.857397)
Access: Lionhead State Park boat ramp
(48.742170, -116.833412)
Access: Lionhead State Park sportsman
access (48.744480, -116.832814)

Shuttle: To get to the Beaver Creek Campground from Priest River, Idaho, go north on ID 57 for 37 miles to the town of Nordman. Bear right onto Reeder Bay Road and follow signs to Beaver Creek Campground, where there's a boat launch and Portage Trail access. To get to Lionhead State Park from Priest River, go north on ID 57 for 22.5 miles. Turn right (east) onto Dickensheet Highway and go 5.4 miles to the town of Coolin. Turn right onto East Shore Road and go 22.5 miles to the northeast end of the lake.

The paddle from Priest Lake to Upper Priest Lake via a 2.8-mile slow-moving thoroughfare (which the locals spell thorofare) is one of the premier open-water paddling trips in the Northwest—if you catch it when it's not overrun with motorboats.

Priest Lake is one of Idaho's most scenic. It's completely surrounded by heavily forested mountains and because of its remote location can be very peaceful as long as you avoid the peak motorboat season. Priest Lake is also among Idaho's largest lakes and boasts more than 23,000 acres and 80 miles of shoreline and is 400 feet deep. During spring and fall—and perhaps midweek during the summer—canoes and kayaks can provide serene and secluded journeys on this beautiful mountain lake.

Priest Lake has well over a dozen access points. The easiest access to the Thorofare is from Beaver Creek Campground, where there's a 0.25-mile portage trail that leads directly to the Thorofare, as well as a boat ramp on Priest Lake less than 0.5 mile from the Thorofare entrance. There's also an excellent sand beach in Mosquito Bay on the northeast flank of Priest Lake in Lionhead State Park. Lionhead has a boat ramp and sportsman access less than a mile across Mosquito Bay from the Thorofare entrance.

Although Beaver Creek and Lionhead are only about a mile away from each other, it's a 55-mile drive around Priest Lake to get from one to the other, so plan your launch site ahead of time.

The Thorofare is very shallow in spots, but generally is about 10 to 20 feet deep and meanders through a peaceful, beautiful forest. It can have strong downstream currents during spring runoff, but by mid- to late June should be a manageable upstream paddle.

Upper Priest Lake is a no-wake zone for motorboats and has four campgrounds with fifteen campsites that are available on a first-come, first-served basis. It is 3 miles long, less than a mile wide, and has no road access.

Kootenai Basin

The Kootenai is unique for an Idaho river. Its headwaters are high in the Canadian Rockies on the border of British Columbia and Alberta, northwest of Calgary. From there it works south and east, eventually crossing into northwest Montana before turning west into Idaho and then north into Canada again. The Kootenai and the landscape that cradles it is more similar to British Columbia than most of Idaho.

The Kootenai basin in Idaho has two basic characteristics of concern to paddlers: mellow and extreme. The Moyie, a tributary that joins the Kootenai at Moyie Springs, has Class I to Class III paddling opportunities, and the Kootenai itself is Class I–II—water level depending. From there, the difficulty jumps more than a couple notches.

The steep creeks that tumble from the nearby mountains are the domain of high-end expert kayakers and aren't detailed here. If you find yourself reading this book and want to poke around, check out Boulder Creek, which joins the Kootenai from the Cabinet Mountains near the Idaho-Montana border. Smith Creek, Cow Creek, and Boundary Creek—all descending from the Selkirks near the US-Canada border—are also established high-end kayak runs.

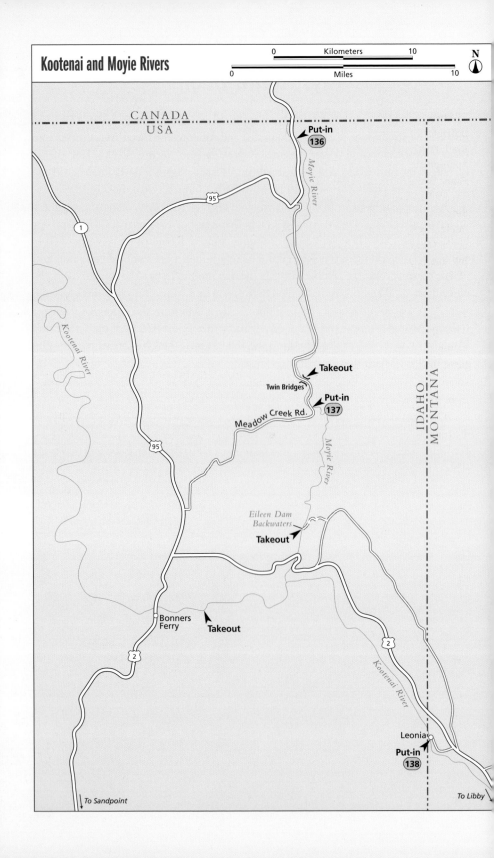

Kootenai and Moyie Rivers

0   Kilometers   10
0   Miles   10

CANADA
USA

Put-in
136

Moyie River

95

1

Kootenai River

Takeout

Twin Bridges

Put-in
137

Meadow Creek Rd.

95

Moyie River

Eileen Dam
Backwaters

Takeout

Bonners
Ferry   Takeout

2

2

Kootenai River

Leonia

Put-in
138

To Sandpoint

To Libby

IDAHO

MONTANA

136 Moyie River, Upper

Distance: 12 miles
Difficulty: Class I–II
Craft: Kayak, raft, canoe
Approximate paddling time: 3–5 hours
Flows: 500–1,000 cfs (**Gauge:** USGS, Moyie River at Eastport)
Season: Apr–June
Put-in: Primitive access near US-Canada border (48.988227, -116.173096)
Takeout: Twin Bridges (48.839116, -116.167586)

Shuttle: From US 95 near the US-Canada border, the takeout is 11.8 miles south on Moyie River Road. It's at the third bridge spanning the Moyie. From the south, it is 12.1 miles from Bonner's Ferry on Meadow Creek Road, which joins Moyie River Road near Meadow Creek Campground. To get to the put-in, go upriver to US 95. Continue north on 95 for 2.9 miles and turn right onto FR 2517. The put-in is about 1,000 feet ahead on the right.

The upper Moyie from above Copper Creek to Meadow Creek is a swift Class II canoe run that's generally floatable during a brief window in early spring. During peak flows the Moyie can flow at 5,000 cfs or more, but as the water comes down to around 1,000 cfs, it's an excellent choice for an open canoe. As the water subsides even further, it becomes Class I.

The put-in is less than a mile south of the US-Canada border, and you'll float 12 miles and take out at the bridge just downstream of McDougal Creek, which is a few miles upstream of Meadow Creek Campground, the put-in for the lower Moyie. The campground could be an alternative takeout, but there are some Class II rapids in between.

137 Moyie River, Lower

Distance: 7.5 miles
Difficulty: Class III–IV
Craft: Kayak, raft, canoe
Approximate paddling time: 2–4 hours
Flows: 1,000–5,000 cfs (**Gauge:** USGS, Moyie River at Eastport)
Season: Apr–June
Put-in: Meadow Creek Road bridge upstream of Meadow Creek Campground (48.823907, -116.163650)
Takeout: Moyie Dam backwaters (48.749762, -116.170362)
Shuttle: To get to the takeout from Bonners Ferry, go east on US 2 for 4.5 miles. (You'll cross a bridge spanning the Moyie at 3.5 miles.) Turn left onto Old US 2 and go 3.1 miles, turning left onto Deer Creek Road. Take another almost immediate left onto FR 2269, which descends to the Moyie Dam backwaters. There are two ways to get to the put-in from here. The shortest and more complicated is to return to Deer Creek Road and turn left. Go 4.4 miles to Placer Creek Connection Road. Turn left and go another 2 miles to Deer Creek Road. Turn left and continue, continuing another mile to the put-in bridge. Alternatively, you can return to US 2, go west 1.3 miles, and turn right onto Eileen Dam Road. This leads directly to Meadow Creek Campground, and offers the opportunity to scout Eileen Dam by turning off onto a small dirt road on the right 4.1 miles after leaving US 2.

The lower Moyie flows through a beautiful constricted gorge and has continuous Class II and III whitewater. It also has two distinct Class III rapids that can become Class IV as flows approach 5,000 cfs.

The Moyie River is swift and beautiful. PHOTO BY KEVIN LEWIS

The first major rapid, at mile 5, is created by the remnants of Eileen Dam. The water pushes against and around the dam to the left (and perhaps under the dam as well, so be careful here).

The second rapid, called Hole in the Wall, is at mile 7. Both can attract wood, and the dam in particular is difficult to river scout. Once you're heading into the rapid, it can be difficult or impossible to stop.

138 Kootenai River

Distance: 14.2 miles
Difficulty: Class II
Craft: Kayak, raft, canoe
Approximate paddling time: 5–8 hours
Flows: 10,000–20,000 cfs (**Gauge:** USGS, Kootenai River at Leonia)
Season: Apr–Oct
Put-in: Leonia, Montana (48.616624, -116.049439)
Takeout: East of Bonners Ferry (48.700957, -116.244343)

Shuttle: To get to the takeout from Bonners Ferry, go 4.7 miles east on Cow Creek Road, which turns off of Ash Street. The takeout is on river-left, the south side of the river, and across the pipeline from the road. To get to the put-in, return to Bonners Ferry and go north 3.2 miles. Turn right (east) onto US 2 and go 17.7 miles to Leonia Road. Turn left and go another 1.5 miles to the river.

The Kootenai River through Idaho is a big, meandering river that's controlled by releases from Libby Dam upstream in Montana. Its flow can vary 10,000 cfs from day to day and 35,000 cfs from season to season. There are no rapids on this section, but at high water the river has very powerful currents that should be treated with respect.

The Purcell Trench was created by a huge glacial lobe that reached south as far as Lake Pend Oreille. The Kootenai River flows into the trench near Bonners Ferry and then works north into Canada.

From the put-in at Leonia the Kootenai works through the final miles of its gorge as it cuts through the Cabinet Mountains and then spills into the Purcell Trench, which leads the river north into Canada.

Additional sections downstream of Bonners Ferry can be paddled as far as Kootenay Lake in British Columbia, although you'll have to contend with Customs if you attempt to go that far.

Paddling Resources

Books

Amaral, Grant. *Idaho the Whitewater State* (Boise, Idaho: 1990).

Blewett, Colby, and Fernald, Rick. *The Playboaters Guide to Idaho* (Bend, Oregon: 2001).

Daly, Katherine, and Watters, Ron. *Kath and Ron's Guide to Idaho Paddling* (Pocatello, Idaho: 1999); www.ronwatters.com.

Hansen, Dan, and Landers, Rich. *Paddle Routes of the Inland Northwest* (Seattle, Washington: 1998); www.mountaineersbooks.org.

Leidecker, Matt. *The Middle Fork of the Salmon River: A Comprehensive Guide* (Hailey, Idaho: 2006); www.idahoriverpublications.com.

McClaran, Don, and Moore, Greg. *Idaho Whitewater* (McCall, Idaho: 1989).

Stuebner, Steve. *Paddling the Payette* (Boise, Idaho: 2014); www.stevestuebner.com.

Websites

American Whitewater—conservation website that includes a nationwide database of rivers.
www.americanwhitewater.org

Boating the Inland Northwest—an online resource featuring flatwater paddling in north Idaho, as well as eastern Washington and northwest Montana.
www.boatingtheinlandnw.blogspot.com

Bureau of Land Management—The BLM maintains a number of excellent online resources for Idaho paddlers. The URL is long, so it might be easier to conduct a search for the "Four Rivers Lottery" or look below for further contact information.

Kayak Idaho—an Idaho-wide paddling resource with more focus on southern and central Idaho.
www.kayakakidaho.com

North Idaho Rivers—excellent write-ups on more than two dozen north Idaho paddling runs.
www.northidahorivers.com

Payette River—a resource for information about the Payette River system.
www.payetteriver.org

River Updates—This new website, launched in spring 2016, includes a forum, flows, and other information pertinent to Idaho paddling.
www.riverupdates.com

Salmon River Guide: Stanley to North Fork—a thorough guide to the upper Salmon River.
www.salmonriveridaho.blogspot.com

River Permit Information

Self-issue permits are required on a number of Idaho rivers, but there are only four rivers where paddling trips, and therefore permits, are limited: the Main Salmon, Middle Fork of the Salmon, Selway, and Snake River through Hells Canyon.

Visit the following internet address or look below for further contact information: www.fs.usda.gov/detail/scnf/passes-permits/recreation/?cid=fsbdev3_029568.

Main Salmon River
North Fork Ranger District
(208) 865-2700

Middle Fork of the Salmon River
Middle Fork Ranger District
(208) 879-4101

Selway River
West Fork Ranger District
(406) 821-3269

Snake River
Hells Canyon National Recreation Area
(888) 785-8037

Nonprofits Advocating for Idaho's Rivers

American Whitewater
PO Box 1540
Cullowhee, NC 2872a3
(828) 586-1930
www.americanwhitewater.org

Idaho Conservation League
PO Box 844
Boise, ID 83701
(208) 345-6933
www.idahoconservation.org

Idaho Rivers United
PO Box 633
Boise, ID 83701
(800) 574-7481
www.idahorivers.org

Idaho Whitewater Association
PO Box 6135
Boise, ID 83707
www.idahowhitewater.net

Paddling Index

About the Author

Greg Stahl took his first swim out of a kayak on a swollen Idaho river on May 23, 1999, and thereafter spent his springs and summers traveling the serpentine meanders of the state's many rivers and creeks. Those journeys have helped him know a different side of Idaho and a different side of himself.

Stahl is also an accomplished writer, editor, and photographer who has focused his work on the politics, people, ecology, and economy of the Rocky Mountain West for more than fifteen years. Before his current position as Communications and Research Director with Boise-based Idaho Rivers United—Idaho's largest river-specific conservation group—he worked as senior editor at *Sun Valley* magazine and as assistant editor at the *Idaho Mountain Express* newspaper in Ketchum, Idaho. In 2005 Stahl was selected for the Ted Scripps Fellowships in Environmental Journalism at the University of Colorado-Boulder, where he concentrated his studies in CU's School of Law. He has been recognized with more than fifty awards for his writing, reporting, and editing. His work can be viewed at www.westernperspective.com.

MIKE MCDONALD